SISTER STORIES

ALSO BY BRENDA PETERSON

River of Light

Becoming the Enemy

Living by Water: True Stories of Nature and Spirit

Nature and Other Mothers: Personal Stories of Women and the Body of Earth

Duck and Cover

Brenda Peterson

Viking

SISTER STORIES

Taking the Journey
Together

VIKING
Published by the Penguin Group
Penguin Books USA Inc., 375 Hudson Street,
New York, New York 10014, U.S.A.
Penguin Books Ltd, 27 Wrights Lane,
London W8 5TZ, England
Penguin Books Australia Ltd, Ringwood,
Victoria, Australia
Penguin Books Canada Ltd, 10 Alcorn Avenue,
Toronto, Ontario, Canada M4V 3B2
Penguin Books (N.Z.) Ltd, 182–190 Wairau Road,
Auckland 10, New Zealand

Penguin Books Ltd, Registered Offices:
Harmondsworth, Middlesex, England

First published in 1996 by Viking Penguin,
a division of Penguin Books USA Inc.

10 9 8 7 6 5 4 3 2 1

AUTHOR'S NOTE
While *Sister Stories* depicts my journey, and the journeys of my own sisters, my chosen sisters, and other women, I have changed the names of certain individuals and, at times, their identifying characteristics, in order to protect their privacy.

A portion of the prologue originally appeared in *The Seattle Weekly* under the title "Harmonic Convergence: Siblings" (November 3, 1992). A portion of the chapter "Our Civil War: Sisters and Abortion" first appeared in *New Age Journal* (September/October 1993) as "Sister Against Sisters" and was later reprinted in *Utne Reader* (May/June 1994) and the *San Francisco Chronicle*'s Sunday magazine, *This World* (July 5, 1994).

Grateful acknowledgment is made for permission to reprint excerpts from the following copyrighted works:
     "The Blanket Around Her" by Joy Harjo. By permission of the author.
     "The Ritual Life of Animals" by Linda Hogan. By permission of the author.
     Selected Poems of Rainer Maria Rilke, edited and translated by Robert Bly. Copyright © 1981 by Robert Bly. Reprinted by permission of HarperCollins Publishers, Inc.
     "Wallpapering to Patsy Cline" from *Open Heart* by Judith Sornberger. © 1993 Judith Sornberger. Reprinted by permission of the publishers, Calyx Books.

LIBRARY OF CONGRESS CATALOGING IN PUBLICATION DATA
Peterson, Brenda.
     Sister Stories: taking the journey together / Brenda Peterson.
          p.   cm.
ISBN 0-670-85296-1
1. Feminism—United States.   2. Femininity (Psychology)—United
States.   3. Women—United States—Psychology.   4. Women—United States—
Social conditions.   I. Title.
HQ1402.P47   1996
305.42—dc20   95 – 4771

This book is printed on acid-free paper.
⊚

Printed in the United States of America
Set in Adobe Garamond 3
Designed by Katy Riegel

for my own sisters,
Paula and Marla

for my chosen sisters
Susan Biskeborn, Beth Vesel, and Peggy Taylor,
who took the journey of this book alongside me

and in honor of all the sisterhoods

Whither thou goest, I will go
and where thou lodgest, I will lodge:
thy people shall be my people, and thy
God my God;
Where thou diest, will I die, and
there will I be buried: the Lord do so
to me, and more also, if ought
but death part thee and me.

—Ruth to Naomi
Book of Ruth, 1:16–17

"WALLPAPERING TO PATSY CLINE"

. . . Sister, *deep within my heart*
lies a melody, one that doesn't twang
with regret. Patsy's right,
we need some loving too.
Yes, we do.
Indeed, we do.
You know we do.

—Judith Mickel Sornberger
Open Heart

Acknowledgments

I would like to gratefully acknowledge the initial vision and support of Joanne Wyckoff; the insightful counsel and kindness of Flor Fernandez Barrios; the astute sisterly scrutiny and help of Christine Lamb, Louise Bode, Marlene Blessing, Linda Hogan, Deena Metzger, Rebecca Romanelli, Susan Colby, and Rebecca Wells; my writer-sisters of WWCRC; and all my nieces, the next generation. I'd also like to thank my Viking Penguin editors Dawn Seferian for her staunch early encouragement, and Jane von Mehren for wholeheartedly and brilliantly meeting me on the page. Finally, I owe deep gratitude to my astonishingly capable assistant, Becca Robinson, for helping me carry this long project. And, as always, I give thanks for the daily comfort and inspiration of Puget Sound.

Contents

Part One

Sisters Mine:
A Lifelong Minuet

1

Sisters Mine

"Promise me," my sister said, taking my hand, "that if the surgery fails, you won't let me linger on without a mind. Promise me you'll let me go."

My middle sister, Paula, knew well the risks of this delicate neurosurgery—she had even diagnosed herself. The youngest surgical instructor in the operating room at Emory University in Atlanta, Georgia, Paula was twenty-two in 1974. With the black humor typical of her OR colleagues, Paula joked that the only reason she'd allow herself to go "under the knife" of her peers was because she needed a job.

"Last time I scrubbed in," she laughed, "I fainted during surgery. When I awoke, the patient and I were lying side by side in the recovery room. 'What happened to you?' the surgeon I was scrubbing in with asked. 'It wasn't my humming, was it?' 'No,' I told him, 'it was my head.' 'Well, you need to get that head of yours fixed before you operate again in this unit.'"

Since childhood, my sister's head had been a source of amazement and, for us sisters, income. Paula and I charged other kids a nickel apiece to touch the base of her skull, which was as soft and eerily yielding as a newborn's. Like an infant's soft spot, my sister's "hole in the head" inspired awe and some tenderness, even among grade schoolers more impressed with species of spiders and snakes than anything human. Touching Paula's soft skull was like entering a forbidden place, an opening in the skull that was supposed to close over any day now, but never did; we children could put our hands on a secret that our bodies understood long before we might grasp it with our minds: Some wounds won't heal, no matter what adults say.

In 1957, when Paula was five, we first discovered the hole in her head. Doctors diagnosed it as a hematoma, or a swelling filled with extravasated blood. A budding science student, I diligently looked up the definition of "extravasate," as my sister gazed over my shoulder.

" ' . . . to force out from the proper vessels, as blood . . .' " Paula read sotto voce with the dramatic flair that would one day make her star of high school plays. "Or, 'to pour forth . . . like lava.' "

"Lava!" my three-year-old sister, Marla, giggled. "A volcano blowed up in her brains!"

From then on it was "brain lava" we advertised in our freak peep show and we upped the charge to a dime for kids to touch Paula's soft skull. Two decades later when Paula called me with news of her impending neurosurgery, she asked, "Remember the brain lava theory of our childhood? Well, I don't think we were too far off, although none of the docs here agree with my diagnosis. I think it's a very rare *sinus para crania,* or an outpouching of the circulatory system of the brain through a hole in the skull."

"Hole in the head," I echoed softly and tried not to cry long distance. "Is it dangerous?" We had become so accustomed to my sister's soft spot. Perhaps her vulnerability was what drove Paula to be the daredevil among us—doing triple flips from high dives while we other sisters played it safer with gymnastics and uneven bars on the ground. In our minds, her hematoma was no more than a birthmark. One doesn't go about risking one's life to fix a birthmark no one could see anyway.

"Very dangerous," she said, "but you can't tell anybody. If it is a brain tumor, I could wake up a vegetable." She paused and laughed. "Do vegetables ever really wake up?"

"You'll wake up," I assured her, but my voice was shaking. I willed myself to be strong for my younger sister, to protect her from my fears for her. All our childhood Paula and I had been each other's bodyguards against the vagaries of a manic-depressive, often violent mother and a father whose long absences we explained to each other as "missing in action." Because our father didn't protect us, Paula and I took the role of pint-sized commanders-in-chief on the home front. Together we older sisters kept the weather watch on Mother's emotional storm. We even had a theory to hold up to the seeming chaos of our home: Mother had water on the brain which ebbed and swelled according to the moon. Sometimes when Mother had her savage migraines, my sister and I massaged her skull searching for soft spots that we girls might have inherited. We never called Mother's episodes madness; everyone from our father to our grandmother to the local Southern Baptist pastor dismissed her rampages as her being simply "high-strung" or "moody." Often my father reminded us, "Be careful with your mother, girls. She's only got two speeds: full speed ahead and stop."

"I'm not telling Mom and Dad the truth," Paula said slowly, as if she'd just made her decision. "I'll only say it's routine surgery. You mustn't let them know how risky this is."

I didn't argue. The last thing my sister needed was to worry about soothing my parents, guarding them when she herself was in danger.

"They'll be no help anyway," Paula finished, her voice cracking. "But I want you there with me, especially since Dad said he's 'just a phone call away' and is only sending Mother. And you know Simon. He says he's got a cold and can't fly up here. I think he doesn't want to marry a woman with a hole in her head. So promise me you'll come."

I made my promises in the three days before that neurosurgery. The first was not to ask so many questions; the last was that I would take responsibility for "pulling the plug," as my sister called it. I also made many promises to my kindhearted boss, Harriet Walden, of *The New Yorker* magazine, who granted me leave from my editorial assistant job without question. This mother hen to our department was one of the few people I told about the seriousness of my sister's surgery. Waving her cigarette and tapping my forehead with a strong forefinger, she said, "You just go. You don't ask 'Why, God?' You just sit in that waiting room and hold on to her with your heart. Look at me, all my friends are so old, their second homes are operating rooms—

that's why I'll never give up smoking." She offered me a Doral cigarette and told me story after successful surgical story. I memorized
these survivors' tales; later, during the twelve hours of waiting to hear
if my sister would survive neurosurgery intact, I repeated Mrs.
Walden's stories back to myself like living mantras.

Though I was well into writing my first novel, though I'd come
from a long line of lively Southern storytellers, it wasn't until I sat in
the pale green waiting room of an Atlanta hospital that I fully felt
the power of stories to hold so fierce a lifeline for myself, for my sister.
And this umbilical cord, this story line, was a strong connection not
only while my sister slept under the scalpel, but also the night before
her surgery.

I flew down that night from New York City to find Paula in her
kitchen, consumed with the chore of repapering her cupboards. "I've
packed for a short stay," she said, cutting huge swatches of bright
contact paper. "Our father is just a phone call away, and our mother
is done in with a migraine over at a church friend's house."

"Out for the count," I said. "Why are you fiddling with your
kitchen? Shouldn't we be . . . well, doing something more meaningful?"

"You want to administer my last rites?" Paula laughed. In the
fluorescent kitchen light her face was full of shadows I'd never seen
before. I shivered inwardly, though the night was humid, clinging.
Everything felt dingy, inside and out. This was not the way I'd imagined we should spend what might be our last night together. I'd
wanted some important event, so we could both face the surgery
girded with the heroic armor of a soldier the night before battle. But
here we were papering her kitchen shelves—what kind of flimsy shield
was this with which to fend off death?

"Simple tasks," my sister said, reading my mind as usual. "They
teach us in nursing school—no heroics, just everyday chores to remind
us that we'll be here tomorrow to finish what we start. I intend to
leave these shelves half done, so I'll have to wake up. God knows,
honey, you'd never paper shelves, even if it was a way of mourning
me, even if I bequested them to you in my will— 'And to my beloved
sister I leave . . . my kitchen shelves!' "

We laughed and slathered the cupboard with SuperGlue in the
corners where the paper was already curling up. I realized this was

the first time we had really laughed since news of the surgery. Soon we were even singing in our familiar two-part harmony as we worked long past midnight.

I picked up a roll of shelf paper as my partner and I began a delicate two-step dance. She joined in the dance from the shelves and we danced for some time before we remembered what awaited us the next morning.

That night we slept together as we had much of our childhood: she curled up with a pillow to her belly where she once held her dolls, my body fitted against her back, one arm lightly encircling her as if I could still spare her the bad dreams, the savage days, of our childhood. She whispered to me as she fell asleep what she would tell me the next morning as the nurses wheeled her to surgery: "I won't die young. We'll be papering kitchen shelves together when we're ninety."

In the waiting room I imagined sharing a kitchen again some seventy years hence with my sisters and brother, seeing us around a table— me at ninety-four, Paula ninety-two, Marla ninety, and my brother eighty-seven. I mark this 1974 waiting room ritual as the first time I consciously understood that I counted on my sisters and brother as lifelong caretakers. The truth was we were only certain of one another in this world—and that was enough. As close as it is, however, my bond with my siblings does not seem more intense than many of my friends' sibling relationships, especially the sisters.

Yet when I first started researching sibling relationships in the 1980s, I was startled at the dearth of research on the sibling relationship, particularly sisters. Psychology has focused on parent-child relations to the exclusion of siblings until only very recently. For many years there was only one definitive book, *The Sibling Bond* (1982), by Stephen P. Bank and Michael D. Kahn. This book was touted as "the first major account of the powerful emotional connections among brothers and sisters throughout life." The authors also noted that while there are multitudinous rituals to mark rites of passage between parents and children, as well as between marital partners, "there are no rituals of church or synagogue that celebrate sibling bonds, nor legal means to make or break them." Yet literature and myth is full of sibling squabbles and bonds. It has taken psychology much longer to grant equal time to sisters and brothers.

Perhaps modern psychology is at last moving past its adolescent phase of preoccupation with parent-child relations—a focus in which separation, rebellion, and self-definition has so long held sway. To swing the spotlight now onto siblings is to grant that psychology itself is ready for the study of peer relations. In a recent *New York Times* article, the startling results of a long-term study of men revealed that their happiness in old age drew not upon the success of their careers, their marriages, their children, or their parents, but on their childhood compatibility with sisters and brothers. The reasoning was that in old age we are past the focus on achievement and more attuned to companionship, to play or leisuretime activities, and to the proverbial mysteries of so-called "second childhood." Those men studied who had strong, cooperative sibling relationships found friendship in old age a familiar and deepening experience; those who grew up with early sibling rivalry, isolation, and misunderstanding continued the same problematic relationship patterns in old age, no matter the success of the marriages, careers, or bonds with their own children.

Given this new research and the recent demographic trends that reveal that by the early twenty-first century we will have a "generation of grown-ups with more siblings than children," the sibling relationship is finally in the 1990s finding itself the focus of intense scrutiny. Siblings as caretakers are "the ultimate insurance policy," comments Dr. Deborah T. Gold, a medical sociologist at Duke University. "They are the only people with the potential to know us from birth to death. They can meet us on an equal footing not possible in a parent-child relationship. And they are the only ones who can help us look over the chaos of our lives and make it make sense."

Current research on siblings is also showing strong evidence that by middle age, "about eighty percent of siblings have positive relationships of varying intensity," that "in old age, pairs of sisters and brother-sister pairs may have more positive relations than pairs of brothers," and that "perception of a close sibling tie with a sister helps preclude depression in elderly women." In the book *Mixed Feelings: Love, Hate, Rivalry, and Reconciliation Among Brothers and Sisters*, Francine Klagsbrun writes that, according to her research, the sister bond was the strongest of all sibling relationships: 61 percent of the sisters reported feeling "close or very close" to their sisters in contrast to 48 percent of the brothers; 67 percent of the sister pairs "saw or spoke to their sisters monthly or more," compared to 48 percent of the brothers; and in response to the survey question "How much do you share your inner feelings?" an overwhelming 77 percent of the sisters responded "some or very much" while the brothers weighed in at 61 percent.

Klagsbrun goes on to note that even though the sister pairs were more intimate, "the closeness sisters enjoy does not necessarily eliminate aggressiveness." Sisters that were interviewed admitted to periods of angry silence more often than other sibling pairs. And the sisters were more likely to be annoyed at habits of or behavior by their sisters. Klagsbrun concludes that sister-sister intimacies may "actually exacerbate their competitive and aggressive feelings," leading to jealousy and fights. In the introduction to a fiction anthology, *Among Sisters*, editor Susan Cahill postulates that a reason for the intensity between sisters is "always the sense that one's sister is a part of one's essential self, an eternal presence of one's heart and soul and memory."

If the sibling bond has long been overlooked, the sister relationship has been ever more hidden. As Christine Downing writes in *Psyche's Sisters: Reimagining the Meaning of Sisterhood*, "sisters matter terribly to adult women. . . . The relationship feels focal, vital, often painful—and most especially untold." I suspect that underlying all of modern society's and psychology's inattention to the sister bond is a deep-seated misogyny and fear of the feminine. This expresses itself in psychology's dreaded fear of "fusion" that threatens individuation. Best-selling psychologist Robert Johnson in *She*, his pervasive study of the feminine, states flatly, "I am personally terrified of the sister quality in a woman." It is ironic that as we turn to Johnson, a male Jungian, to define femininity, we find such archetypal fear of what he intended to praise—it's like getting patriarchal poison mixed in with the mother's milk. This inherited fear of the feminine as fusion has left a true gender gap not between men and women, but between women and women. We know that men are afraid of women; but are women afraid of women, too? And does this reflect some deep terror of being devoured by the feminine that is within ourselves? Or is it

simply the product of thousands of years of the dominant masculine
model? Is there a way to heal this fear, to come closer to our sisters
and our true selves while still balancing our individual growth?

For centuries women have gazed into the masculine mirror—and
we have been told we were the "weaker sex," "hysterical," "irrational,"
"second-class." Even our language betrays us; the root of the word
"hysteria" is "womb," while the origin of the word "testament," the
word that signifies reliability, is "testicle."

In choosing to focus on the intricate dance of sisters in this book,
I hope to celebrate the bond as well as explore the shadows between
sisters. My approach is listening and storytelling, the very fabric of
feminine *gnosis*. This book is narrative nonfiction with continuing
characters from my own life and interviews with women whose relationships with their sisters are a complex and continuing journey. In
the stories told here, many of the sisters, both blood and chosen, are
women I've known intimately over time; I've witnessed the complicated, shifting alliances of these sister bonds from within the inner
circle. Several women even lent me their letters, diaries, and deepest
confidences—a gift that opened up for me the world of sisters in both
its archetypal power and personal secrets. Some of the women's names
have been changed to respect their privacy, but the stories are true to
their characters and how they've understood the complex society of
their sisters.

I am also interested in societies of sisters—from ancient priestesses
to nuns to secret tribal societies—in which the whole stratum of
women exists quite independently of their brothers'. In these societies
of women we can witness every power, intrigue, and lesson humans
have to learn. Finally, I see sisterhood as complete unto itself, not a
stage of development out of which we women are supposed to evolve
or grow. Nor is the sister bond a prelude to or training for the "real"
relationships with men. Because it is a lifelong bond, sisters' intimacy
illumines and teaches us as much about ourselves as does motherhood,
marriage, career, or society.

In her book *Among Women*, Louise Berkinow makes the telling observation that "we have died in each other's arms far more than the
romantic novel or cinema would lead us to believe." What would
happen if our stories, from novels to poetry to movies, really portrayed
the sister bond in all its lifelong complexity? Would the rich mirrors

of sisterhood reflect to us a feminine face that is as many-faceted as that allowed men?

Of course literature is replete with complex sister relationships, from Chekhov's *Three Sisters* to Shakespeare's *King Lear* siblings (recently echoed in Jane Smiley's *A Thousand Acres*); then there is my own favorite trilogy by Rebecca West, *The Fountain Overflows*, based on her own remarkable sisters.

I am also heartened by the very recent movies and books offered, such as *Having Our Say: The Delaney Sisters' First 100 Years*, that celebrate the bond between centenarians. On a cross-country trip in 1992 the airline offered the films *Sister Act* on the eastbound flight and *Fried Green Tomatoes* on the return. Perhaps this was the feminine fallout of the successful and controversial movie *Thelma and Louise*, but it has sparked a trend that only increases as we move into a new decade. In 1994 the media discovered siblings: *Family Therapy Networker*, *New Age Journal*, and *Utne Reader* all ran cover stories on the sibling bond. On the screen, sisters especially sprang up like wildflowers—from the successful British television serial "House of Elliot" with its fashion designer sisters, to the popular American series "Sisters," to the plethora of new sister movies, including *Sister Act II*, *Bad Girls*, *A League of Their Own*, *The House of the Spirits*, *La Belle Époque*, *Boys on the Side*, and even *Little Women*. This sudden rediscovery of sisterhood in our mainstream media is a hopeful sign that the next generation of sisters will enjoy many mirrors of lifelong female bonds.

What will change now on the threshold of a new century as we hold up the feminine mirror to study ourselves by our own standards? The sister mirror—both our biological and chosen sisterhoods—is a lens with which to see and know ourselves better. In turning to my own and others' sister stories, I can tap a wellspring of long-devalued wisdom and healing. In recording these stories, I have listened to women speaking about their sisters and I've been struck by the extreme emotions. Many wept over their sisters; others suddenly felt missing pieces of their deepest selves come together by exploring this uncharted territory. We sisters are only now beginning to see each other whole—and it may well be a new world we will make from this vision.

Among many visions of sisterhood, I have found one constant: the search for Self, the claiming of one's feminine identity not in contrast to our brothers, but within the wide world of women. Society is only now recognizing the sisterhoods as separate but equal to the brotherhoods. I offer this book in that spirit: If we reconcile and truly know our sisters in all their shades of light and dark, then we can recognize who we are and what we bring to a world too long without its true, feminine peers.

2

Three Sisters:
Another Eternal Triangle

My sister Paula had indeed diagnosed herself. When the neurosurgeon and a doctor friend of my sister's returned after the eight-hour operation, they were subdued, their faces dark. My heart pounded so hard I could barely hear the neurosurgeon, who seemed to be very angry at his young associate.

"Well," he growled. "She did it, all right!"

"Did what?" I could barely get enough oxygen in my lungs to ask the question. I dared not ask, *Did she die?*

"*Sinus para crania,* vascular tumor. She figured it out, all right. But who's to know, it's so rare. . . . I mean, I've only read about half-a-dozen cases." The neurosurgeon turned to glare at the other doctor, whom my sister had asked to scrub in as witness to the surgery. The neurosurgeon grudgingly admitted him as one might a spy.

"What Dr. Carkeek means," my sister's friend, Frank, explained to me wearily as if he'd been through it many times before, "is that it wasn't what we expected, so we did the best we could . . ."

"Quite a mess." Dr. Carkeek shook his head.

"But did she . . . is she okay?" I grabbed the bedstand and felt faint. A post-op nurse had called my mother and me in the waiting room to say there was some problem; we should return to Paula's hospital room and wait for her until further report. My anxious mother succumbed to a migraine, which kept her groggy, vague.

"The surgery itself was successful." Dr. Carkeek bristled.

"She did have an episode of respiratory arrest due to her extremely low blood pressure," Frank interrupted softly. "But we brought her back."

Dr. Carkeek took this as a direct insult. Turning on his heels to leave, he snapped, "You explain it, Doctor, since you know so much. I've requested an angiogram for tomorrow just to make sure there are no more complications." Then he strode out, stethoscope dangling like a steel talisman.

"You'll have to pardon the guy," Frank sighed. "Nurses shouldn't out-diagnose neurosurgeons. His pride, and the pecking order, is deeply wounded."

Only then could I rouse myself from my stupor of fear and demand, "And what about my sister? What the hell is going on with her now?"

"Surgery was difficult," Frank admitted. "We really thought it was a tumor, not her circulatory system outpouching through the skull. We sewed up the hole in the head with steel. If that's all that was really the matter . . ."

"What else could it be?"

"Don't know. The angiogram will tell us more. If you just wait a little, post-op nurses will bring her back to the room. She's asked that you spend the night here with her . . ." He stopped, embarrassed. "Just you."

My mother took her cue gratefully and volunteered to return to her friend's house. When they at last wheeled Paula in, I was unprepared for the sight of her: lips swollen blue-black from the breathing tubes, bruises all over her arms from the IVs and elbows of operating room staff; but the worst was her head. They'd shaved a wide patch of her long hair and bandaged the back of her skull; but my sister had already hidden her wound under a swatch of her abundant blond hair.

"Bride of Frankenstein, Behba," my sister managed to say through thick lips, using her pet name for me. "Eight-inch incision, like somebody hit me over the head with a pickax. Not a pretty sight these wire stitches . . . but I'm awake, ain't I?"

She didn't stay awake for long. Dr. Carkeek was worried about post-op seizure, so he prescribed a heavy dose of Valium for the night. Whether it was the drugs, to which all of my family are extremely sensitive, or post-op psychosis common in these cases, my sister's first night after surgery was horrific. Incoherently she thrashed about in her bed until the night-shift nurses tied her down. Paula wept and ground her teeth like an animal clamped tight in a steel trap. I held her hand as I wondered—was the trap also the steel sutures tugging tightly in a crisscross gash down her skull? I tried to calm her by massaging her feet, the only part of her body not bruised. About midnight she grew very still, her eyes wide open with terror.

"Don't let her in!" my sister screamed and twisted her head violently back and forth. I was terrified her movements would rupture the sutures, so I held her shoulders down, shushing her. As often happens, I sensed her thoughts through our sibling telepathy before she said them. "Don't let Mother get in!" she screamed. I knew what haunted Paula's hallucinatory post-op psychosis. It was not her imaginings.

"We're safe, we're really safe here, aren't we?" Paula whispered, pupils dilated from wide blue to big black. "Where's Mosby, Behba?"

She meant our third sister, Marla, whom we'd nicknamed Mosby after the wily Confederate Captain John B. Mosby, whom the Yankees called "The Gray Ghost." It was a common habit of our sisterhood, especially when we lived in the South, to hide from our mother's bad spells in an upstairs attic or closet. Which house, what state—it didn't matter. Our father's Forest Service job had moved us so often that sometimes we never even bothered to unpack our clothes from their cardboard boxes with their convenient hanging poles. Our mother's bad spells were not simply migraine headaches, they were hurricanes. Whenever our sisterly storm watches sighted a big one brewing, we evacuated ourselves straight to the closet shelters. We imagined malevolent winds howling through my mother's head, at gale force. That must be why everything from kitchenware to plants to my siblings and myself were thrown about in Mother's violent wake. Those days, we kids were so much detritus spun round after a whirlwind. We knew what to look for as early warning signs of Mother's madness: electric gray eyes so bright they hurt to stare into, those lightning fast hands striking like heat-sensor missiles. We wondered if my mother's hands held any memories of hitting us. That night in the hospital as I sat with my sister Paula, watching her thrash about in her drugged sleep, I sang her the songs of our shared childhood. I had to imagine my sister's harmonies to support me. And in that deep dark with my moaning sister, I comforted myself with the memory of Paula telling me, "When I sing, Behba, I always hear you, too, even if you're not with me."

The next morning's angiogram extended Paula's trauma. Dr. Carkeek had neglected to inform the technicians that my sister had already undergone surgery and so was extremely vulnerable to any movement to the base of her skull. Without this warning, the techs proceeded to cut a slit in Paula's thigh at the femoral artery to insert colored dye. Then with a series of rapid twists, they positioned her skull for the photographic scan to see how the dye moved through the circulatory system of her brain. My sister, still not yet fully conscious after the previous night's Valium dose, screamed out in pain and fought the technicians who, without doctor's orders, followed normal procedure for someone presurgery, injecting her with an IV push—an intravenous dose of Valium made much stronger by the direct influx of drug into the bloodstream. Immediately my sister calmed, but the IV push sent her into a Valium overdose and a semicoma. Because Paula had chosen to have this neurosurgery performed at a hospital in Tennessee, she was not safeguarded by the usual insider status accorded a staff nurse at her own Emory Hospital in Georgia.

When they wheeled her back to her room semicomatose, the nurse explained to me that Paula would soon "pull out of it before surgery."

"What?" I shouted. "She's already had her neurosurgery!"

The nurse was shocked. "Oh, we had no idea . . ." she began. "We didn't see any signs of surgery or we never would have administered the Valium IV push."

Since we couldn't get ahold of Paula's neurosurgeon, it was to my sister's doctor and nurse friends I now turned for advice and treatment, though they had no power to prescribe or take over her case. Paula was not only in a coma, she was also in a medical limbo in which we all had to wait until we found her doctor to take any action to help her.

I was in a rage of confusion and fear. The first call was to my sister Marla, whose gift at explaining the medical word-salad to a layperson is unparalleled from her years working as an intensive care nurse.

"Talk to her, sis!" Marla ordered. "Hearing and touch are the last to go. So hold on to her and talk, sing, tell dirty doctor jokes—anything to anchor her attention. Don't let her just float. That's when they all take off. You know, comas are strange. Sometimes I think a coma is like mandatory attendance in some class you skipped out of in daily life. It's not just time out. I think coma patients are in an unconscious study hall." Marla paused, then said gently, "She's not going to die, Behba. I can feel her still kicking, all the way up here in Pittsburgh! Besides, what would we do without our middle sister—it's supposed to be this way: the Three Musketeers, the three-legged stool, third time's the charm. The numbers ain't right for Pooh to go. She's got to stay with us, it's natural."

As Marla said it, I felt the truth of it. We three sisters were another eternal triangle, as strong and profound a balancing act as the triangle of mother, father, and child. Because our mother was so volatile and our father absent, we three sisters had bonded more profoundly than most sisters. And yet perhaps we expected a close relationship with one another because it was a family tradition. We were deeply influenced by my three aunts on my father's side, Nettie Mae, Mary Leola, and Donna Ruth. These aunts share my father's Seminole and French Canadian Indian blood with a little black Swede thrown in, "just so we can pass," as Mary Leola teases.

Swarthy, ribald, and tribal, these three aunts kept their fond, dark eyes on us sisters every summer when we joined my father's family in the Ozarks at Grandfather's farm. From these aunts we sisters learned to smoke, drink, and decide for ourselves what we wanted, with or without the menfolk's permission.

"Sisters stick together," Aunt Donna Ruth would confide in us over a cigarette behind the barn. In her own life she had run away to her big sister after a teenage marriage was annulled. And after other heartbreaks, Donna Ruth sought out her sisters as allies, often moving in until, as she said, "the next catastrophe called a good-looking man came along." She finally married a Methodist minister whose lively black humor matches her own. "Happily ever after, girls"—she'll wink at us now—"nothing like a minister and an ex-sinner!"

Our aunts are dark-skinned and their black, curly hair was a wonder to us as children. "White gals," was what Mary Leola called us—we, who had inherited her mother's Dutch and our mother's British blue eyes and fair skin. "Sun just eats y'all up and leaves us be. That's 'cause we got a touch of tarbrush and a touch of the tepee." And when she saw how crushed we were by what we believed was her criticism, how ashamed we were that we couldn't carry on the dark good looks of my father's family, she'd add very gently, "Maybe you gals belong to the moon. Moon can shine on y'all all night and never do nothing but make you brighter. Y'all're goddamn moonbeams."

It was that old, kind teasing that I recalled the night I called Marla Mosby for comfort while our third sister lay comatose. "Hey, Mo," I asked, "remember Aunt Mary telling us we belonged most to the moon?"

Marla laughed. Having lived half her high school years and all her college years in Georgia, she'd spent a lot more time with Aunt Mary Leola and her sprawl of kinfolk in North Georgia than I had. "That's a funny thing to think about now." She faded off. For a long moment we both fell into silence during which I could hear her breathing. It comforted me, listening to Marla's steady breath in my ear and watching the rhythm of Paula's white-clad chest rise and fall in her deep detour away from consciousness. I remembered reading that whole pods of whales breathe in synch in semi-sleep as they rest half their minds and float out upon midnight waves in full moonlight.

I took a deep breath and gazed at Paula's unconscious, upturned face. In the small halo thrown from the bed lamp, her pale hair pulled back to cover a white head bandage, she looked at last peaceful, even radiant. "She's a goddamn moonbeam," I said softly, leaning close to whisper in Paula's ear. Then for the first time since she'd come out of surgery I began to weep. I knew that it was safe now to cry with my other sister on the phone, holding the lifeline that I hadn't been able to let go ever since they wheeled Paula into the operating room.

Marla's voice was so soothing as she said, "Put the phone in Pooh's ear, Behba, and let me talk to that girl. I've got a few things to say might wake her up!"

I held the phone to Paula's unconscious ear and shook with quiet sobs. At last, someone else to help me keep my sister in the world. My other sister. I watched Paula's eyelids flickering, the rapid eye movements of otherworldly dreams, as deep inside her coma she listened.

It was only then, when the tears had relaxed me enough to ease my terror and help me think straight, that I remembered Paula herself had had notable success in her own neurosurgical nursing work with coma victims; she always talked and read to them, touched them and told them it was time to come back. Once she established a code system of squeezing fingers with a small comatose boy who over a period of six months kept contact with her until he at last opened his eyes. "I watched you from up there," he had told Paula. "I was floating on the ceiling and I didn't want to come back down to my body. It hurt."

As Marla talked a blue streak into Paula's ear, I tried to remember that finger code to crack this coma. Right then I actually longed for our mother to be in this hospital room. She had been a telegrapher during the war for the Wabash railroad and her fast, brilliant fingers were the talk of the rails. Maybe her Morse code would rouse Paula? As I gently tapped Paula's open palm, I heard Marla's tiny voice calling my name.

"Listen," she said when I cradled the phone on my shoulder. "Tonight is crucial. If we can catch her before she slips too deep, we've got her. Can you stay awake another night? Do you want me to fly down tomorrow morning?"

"Yes," I said, again giving way to tears. "I'm so sleepy . . ."

Then Marla went into action. She arranged for some of Paula's nurse friends to travel up to that Tennessee hospital and set up round-the-clock shifts with Paula. I don't remember much of that night except sitting with Sherrie Scott, Paula's best friend from college, and the radiator hissing. Sherrie talked a blue streak to Paula, telling her stories of their college days as bawdy and entertaining as *The Canterbury Tales*. There were others who relieved me, young doctors and nurses, Paula's hospital colleagues; they set up a professional circle to protect Paula from the limbo left by Dr. Carkeek's disappearance. By the next evening, Paula began to tremble like an animal in the twitches and horizontal kicks of a running dream. Within minutes, her luminous blue eyes shot open and she bounded halfway out of bed like a prisoner escaping. Sherrie and I caught her in our arms, laughing and screaming for joy.

"Not so fast, there, cowgirl," Sherrie said. "This ain't no rodeo!"

Paula looked around defiantly. "I've got to get going!" she insisted. "I'm late!" Then she shook her head, surprised to find herself in a hospital bed, her head bandaged, her legs strapped to the iron railings to keep her from thrashing. "What . . . ?" Then the nurse in her momentarily took up residence and she let out a sigh. "How long have I been under?"

"Little over a day," I answered, grinning. I could hardly keep myself from jumping up and down on the bed as we did as kids, playing circus trampoline. But I tamped down my joy when I saw Paula's dilated eyes waver and she lay back in the bed with an exhausted sigh.

"I'm in and out," she murmured, eyes closing again. Slipping away. "I'm not tracking . . ." Then she was gone again, but this time only for several hours, before she bolted upright and tried to escape. We held her down. Sherrie lectured my sister. "You're going to rupture your stitches and the angiogram incision," she said firmly. "You have to stay flat and let the catheter do its work."

"Let me go!" Paula screamed, her eyes shut tightly. "Let me up!"

For another half a day Paula would lapse into coma and then leap out of it like the old gymnast that she was. Sometimes we simply sat on her legs to keep her in the bed. She murmured and moaned to herself and yelled at us for keeping her flat. Then, very slowly as we entered the second evening of coma alternating with incoherent consciousness, Paula suddenly sat up in bed and did not try to run away. We were watching *M*A*S*H* (her favorite program), and she peered intently at the television before sinking back into her pillows. Now she was more drowsy and drugged than comatose. "I don't get it," she'd say in frustration, "how come nobody is finishing their sentences?"

Sherrie and I sat on either side of my sister, holding her hands and interpreting the story for her. Paula nodded, sighing and smiling. "It's no use," she said. "Brain lava."

But she didn't ever disappear again into the deep coma. Now she even had lucid hours when she made perfect sense. When one of the residents on call came in to check her swollen labia and the swelling hematoma in her thigh's femoral artery where they'd inserted the angiogram needle, Paula recognized him immediately from when he had been in training at the hospital where she worked, and said slyly, "Scott, if you didn't get to see my private parts when we were dating, you're not going to see them now."

"Come on, Paula, give me a break," Scott said good-naturedly. "It's my job. Let me do it. If you hadn't kept acting *The Great Escape*, you wouldn't be bleeding like this."

"No," Paula insisted, her smile still quite sensible. "I want an older doctor—and an uglier one." Then she threw her pillow at him.

At that moment we all knew my sister had returned to herself. From then on it was a daily process of rest and reunion.

I lived in the hospital with her all week while she recovered from both the neurosurgery and its aftermath. Marla decided another nurse was unnecessary and she would come be with Paula after she was released from the hospital. My mother visited daily before returning to play with her friends; and my father, as always, was just "a phone call away."

During one of her better days, I asked Paula, "Did you hear us talking to you in your coma?"

Then Paula grinned. "Yeah, it was a real talk show in there, Behba. I thought you'd never shut up. And Mo . . . if I weren't in a coma I'd be downright embarrassed by some of those traveling salesmen dirty jokes she told me. I was laughing my head off. . . ." She gingerly touched her bandage. "Oops, wrong metaphor."

"Did you feel my finger codes?" I asked.

Paula nodded and gave me a fond look. "You remembered, Behba. Do you know what your message was saying?"

"No, just gibberish, I suppose."

"You were saying, yes, yes, yes, yes, yes, yes, yes!" Paula laughed. "My finger code with that coma kid was simple: yes and no. 'Yes.' was a quick squeeze and 'no' was a long squeeze. Next time I think I'll teach you sign language so at least you can be more eloquent." She grew more serious and held out her arms to embrace me. "Although," she murmured, holding me tight, " 'yes' says it all, doesn't it, honey?"

My sister didn't say "yes" to life for long after that traumatic neuro-surgery. When her fiancé, Simon, arrived post-surgery, I was quietly appalled at his criticism of Paula's appearance—the deep bruises beneath her eyes, her pallor, her shaved head—and distracted manner, which was simply disorientation from the anesthetic, the Valium overdose, and the various post-op drugs.

"Oh, it's just his doctor's black humor," Paula said, dismissing Simon's comments, and assured me she was fine enough for me to fly back to New York.

But she was not fine at all and I knew it, though I had no medical evidence, only that sister telepathy. At the four-year point in their relationship, Paula was changing her life to follow Simon down to Miami, against all the advice of her sisters and friends. Ten days after her neurosurgery, Simon picked up Paula, who had packed her belongings for a move out of the apartment she shared with her best friend and Marla. Paula and Simon left, bound for Miami, where Simon was in medical school, and where Paula had a new apartment to be near him and her new nursing job.

Whenever I tried to tune into Paula in her Miami apartment, all I got was static, the kind of wayward signal I had felt when she was semicomatose post-surgery. When I called Paula at her new home, her vague politeness, the fact that she told me not a single story about her new life, disturbed me deeply. One night very late, in the middle of a snowstorm, I felt such a bolt of panic through my body that I jumped up and began pacing the studio. I didn't have a phone in my apartment, preferring to do all my talking at work, and at night, enjoying what passed for quiet in Manhattan.

But I felt no quietude, only a buzzing in my ears, my heart throbbing so fast I thought it might be cardiac arrest. Very purposefully I steadied my breathing and closed my eyes, trying to figure out what was going on. And then, in a moment of frightening calm, I knew: It was not my body that was in trouble, it was my sister's.

Where was she? What was happening? I scrambled for her new phone number in Miami and threw on my parka to run the five blocks up the street to a phone booth. As the phone rang and rang, I sent my sister every telepathic alarm signal I could imagine, willing her to pick up that phone.

Years later Paula would finally write me about exactly what happened that night as I stood in my snow-covered phone booth praying for her to answer. It seems that Simon had finally broken the news to Paula that he was in love with a nineteen-year-old girl. He couldn't decide whether he still loved my sister or this other girl; and until he could work out his decision with his therapist, he'd moved Paula down to Miami. Paula and Simon had a terrible fight, then Paula hurled a framed picture of herself at the wall and drove back to her apartment. She was utterly humiliated that she had believed Simon rather than her own sisters, her friends, and her inner radar. How, she wondered, could she ever face her friends or return to her university medical life in Atlanta? She believed she had not only lost face, but faith in her own judgment. After giving up her career, family, and friends to follow Simon, it seemed a logical next step to simply give up on her own life:

"Remember, Behba," she wrote me those many years later, telling me her side of that terrible night's actions, "I was still post-op, drugged and not really tracking. I felt all alone down there without my supportive sisters and friends. Simon's declaration was too much to fathom. The following week at the hospital I faked my way through the orientation for my new job; and I carefully removed two vials of Sublimase from the anesthesiologist's cart in the operating room. The night of your call, I felt a blackness that only a few have ever known overtake any reasonable thoughts I had of staying alive. I withdrew all the Sublimase into a syringe and lay on my bed to identify a vein with which to kill myself. I had read books about *seppuku,* the Japanese form of suicide; and I went to that plane where one's life on this earth is left behind. I wasn't afraid like I had been weeks before facing a major operation. But instead I felt a sense of peace, knowing that I would no longer have to explain my crazy choices of moving for a man who loved someone else.

"I wish I could say that I remembered there were people out there who loved me or that I was being selfish and not caring about my friends and family; but the truth is that I only wanted OUT. I did not feel much anger, but more a feeling of 'you should have known better . . . your loyalty was wasted.'

"But it was all going to be okay, because very soon I would be floating in a deep sleep, the essence of denial and sweet bliss. I had watched many patients going calmly into that deep sleep where the cut of the knife was no longer felt. After all, I was going to take an overdose of anesthetic . . . to kill the pain. The darkness that had surrounded me during my own neurosurgery comforted me now as I knew there would be no way to reverse the anesthesia about to enter my veins. I would simply be able to sleep and someone else could explain it all.

"As I searched out a vein in my arm, the nurse in me took over as if it were someone else's arm. But the phone interrupted me with its shrill rings, insulting my peace, annoying me more than anything else. I finally grabbed the phone, thinking it might be a message for my Cuban roommate and her overprotective family would come check if there was no answer on a Friday night.

"Instead it was you, my screaming sister, calling from that New York phone booth. 'What the hell is the matter with you!' That's what you screamed into my ear. 'What on earth are you doing to make me walk half a mile in this pouring snowstorm to a pay phone to call you?'

"I simply burst into tears and told you that there was not much going on except that I was about to kill myself. Oh, I hated you at that moment for interfering and making me face the pain that I had almost escaped. Then you told me that you loved me, other people loved me, and that you would personally kill the jerk who'd brought me to this horrible end of my life. Well, *that* thought really started to cheer me up a bit!

"I don't know what you said that finally clicked but it had something to do with staying in this world with you. We had been such a sweet tribe of sisters through all the moves, hurts, parental rejection, and sadness that I couldn't bear for you to do battle without *my* wisdom and humor.

"I'm so glad that I stayed in this world. I would never have known the wonder of a child nursing at my breast or experience real love as I do now. I know I sometimes forget all this when you and I are cross with each other or ignore the obvious needs that one would give to a friend without a thought. But you gave me back this life with all its beauty, ugliness, pain, and joy. Most of all I now have my new tribe of daughters, these little sisters."

My own sisters and I often tease one another about the family roles we play. If I am the older sister protector, the Mad Dog, as they call me, then Paula is the Princess and Marla the Angel Unaware. Our roles belie our looks. Though she is so often my opposite politically and spiritually, Marla is built more like me—reedy and slight on top with stronger hips and long legs. Marla and Paula share the same coloring, towheads with straight Palomino manes of hair; they are considered very beautiful with their broad Dutch brows and full lips. I am ash blond with what my father calls "unmanageable curls" and finer features like my little brother, who is the darkest of us all. Marla has my father's deep, midnight blue eyes, while Paula and I inherited my mother's pale blue eyes, what we call her "wolf eyes." Our sibling bond is sometimes much like a wolf pack, for we are fiercely loyal and sometimes exclusive. But unlike that animal pack, there is no alpha male or female among us siblings; our roles are more about shifting sibling strategy than dominion. In my sister triangle, we play many roles with one another—from confidante to counselor, from parent surrogate to child. As the older sister it has taken me many years to wriggle out of my overly protective role, just as it has taken my younger sisters decades to successfully topple my assumed authority as eldest. We three sisters all have had to give up some of our natural power and surrender to one another's authority.

More often than not, we take one another's advice. But there have been several times when we vehemently disagreed with one another's counsel, especially on the subject of abortion. The worst argument in the history of my sister bond with Paula was in 1977 and is only now, some two decades later, after I have given up trying to be her long-distance bodyguard, that it is at last resolved.

When my sister met her husband, Aaron, she was living and working in Miami at a large city hospital. After two years of healing over Simon and dating extensively, Paula was thriving. She was, as always, a bit of a nursing star, the Belle of the ER, as I teasingly called her. I was not far from wrong. Her vivacity and expertise made her a head surgical nurse much in demand. Sometimes she'd call me with miracle stories of surgical wonders. Her photographic memory made her a necessity for those original groundbreaking procedures done during emergencies and later in need of documentation for future surgeries.

The surgeons used to fight over my sister as their scrub nurse. One trauma surgeon in particular, Aaron, claimed her not only as his surgical partner, but also as his wife. Paula prepared the family to meet her fiancé by explaining, "Aaron is Cuban and a genius of a surgeon so . . . well, he's not modest."

What she did not tell us is that she had specifically admonished Aaron that without her eldest sister's blessing, she would not marry him. We were all nervous about the first meeting with Paula's financé. Whose bright idea it was to introduce him at Marla's graduation from nursing school, we'll never really know. But it was typical between Paula and Marla that on one sister's big day, the other would up-stage her.

The whole family flew to Atlanta from various parts of the country to gather at Emory University in 1977. There are photos of that grad-uation day that tell the story: Marla smiles proudly, standing in front of the family in cap and gown; behind her my parents look distracted and my sister Paula and I have our heads together, faces drawn as we whisper what I still remember was a terse conversation. What we were discussing with such troubled expressions was the same discussion that would sadden much of our dialogue for the next fourteen years—her fiancé, later her husband.

But on that day he was still her fiancé and the subject still seemed negotiable. I was protesting with every Mad Dog elder sister instinct in me and Paula was resisting. But at least we were still talking to each other. By the next day we were stony silent, refusing to acknowl-edge each other's existence, and Marla—when she was not fuming over her upstaged graduation—was playing peacemaker.

Upon first arriving at the graduation ceremony, fiancé in tow, Paula introduced Aaron by launching into what she described as "our own version of Bonnie and Clyde." We listened, ashen-faced, as Paula de-lightedly told us about her journey to Marla's graduation.

"Aaron and I were driving on the Georgia interstate behind this huge semi-truck when suddenly it slammed on its air brakes. Smoke swirled up and Aaron had to fishtail or else we would have been decapitated," Paula told us. "Well, Aaron wanted to show that trucker just who he was dealing with so he reached for his gun, a Smith and Wesson 38, and said, 'I'm going to pass this asshole and point my gun at him to say *Hey, Bucko, don't mess with me!*' I put down my knitting and told Aaron this was crazy, that truckers had guns, too, and maybe the guy was on speed. But Aaron was furious and ignored me. He had his gun in his right hand and we started passing the trucker. I used both my hands to struggle with him and overpower him, to try and keep the gun out of sight. Who knows what the trucker saw that first pass-by? Aaron and I were still arguing and then we compromised: He'd make a second pass and just lay the gun on his right thigh to let the trucker see it clearly as we drove by. The trucker saw that gun, all right. Soon after we passed him we noticed there were six highway patrol cars, an ambulance, and a fire engine following us. They followed us for a long time, then, all at once, every cop car turned on its red lights and sirens to pull us to the shoulder. Then a bullhorn shouting: 'Driver and passenger, out of the car with your hands up!' Aaron got out, but I had to bend down and search for my shoes. The bullhorn bellowed, 'Passenger, get out of that car!' So I scooted out and suddenly they had us separated and spread-legged, searching for weapons. Every one of those cops had his gun pointed straight at us like we were criminals or something. I was in a summer tank top and shorts, but Aaron was in white jeans and T-shirt and shades with his black, curly hair. It occurred to me then that he did look a little like a hood. Anyway, the cops kept yelling about our gun and Aaron kept trying to tell them he was a trauma surgeon from Miami and he'd saved lots of cops from gunshot wounds. The cops started to calm down then after they checked his ID and secured his gun. And then this amazing thing happened: They started admiring his gun and exchanging good-old-boy stories about their weapons like they were hunting buddies. They didn't even give us a speeding ticket. So here we are, safe and sound."

When Paula finished her story there was some nervous laughter and my father nodded to Aaron, though his face was inscrutable. Did he approve of his future son-in-law's highway brinksmanship with a loaded gun? Did Father, himself a hunter, find Paula's story as hilarious as Mother did?

I sat very still and eyed my future brother-in-law in despair. Then I asked, directing my question only to my sister Paula, "And what do you think that trucker reported to the cops? That he felt himself threatened or that he'd witnessed a man and woman fighting over a gun?"

Paula shrugged with a smile. "Who knows?" she said.

I remember exactly the look on my sister Paula's face: She was exhilarated, almost giddy, and yet her face was frozen, like a deer in the headlights. I recognized that face. I'd felt it only a year before when I'd found myself with a man who so aroused me I had to leave for the ladies' room to compose myself. In the ladies' room, I had placed a hand on my chest and felt my heart thudding with what I took for excitement. I didn't then understand that adrenaline rush for what it was—the fear that comes from real danger: dancing in the lion's mouth. But it was so familiar, so seductive.

After my sister told her highway patrol story, I was horrified to hear how Aaron had risked their lives and captured my sister's heart with his violent bravado. Where was my sister's wild nature now— the daredevil, the tomboy, the high-flying gymnast and brilliant nursing instructor? There she sat, subsumed in his story, not seeing the danger, not seeing that when she was in his shadow she was dominated, almost tamed. Of course, he was acting out her violence and the familiar dangers of our upbringing. But there was something else—he was contemptuous of women, from his mother to his pediatrician sister, even to his fiancée. And it was this bold contempt that troubled me the most. How would we sisters fare with such a possessive brother-in-law? It is a great statement of our sister bond that it was not destroyed during Paula's marriage. It survived through subterfuge, dogged commitment, and feminine guile, for there is nothing more suspect than a sister to a jealous, controlling husband.

That Aaron was theatened by Paula's sisters, especially me, became obvious. In a way Paula had set him up. For by insisting he achieve my approval and then telling me the horrific highway story, she insured that he would certainly never get my blessing. Add to that the fact that Aaron immediately resented my so-called "power" and that it was in his character to try to overthrow it.

But I was powerless to stop my sister's marriage at that family reunion. I saw it would happen all over again—my sister would marry our mother; she would suffer and practice surviving, because that's what she knew best: that trapped cunning and hiding was what we both then often mistook for love.

I could not save her. I barely knew how to save myself. And the truth was that whether I gave my blessing or not, she would marry him. Even so, at the end of our family reunion I had to plead, "Please don't do this, Pooh." I took her aside from the others.

She knew exactly what I was saying and she bent her head, weeping.

Then Aaron glared over at her and asked, "Are you coming with me?"

As if hypnotized, my sister, who had always fought back against

Mother, who had of all us sisters been the bravest, the most physically and vocally brazen, who had shouted and cursed and told the truth against my mother when I was placating or Marla was crying to herself—this courageous sister simply hung her head and followed this man into the parking lot, into her married life, which would only end fourteen years later when she, in the middle of the night, would finally walk away with her three daughters and never go back.

But in 1979 when my sister at last married Aaron there was nervous family approval. Aaron and I had made a tentative truce. He had in fact operated on me—a delicate and expert hernia surgery for which I am grateful. But even as I lay under his knife on the operating table, fully conscious during this major surgery because we'd decided on a local anesthetic, I looked up into his skillful eyes and still knew this: that he was both a healer and dangerous.

At Paula and Aaron's wedding reception he regaled the queasy family gathering with operating room tales. My relatives weren't the only queasy ones. Marla did not attend Paula's wedding because she'd found herself pregnant months before and my parents objected to her appearing pregnant at the wedding. The night before the ceremony Paula had sobbed over our little sister's absence.

"I'll never forget this, Behba," she said softly. "I'll never forget that my sister isn't here." She did not say it vengefully; she said it miserably, as if this rite of passage were incomplete without Marla.

And it was. Though the big wedding was elegant, lavish even, the weather seemed to pick up an undercurrent of my sister's mood and a freak ice storm savaged the reception. Ice sleet pinged against the windows at the wedding reception where we danced, spinning inside a hotel that would soon be covered in solid swirls like frosting on the many-tiered wedding cake. Delicate and treacherous, the ice prevented anyone from leaving the parking lot; my uncle, who prides himself on his Midwest winter driving, endured three hours sliding around solid ice ruts in his car before he gave up and joined the rest of the wedding guests whom my father had to house in the Atlanta Hilton. During those expensive, icy days at the Hilton, we continued the celebration with a skeleton hotel staff bringing us room service. It was a riotous good time, except we still missed our third sister.

"We're just not complete without you," Paula called to tell Marla.

"Well, I wish I was there with y'all," she said wistfully. "I really do. I wish we were together." She was silent a moment, then asked, "When do you think we'll all be together again?"

I stared at Paula, who was on the extension phone. And I knew somehow that we three sisters would not be in synch again, not for a long while. Even though we might attend family reunions, even travel together, we were all headed in different directions—Paula to her difficult marriage, Marla into single motherhood, and I into a permanent Western retreat from my family, first in Colorado, then Arizona, and at last the Northwest tip of the continent in Seattle. "If you run any farther away from us," Paula often jokes, "you'll be in the Pacific Ocean."

Have I really run away from my sisters? If so, distance has not resolved any of the difficult or deeply ingrained dance steps in the lifelong movement of these sisters of mine. They challenge and disconcert me, they embrace and astonish me. Most of all, they keep me on my toes in this triangle, this sisters' minuet.

Part Two

Sisterhoods:
A Natural History

3

Other Species,
Other Sisters

There were a few advantages to my sister Paula's marrying a man who was almost always at odds with her sisters. The first was the three remarkable daughters they created together and the second was the fact that Aaron's family had lived in Key West for generations—so those turquoise coral Keys and lush Everglades, the territory of my own family's Seminole ancestors, became a second home to us. What we also discovered there in the Florida Keys was a second sisterhood, what my nieces call our "other family." By this they mean the group of bottlenose dolphins we've been visiting with for the past decade at a research center in Key Largo. My search for sisterhood would not be complete without beginning with the biology and natural history of the female bonding which, for many species other than our own, is the basis of group stability and survival.

There is a strong sisterhood among the animals and the study of this female bonding has recently been the focus of more research as women scientists themselves take to the field, living alongside animals as diverse as elephants, hyenas, lions, dolphins, and chimpanzees. Just as human psychology has finally turned to the study of the sibling bonds, so animal research has begun to study the complex female-

female relationships among our fellow, or perhaps I should say, *sister* creatures.

In my own family, these sister creatures are as beloved as any of our relatives. In fact, we owe the survival of Paula's youngest daughter to the dolphins. It all began in a hurricane in 1987 when Paula and Aaron, with their two daugthers, Lauren and Lindsay, got waylaid en route to a family reunion in Key West. Paula called me in Seattle where I sat reading an article about a marine mammal research and education center in Key Largo, Florida. Dolphins and other cetaceans have long fascinated me; as a child I had an imaginary friend who was an ichthyosaurus, the early ancestor of dolphins.

"I'm bummed and bored, sis," Paula sighed on the phone. "Aaron's out windsurfing in the tail end of this hurricane, of course. The girls and I are stuck here in this motel. They're bouncing on the beds but I can hardly move. I'm so big, so 'bout-to-bust, I can't remember the last time I saw my toes."

My sister was eight months pregnant with Lissy; she'd stopped windsurfing with her daredevil husband only in her seventh month. Stillness and waiting have never been my sister's strong suits. I could hear her restlessness all the way across the continent.

"Where are you?" I asked.

"Key Largo." Her voice was laconic.

I started screaming, flapping my newspaper in excitement. "This is incredible! You've got to go see these dolphins. I was just reading about them. Oh, do it for me . . . please, sis!"

"Whoa, there, gal," Paula laughed. "We'll do our best. Give me the scoop."

As it turned out, the research education center was within walking distance of their motel. By that evening Paula and the girls were on their car phone calling me. "You've got to come, Behba!" Lauren, the elder daughter, cried. "The dolphins are in this big saltwater lagoon off the ocean. They swim out into the ocean every couple days—not like those concrete prisons in zoos. These dolphins are still just girls, like us."

"Yeah, their names are Samantha, Dreamer, Nikki, Sarah . . . Dinghy, Genie, Squirt, and Spunky," chimed in her sister, Lindsay.

"Right," Lauren continued, "and those dolphins never blink. They look you right in the eyes. They like kids best, not grown-ups! They ditch most of the adults and hang out together in the lagoon's human-free zones."

"But they did choose Mom," Lindsay reminded her older sister. Lindsay is the little scientist, the calm and contemplative middle sister often in the wings of her older sister's passionate daily dramas. "That's because she's pregnant and they wanted to be Mom's midwives."

"The dolphin chased everyone out of the lagoon after a while," Paula explained. "Then the females circled me so fast I was frightened, but the researchers told me it was a protective response to my late-term pregnancy. Dolphins use sonar and echolocation like our ultrasound to hear the fetal heartbeat." She laughed. "The dolphin midwives were ready; but I'm not . . . not yet, I don't think."

As a nurse, Paula was more than casually interested in this other species' behavior around her pregnancy. The researchers had told her that dolphins have often deciphered the pregnant condition of women before they know it themselves. Dolphins have been known to signal, through repeated probing of their sensitive beaks and echolocation scanning, the tumors, heart conditions, and nervous system problems in humans who enter their watery element.

I could sense something my sister wasn't telling me—an echo of her concern. There was a gravity in Paula like an almost imperceptible ripple on a placid pool. "What's wrong," I asked and there was sudden silence from all on the car phone.

"Well, it's kind of strange . . ." Paula hesitated. "The nurse in me doesn't really believe it, but the mother in me says *listen up!*"

"To what? Listen to what?" I demanded. There are times when Paula draws out her stories for optimum suspense; as a storyteller I understand her technique, but I rarely appreciate it when I am on the receiving end.

"The researchers were concerned with the way the female dolphins were behaving around me. The dolphins seemed very upset by my condition, as if . . . as if there were something wrong with my fetus. The researchers said maybe I should check it out . . . that the dolphins' concern indicated something not quite right."

The researcher in my medical sister did check it out; but all ultrasounds seemed normal. Normal up until the birth when it was discovered that newborn Lissy had a rare blood incompatibility requiring transfusion. Paula had heeded the dolphin midwives' concern, and remembering that her second child had been born with a milder form of this ABO-negative blood incompatibility, Paula asked a woman friend to stand by to donate compatible blood if needed. "The dolphins' alarm was not lost on me," Paula said. "I knew they could sonar the baby's placenta better than any of our ultrasound equipment. Their good midwifing made me extra careful."

Because of this caution, the transfusion from Paula's friend was on hand to be given the day after Lissy was born. "She was so lethargic and pale lying in my arms," Paula remembered. "Her tiny lips were white and she was so sickly she didn't nurse. Her bilirubin was rising at an alarming rate. After the transfusion, it was astonishing to watch Lissy just turn pink and start glowing with health as my girlfriend's new blood coursed through her little veins, healing her." Lissy was in intensive care for two weeks, all went well, and she survived. In her newborn photo she was, like all my sister's C-section daughters, beautifully round in her face, with brilliant blue-green eyes, the luminous color of tropical lagoons. She has her Cuban father's dark skin and her mother's delicate mouth. The only sign of her dangerous birth condition was a slight jaundice, which disappeared soon after she left the hospital.

That first encounter with the dolphin midwives may have saved Lissy's life; it certainly changed our lives. For almost a decade my sister and nieces and I have returned to this same group of female dolphins like an extended family. This embrace of another species, another sisterhood, has taught me that we humans are not here alone, that there are other minds and skills to which our species can apprentice ourselves. While my first and lifelong commitment will always be to the dolphin sisters at that Florida Keys research center, my family's fascination with dolphins and other whales has grown to include many encounters with wild cetaceans in their natural habitat— from watching gray whale migrations off California coasts with my brother's daughters to listening to humpback whales in the South Pacific to zipping full-speed along with wild bottlenose dolphins while boating in the Everglades. I know I'll spend the rest of my life exploring this cetacean bond. And a few of my nieces and nephews claim they'll be marine mammal biologists when they grow up. "Should we call ourselves a pod, do you think?" Lindsay has asked in all seriousness.

In the fall of 1993 when we journeyed to visit our extended animal family, an extraordinary blessing awaited us. We were in need of gifts that year, because that was when Paula at last filed for divorce from Aaron. She'd left him six months earlier. But this time she did not return to him. This time she would never return to Aaron. Their divorce was a grueling process and as we journeyed to the dolphins, we were all somewhat subdued. We arrived at the research center, to be met by the director who embraced us with a smile. "Guess what?" he asked the girls.

They were suspicious of surprises, with their lives turned upside down in this messy divorce, so they hesitated just a moment before asking in a chorus, "What?"

"Dinghy just gave birth today to her newborn—the calf is only eight hours old. And because Dinghy knows you all so well, you can come sit by the lagoon and pay your respects."

Very quietly we sat by the edge of the lagoon. "It's off limits to all but family," Lauren informed us proudly.

In the same green lagoon swam Genie with a calf delivered just weeks earlier. Protectively the two new mothers swam with their small calves all but hidden beneath their pectoral fins. It was astonishing to see such tiny dolphins and we felt blessed to witness and welcome these new calves.

"Look," one of the researchers whispered to us. "The newborn is still wrinkled from being folded up inside the womb."

Wonderingly, we watched as the mothers and calves swam slowly nearer and nearer to us. It was obvious that Genie's weeks-old calf had already mastered the most crucial element of all dolphin life—breathing. Dolphins are conscious breathers, which means if they are caught in a tuna net or knocked out, they will drown; their autonomic nervous system does not breathe for them as ours does. Learning to breathe in synch with the mother is a vital survival skill which Dinghy's brand-new dolphin calf had not yet perfected. Often a sister or aunt to the newborn dolphin will aide in the birthing process by lifting the newborn to the surface for air after it corkscrews out, tail flukes first, from the mother. In this way other females in the pod are crucial to the survival of the young. They also babysit and teach the newborns, alongside the mother.

We had to laugh as we saw Dinghy's brand-new baby dolphin

trying to learn the dolphin art of breathing in synch with the mother. Gone was the gliding arc and usual flow of the dolphin dance of surfacing, breathing, and diving together. Instead this little one shot up out of the lagoon, snout-first, took a tiny gasp, and then dove back under Dinghy's mothering fin. It was almost comical to see the youngster so awkwardly astride his mother; yet we all knew the gravity of this newborn's life. Half of firstborn dolphins die, even in the wild, because their mother's milk is poisoned with PCBs and other human pollution dumped into the oceans. If a newborn calf dies, the mother will carry the tiny corpse until it disintegrates. What does this tell us about a dolphin mother's capacity for grieving? This calf was Dinghy's second-born and his chances for survival increased, since Dinghy had already purged much of the toxins stored in her blubber when her firstborn calf had died. This lactating purge is what researchers believe accounts for the female dolphins' longer life span.

"Be very, very quiet," the researcher hushed us. "Dinghy is really nervous, especially after what happened with her last newborn . . . but she doesn't seem to mind you all around her and the calf."

Lissy and I sat down gingerly on the edge of the lagoon, Lissy perched in my lap.

"Let's breathe with them," Lissy said suddenly. "We'll help teach that baby how to breathe, too."

It was an inspired idea and I told Lissy so, reminding myself that the word *inspire* also meant "to breathe in." We sat silent, except for our deep breathing in synch as Dinghy and her newborn circled the lagoon, keeping their distance. But Genie suddenly veered right toward us, full speed. At the last moment she turned her head sideways in that familiar wide-angle dolphin gaze—unblinking, brown, and benevolent eye holding ours, considering us deeply.

"She recognizes us," Lissy whispered happily, eyeing Genie. "You know me, don't you, Genie? You knew me before I was born!"

As if sounding Lissy's small heart, Genie emitted a short burst of creaking whistles from her glossy blowhole and suddenly her calf leapt out from under her fin, over her body, splashing our feet. Lissy and I laughed and whistled in delight, which sent the young calf skittering around the lagoon in a series of tiny leaps, like a victory lap, before returning dutifully to Genie's sensitive side and again taking up their breathing duet in perfect synchrony.

On her side of the lagoon, Dinghy watched this land-sea dance of human and her own kind. She circled closer and with each sweep by us, she turned sideways, held our gaze. This was Dinghy as we had never seen her—tender and inward-turning, when before motherhood she had been high-spirited and wildly engaging, especially with children. Lissy and I grew very still, breathing now in deep meditation, as if we were swimming with Dinghy again in our dreamtime. The fragrant autumn heat, the smell of herring and saltwater, the hoarse pelicans flying overhead—it all slowed into this: We breathe in and out together, the dolphin and calf surface and exhale their fast *twoosh,* then dive and disappear. There was one moment when I realized we were all breathing in ensemble, woman, child, dolphin mother, newborn. And the next moment, Dinghy was before us, turning slow motion in the water, her fin lifted to reveal the tiniest dolphin I have ever seen. The newborn was only three feet long, its tiny tail flukes splashing awkwardly as it shot to the surface, took a little breath, then dived back beneath Dinghy's fin like a tadpole.

My eyes blurred and Lissy was crying softly, too. "She *showed* us her baby like we're really family now." Lissy told Dinghy, "We love your baby, too. Like you loved me when I wasn't born yet."

Dinghy floated a moment more near our feet, her eye holding Lissy's gaze. "I'm not just a girl," Lissy breathed. I'm a midwife." Once again Dinghy lifted her fin for our last look at her newborn. Then she continued her slow circles. She had allowed us that intimate glimpse and now she seemed to rest and let us just keep breathing with her, with her tiny calf.

Lissy, Lauren, and Lindsay resolved to pray for the newborn dolphins every day. They well knew the dim survival rates for cetacean calves. Every night when the girls said their bedtime prayers, they included the dolphins and their newborn calves in the same breath as they did me, their parents, and friends.

"Well," my sister Paula still teases when she calls to report on the nightly prayers, "we may be a broken family but we're still a pod." And those new dolphins are still surviving, still very much with us.

Believing myself part of a human and cetacean pod, I often wonder about these deep alliances with animals and how they shape our lives. Having opened to another species, entered their element, I've yielded to their experience and control, and this surrender has completely changed the way I see interspecies relationships. I feel profoundly imprinted by another animal intelligence that is equal to my own, as well as unfathomable. As I have studied the marine biology of these animals, I've grown impatient with the detached, so-called objective scrutiny of the mostly male scientists. For too long their research has overlooked the essential female bonding for group survival, this animal sisterhood.

As Denise Herzing, director of the Wild Dolphin Project, says, "All observation is intimate." Herzing has studied the same pod of spotted dolphins off the Bahamas for the past twelve years. She continues, "Sure, we have the hard data, but what this research is really about is connections between animals, and then with humans. Have you ever noticed that particularly women researchers will name the animals they study?" Herzing and I have often discussed the sisterhood of animals, as well as the growing sisterhood of researchers who bring their distinctly female point of view to studying animal behavior. When we look at the natural world around us from a feminine perspective, one that values relationship, connection, and female bonding, we see other species have much to teach us about survival, cooperation, and long-term intimacy.

It's natural for women to have a history, a biology, and a spiritual tradition. Sisterhood has had so long to wait to rediscover these lost parts of our bond; but they are there—whether among animals or humans. If we can remember ourselves, we won't lose the natural history of our sisterhoods ever again.

4

Sister as Pod and Pachyderm

My decade of swimming with dolphins has confirmed my belief that strong sisterhood is essential to the survival of a species. In the wild, dolphin pods are highly socialized groups in which complex female bonding assures the well-being and nurturance not only of the young, but also of the entire pod. Denise Herzing has focused intently on the female relationships in one pod of more than seventy-five dolphins and as a result, these wild dolphins have accepted and socialized her into their pod, allowing her access and intimacy unusual in cetacean studies.

Herzing cites three female dolphins in particular as examples of evolving sisterhood. Rosemole, Little Gash, and Mugsy were companions from infancy, raised under the close watch of their mothers and the elder females who make up an essential element of all dolphin pods. Almost inseparable, all three young females found their relationship shifting when Rosemole and Mugsy became pregnant. They bonded with other pregnant and mothering dolphins, shifting alliances away from Little Gash, their former playmate. Rosemole and Mugsy were busy participating in the complex nurturance of newborns. Not only must the newborns be taught to breathe, fish, and understand the sophisticated structures of dolphin society and communication, but newborns often stay all their lives near their mothers to become doting aunts and later elders in the pod's highly socialized female infrastructure. The males in adolescence often travel together as bachelor pods which keep in loose contact with the female primary group. When Little Gash herself got pregnant, she again resumed her sisterly bond with Rosemole and Mugsy. The three are now as devoted to one another as they are to the welfare and safety of their young and the whole pod.

Keeping their offspring and pod safe is a job that falls to females of many species, especially cetaceans. And this is a vocation for which animals train all their lives. Consider the lifelong alliance within pods of orca and pilot whales. Male and female orcas will stay with their mother and her extended family from birth to death, an average life span of up to seventy years. This strong sisterhood is all about ensuring the survival of everyone. In an article by renowned cetacean scientists Kenneth S. Norris and Karen Pryor entitled, "Some Thoughts on Grandmothers," the researchers cite the new studies on a pilot whale phenomenon: There are large groups of postreproductive females, some more than a decade past possible reproduction—and some of them are still lactating. Norris and Pryor wonder if this is explained only by the theory that these older females are nursing other female orcas' young while the mothers dive deep for food. But there must be something else at work here, Karen Pryor adds in a note all her own: "So the only use for postreproductive females is babysitting? I suggest that the role of postreproductive females in pilot whale schools may be as a repository of cultural information, such as the whereabouts of feeding grounds. . . . A dominant male may be replaced by a rival at any time. If long-term experience is necessary, for example to learn and remember the terrain beneath your feet or fins, then continuity of individuals in the group is vital: and older females can provide it." Pryor concludes that these postreproductive females provide an invaluable survival skill: "Their principle biological contribution might be to learn, remember, and transmit what pilot whales need to know."

Orca researcher Sara Heimlich-Boran notes, in the textbook *Behavioral Biology of Killer Whales*, that the close sisterhood of juvenile females suggests that "same sex may be as important as age in determining relationships" and that "associations between mothers and barren females showed the most stability over time." Because the mother-progeny bond is of primary importance, the strong alliance between barren females and mothers implies that the "relationship is one of kinship." And kinship among aunts and sisters and mothers is centered on cooperation and caretaking.

This cooperation is so extremely close that it even involves the most basic element of life: breath. Orca pods, like many cetacean societies, form respiratory units to teach their offspring the crucial skill of conscious breathing. Especially among orcas, these respiratory units—surfacing and inhaling in synch—are responsible for the survival of the entire pod. Imagine timing one's every breath to that of the mother, who in her turn is synchronizing her swimming with others in the maternal subgroup.

What might happen in our own species if we patterned ourselves on the intimate breathing relations of the orcas? As a corollary here, the statistics on Sudden Infant Death Syndrome in this country are staggering, the highest in the world. In Third World countries, the incidence of SIDS is minimal. One reason, scientists theorize, is that in the less industrial nations, babies often sleep with mothers or in a family bed. When the infant stops breathing, as if simply forgetting this strange new respiratory chore, the sound of adult breathing nearby reminds or stimulates the newborn to continue breathing. Perhaps human mothers can learn from maternal orcas about how to keep our newborns alive.

There is something else we might emulate about orcas in our human society. The male orca, unlike dolphins, will more often than not remain with his mother for his entire life; the mother's daughter will also stay near, breeding and bringing her calves into the maternal group. Among dolphins, when the male calf leaves to join his adolescent male buddies, he will carry with him his mother's signature whistle which will allow him to easily reaccess the maternal subgroup. Some researchers believe that the mother's signature whistle does, in fact, establish the male calf's status in the matrilinear hierarchy of the whole pod. The female calf, while knowing her mother's whistle, will develop a signature whistle all her own, thus allowing her to stay in the maternal group alongside her mother without confusing herself with that mother, and forming her own identity.

Female animals are most responsible for the identity, survival, and long-term stability of the pod. The intricate female-female bonding of grandmothers, aunts, mothers, and barren companions to nurse, caretake, and teach the next generation is called *allomothering*. It is an essential practice not only among dolphins, but among many species. And it is particularly poignant in the remarkable endangered species elephants.

Among elephants, as among cetaceans, the real story of survival is not about survival of the fittest, but survival of the whole group. And it is the females who assure this group survival the most dramatically. Female elephants are the most stable element in the elephant society, while the males form nomadic, homo-exclusive subgroups that appear only for reproduction and then rove off again, leaving the females to protect the next generation.

Cynthia Moss has spent the past twenty years living side by side with African elephants. Her study of one particular herd and its matriarch, Echo, gives us an intimate window on this species, as well as an illuminating look at the sisterhood among elephants. As Moss muses in her book *Echo of the Elephants:* "In more frivolous moments I think of the bull areas as all-male clubs." The elephant bulls "hang out with a few buddies or move about on their own. . . . I can sometimes almost picture them sitting around in leather armchairs reading *Wall Street Journal*s."

Elephant society is composed of family units of about eleven members; "a family consists of related adult females and their offspring, ranging from newborn calves to adolescent males and females up to about ten or eleven years old. Families are tight-knit with strong bonds between the adult females. Each family is led by the oldest female—the matriarch." Echo, matriarch of the African EB family, whom Moss has observed from her Land Rover and camps, has proven herself to be a mastermind of migrations, locating watering holes and protecting newborn and adolescent elephants. The males will stay within this female family until they are about fourteen and reach sexual maturity; the females remain within the same family and form intimate bonds with cousins, aunts, offspring. Moss remarks that "Females are rarely if ever alone, spending their whole lives surrounded by close relatives . . . mother and daughter, grandmother and granddaughter, sisters, aunt and niece, and cousins." The female elephants form fond bonds of affection and alliance and when they greet each other after being apart for brief periods, the females will elatedly trumpet, spin, flap ears, and release a tear-like substance from their eyes as if weeping with joy. These intense bonds of affection serve to strengthen the female group's chances of survival as they are ever-attuned to one another's needs and those of the offspring. There are several poignant photos in Moss's book of a tiny newborn huddling between the huge tree-trunk legs of maternal elephants standing like a forest of females against the predatory circling of lions or hyenas.

Death rituals in the elephant family are eerily reminiscent of our own rites. It's ironic that anthropologists have long maintained that the first sign of our species' humanness was Neanderthal man's burial of the dead. What does this mean when we now discover elephants burying their fallen companions? These massive creatures show deep grief over a fallen family member. They recognize bones of their own kind, often staying by their dead for days, performing a haunting dance with their feet, flinging dirt over the carcass, and placing palm fronds over it as if in burial.

When Echo's family came across the bleached bones of her daughter Emily—a very important female in their group—Emily's daughter and granddaughter examined the bones. "There was a palpable tension among them," Moss writes. "Eudora concentrated on Emily's skull, caressing the smooth cranium and slipping her trunk into the hollows in the skull. Echo was feeling the lower jaw, running her trunk along the teeth—the area used in greeting when elephants place their trunks in each other's mouths." This communion with the bones of their beloved Emily, who would have been matriarch after Echo's death, is a moving evocation of the rituals and intelligence of elephants, brought to us by a woman simply observing day after day in the field. This kind of research helps us know in a personal, connected way the cause and effect of poaching, culling elephant populations, and the wounds we inflict on families when we disrupt the intricate relationships of elephant societies. In fact, research has shown that if an elephant matriarch dies, her family suffers extreme trauma. The book *Dolphin Conferences, Elephant Midwives, and Other Astonishing Facts About Animals* reports that if a matriarch elephant dies, "survivors will mill around her body in panic. There can be total troupe disorganization, and sometimes familes never recover."

In a moving and eloquent essay on elephants in a recent *New York*

Review of Books, Elizabeth Marshall Thomas, author of *The Hidden Life of Dogs*, soundly takes to task the African game managers' policy of culling old elephants who are past their reproductive years. The natural world is not our farm, she argues, and agricultural production theories do not apply to wild animals, who do not require human control. Elephants are not simply commodities who yield ivory and elephant-foot wastebaskets. They, like our species, have an equal right to exist alongside us. The game wardens' management strategies of killing old elephants is woefully shortsighted, says Thomas. "Analogous in human beings would be to slaughter all CEOs and managers, all teachers, coaches, and librarians, all elected political leaders" and, one might add, all matriarchs. In fact, Thomas notes, elephants up to sixty years old were discovered to be either lactating (allomothering) or pregnant. And even when they do stop reproducing, what might an elephant matriarch still offer her family? It is just this question that such female scientists as Cynthia Moss have amply answered in their patient long-term research of elephants. When an extended elephant family loses its elders, especially its matriarchs, it is losing its grandmother guardians of survival.

Katharine Payne, who also researches the lives of elephants, dreams of a day when "people will value wild animals not for money but for who they are and what we can learn from them." With the matriarchal memory and sisterhood wisdom that guides a family to survive, the elephants not only offer humans a lesson in remembering the past and assuring the future, but also become a fascinating mirror as to how communication among animals reflects our own same-sex bondings.

Katharine Payne's research is a prime example of how women looking at the animal world can drastically change the way we view other species. Payne's particularly feminine skills of intimate observation revolutionized elephant research with her discovery of elephant communication. She found that elephants use a subtle subsonic or infrasound (below human hearing) language. Payne, who had studied music and biology and made many humpback whale song recordings with her husband, was in the Metro Washington Park Zoo in Portland, Oregon, when she noticed something odd about the elephant cage. "I repeatedly noticed a palpable throbbing in the air like distant thunder, yet all around me was silent," she wrote in her groundbreaking *National Geographic* article in 1989. Elephant researchers had

long been stymied by the fact that migrating elephants will suddenly
freeze midstep as one herd and lift their ears to the air, as if listening.
But what do they hear that humans can't? And how do the males
locate with uncanny accuracy a female elephant in estrus when she is
receptive only a few days every four or five years? Was there, in fact,
some communication among elephants that we hadn't yet discovered?

When Katharine Payne sensed the air throbbing around those cap-
tive elephants, she remembered the church pipe organ of her childhood
and how "the whole chapel would throb, just as the elephant room
did at the zoo." So she asked a very pragmatic, but inspired, question,
"Suppose the elephants communicate with one another by means of
calls too low-pitched for humans to hear?" With a research grant, she
recorded many of the same elephant populations currently being studied by her colleagues Cynthia Moss, Joyce Poole, and Iain and Oria
Douglas-Hamilton in Tanzania and Kenya. Payne discovered that
indeed the elephants were talking far below the level of human au-
ditory range. Imagine the rumbles of thunder just out of earshot, of
windy trumpets, volcano rumbles, and earthquake roars—that is the
language of elephants. And that explains why males come running
when the female broadcasts her receptivity, why there may be parallel
herds sounding each other over the African savannahs so they don't
all converge on the same watering hole at once. Imagine the elephants'
songs of estrus and migration booming a mile away, and being answered in a language so low we can only sense its hum like far-off
heat lightning. "The great majority of our recorded calls were made
by females," Payne reported. "Female behavior is richly illustrated by
their calls—mothers, calves, and baby-sitting sisters settling questions
of when to nurse or how far to wander. Probably the noisiness of
female groups enables males to learn much about the latter's location
and sexual state simply by listening . . ." And what the elephants are
listening to most is their "matriarchs with generations of memory in
their heads."

Listening intently to feminine wisdom, plotting subtle communication, societal and survival plans—this is what the sisterhood of animals and humans is all about. And much of this female-female
bonding and communication has been dismissed in all species by traditionally male scientists more interested in ranking top predators,

or recording male aggression and rivalry, than in studying the nurturance and stability of the entire group.

Many women scientists are still fighting to find funding for studies of female animal relationships. It seems that the sisterhoods of animals, like the sisterhood of humans, is often given less stature. As Sarah Blaffer Hrdy and George C. Williams have written in their 1983 article "Behavioral Biology and the Double Standard," there is a sociobiological myth of the passive female: "Males are depicted as active, enterprising and adventurous, as well as aggressive and promiscuous; females as passive, reactive, and coy." This bias has perpetuated many popular misapprehensions about primate as well as human behavior. This sexist double standard, say the scientists, promotes a Victorian (and earlier) attitude which, in turn, reflects our human gender bias. Overly focused on male interaction, the scientific double standard limited its female research to mother-infant relations, overlooking the intricate web of grandmother, aunt, and sibling females, many of whom practice profound and crucial allomothering.

This sexist bias on the part of scientists also perpetuates the myth that an animal hierarchy is strictly dependent upon the dominance of the male members. Primate research has been particularly guilty of such male-oriented bias: "In spite of findings on the relative permanence of female relationships . . . the conviction persisted that males had to be the prevailing influence upon primate social life," say Hrdy and Williams. Such phenomena as allomothering, female cooperation and hierarchy, and female reproductive choice were simply overlooked. "Traditions of male-focused behavioral research have not merely meant a detour in our efforts to understand female behaviors, but also a temporary block for understanding the full complexity of animal mating systems. They have also led to a misuse of the biological evidence to bolster sexist preconceptions."

Fortunately, even as Hrdy and Williams were writing this article, more women were entering the field and publishing research on animal behavior. In contemporary primatology, there are the studies of the three founding mothers, the "Trimates": Jane Goodall's monumental study of chimpanzees, the late Dian Fossey's passionate protection of gorillas, and Birute Galdikas's study of orangutans. Because these women patiently lived many years alongside primates—for example, it took Galdikas twelve years to habituate a single orangutan to accept her presence—they gleaned radically new insights into primate behavior. Tracing the history of how the Trimates changed primatology, a recent issue of *Science* devoted to women in science celebrates "the women's capacity to empathize with their subjects, seeing them as individuals whose life histories influenced the structure of the group." Though some scientists invariably dismissed Goodall's early findings as sentimental, she is today considered a pathfinder. As another prominent primatologist, Alison Jolly of Princeton University, says of Goodall, "She essentially redefined what it is to be a human being." Goodall herself notes, "Letting nature, including the animal, go its own way, I think is more female—at least in our society. It requires a certain kind of patience to put up with something you can't control."

Patience, empathy, long-term alliances, these skills also describe the research styles of many of the female scientists now at work in the field of animal behavior and research. As Sir David Attenborough wrote in his foreword to Cynthia Moss's book, "Watching animals in cages running round mazes and solving problems devised for them by experimenters . . ." was the generalized tradition of old-school orthodox scientists. Attenborough declares that Moss "has demonstrated that a scientist can be both objective and—using the word in its most literal sense—compassionate."

Denise Herzing of the Wild Dolphin Project echoes this particularly feminine trait of forming empathetic relations with the animals we study. "When you consider that the first science was that of astronomy, studying distant objects," Herzing exlains, "you can easily trace how we've perpetuated an old system of objectifying what we observe. But studying the far-off solar systems is not a good model for understanding animals who coexist with us in a complicated, interactive system. That research requires closeness and relationship, as well as long-term observation."

The rational mind with its telescopes and scientific distancing has dominated science for so long that we've lost our connection with nature and so ourselves, says Herzing. "It's the same problem with how we're treating the planet," Herzing commented. "Our objective, detached, unrelated scientific stance has allowed us to exploit nature for ourselves, as if we were not part of the whole system."

Biochemist Dr. Linda Jean Shepherd notes in her book *Lifting the*

Veil: The Feminine Face of Science, that Aristotle wrote that a woman was basically an "infertile man with an animal soul . . ." Since Aristotle, science has often limited itself to measuring and quantifying, rather than intuiting the whole. In strong contrast, Shepherd's book explores the new scientists, many of them female, who integrate receptivity, feeling, and relatedness into their research. In describing a gathering of female cell biologists, Shepherd portrays their discussion as "warm, personal . . . passionate. When they talked about cells, they became positively rapturous. Their voices were alternately enthusiastic and spirited, then hushed, tender, and awed." The scientists declared that under the microscope the intricate world, from keratin fibers to cancer cells, was pretty. Concludes Shepherd, "these researchers felt related to the object of their investigation, touched by the beauty of nature, rather than coldly observing nature from a superior position. Such feelings of awe and reverence do not prejudice or bias results. Instead, they create an openness to learning." And finally, "this passion to know nature as a beloved continues to motivate an underground of modern scientists in all disciplines."

Love, relationship, intimate observation—these are what the feminine brings to the hard sciences. And this point of view balances the biased preoccupation with competition and male aggression which is part of, but not the whole story. The whole story is that of interdependence, collaboration, and long-term commitment—exactly what the sisterhood of animals shows us.

If female animals are often responsible for the survival and stability of their species, perhaps we humans can model ourselves on this sisterhood, which embraces the grandmothers down to the daughters. When we look around at human societies we see some very dim chances for our own survival. Medical experts estimate that by the year 2000 there will be forty million people infected with the AIDS virus. A *Newsweek* report in the spring of 1994 linked the 50 percent drop in male sperm count since 1938 to pollution in our waters, and PCBs, when decomposing, affect the body like estrogen. Testicular and breast cancers, shriveling penises among humans and animals, says *Newsweek*, are only some of the known effects of this pollution. If we are going to survive such ravages as a species, we might consider the idea of allomothering ourselves as well as our sister creatures.

Already the roles of extended families and nontraditional families are showing how allomothering can benefit and protect our next generation. Social historian Stephanie Coontz, whose 1992 book *The Way We Never Were: American Families and the Nostalgia Trap*, disinvested us of our illusions about the "normal" or nuclear family, told a *New Age Journal* interviewer: "There are plenty of studies done that suggest that a variety of caregivers, if they're consistent, and a variety of exposure to many adults, is extremely healthy for children." Coontz cites other cultures, such as Hawaiian, in which an adoption system, *hanai,* links "extended kin and neighbors even more tightly" than any nuclear family. "If you were my sister," Coontz said, "and didn't have a child, I might say, oh, take one of mine and raise it as the *hanai* mom." The insistence, especially in this country, on an idealized nuclear family is "a tragically limited sense of love," according to Coontz, herself a single mother who has called upon the alliance of close friends and family to assist in parenting her children. Coontz commented that she finds herself better off with such allomothering than many mothers in a traditional nuclear family. For example, when she had a C-section, she had many friends offer sustained, long-term help in caring for her and her children. In contrast, she saw new mothers around her suffer greatly because everyone assumed they were in a relationship and the husband was helping out. But the husband was working and too often the new mother was left to fend for herself. Concluded Coontz, "Most societies in human history have felt that parenting is far too large a job to even be entrusted to two people, no less one—and so they have lots of wider networks."

Such a wide net is that of the sisterhood bond. It has worked so well for animals, but has been devalued in humans in favor of some notion of a nuclear family that is more and more of a myth. The fact is that with divorce rates soaring, sisterhoods are what keep many American families afloat.

Whenever I visit my sister before our dolphin swims, I am caught up in the dizzying and deeply organized daily life of her sister society. To her credit, my sister managed to keep her sisterhood intact during the long years of her marriage in which her husband was jealous of and resented her strong female friendships. When she was divorced, that sisterhood took up its unashamed, rightful residence in Paula's routine. On any given day there will be some three to five friends dropping by with their children, doing chores, baby-sitting, helping out in every crisis. Many of my sister's friends are women doctors, lawyers, real estate agents, hospital administrators, and teachers. Together they coordinate and raise money for their children's school. They advise each other on everything from surgery to lawsuits. And most of all they embrace each other and each other's children like allomothers, with a fond, careful eye on the future.

It is not too big a leap, then, to imagine that allomothering can occur between species—that nurturing and altruism don't have to be confined to our own kind. Can our definition of a pod expand to embrace other nonhuman alliances? What would happen if we reconnected with our animal sisterhoods to work for the survival of all species and of this planet we share? We can forge sisterly bonds between species, bonds which focus on empathy, communication, species stability, and survival.

The first lesson the animal sisterhood teaches us is to bond deeply with one another and to develop strong female alliances as a basic survival skill. The second lesson is about connection to the whole, the environment, this Sister Earth that directly nurtures all her species. This conscious connection to the earth and animal knowledge might at first be painful—for as we reconnect with nature, we often feel her devastation.

A psychologist friend of mine told me that after the vast oil spill in Prince William Sound in Alaska, every one of her clients, particularly the women, brought their grief over this environmental disaster into their therapy sessions. "Their despair was deeply personal," my friend said, "because they know it's all connected—that what happens to the wildlife and waters happens eventually to us." What my friend told her clients as they talked about their pain over the ravages of our natural world is that it is healing to grieve, to praise, to connect emotionally with nature; that nature itself is exactly what therapy is all about: finding balance and well-being within the Self and within the whole world.

Connecting nature and our own inner worlds is what indigenous peoples have always taught—from the aborigines to the Native Americans. Recently there is a new movement called "ecopsychology," which finds a profound resonance and healing between nature and psychology. Two articulate voices for this movement are Theodore Roszak, the author of *The Voice of the Earth*, and Melissa Nelson, the editor of *Ecopsychology Newsletter* in Berkeley, California. Roszak talks about "the ecological unconscious" as being that sympathetic bond between ourselves and nature. By merging our own psychological health with that of the environment, we are participating in a survival strategy very similar to that of the animals who have never had the illusion of separation or dominion over nature that our sciences have lent us. As Melissa Nelson comments, "What I am discovering is that the health of the mind and the health of the earth cannot be seen as different." She adds, "In indigenous thinking, certain knowledge, certain stories, and certain places are known only by a few, or maybe only one person. That person has been specially trained and prepared to receive those stories or to go to special places."

This reminds me of those elder female elephants who have memorized the migration paths, the watering holes, the nurturing or healing techniques to assure the survival of their whole herd. Knowing the stories of one's sisterhood—whether herd, pod, or human tribe—is a vital survival skill. What we need now are Sister Pods consciously reconnecting, telling the stories between species, and working together to include all species.

Women don't have to be living in the field with wild animals to connect on a daily level with the animal sisterhood. Simple acts in one's own local ecosystem are as important as discovering the language of elephants. For example, at a grassroots level we can get involved in preservation of habitat or ecological education, or volunteer for raptor rehabilitation or even feral cat rescue.

Every time I visit my sister Paula and my nieces, we all reunite with our dolphin sister pod. It is a relationship that will last as long as we are all alive. And someday, if possible, I'd like to be part of these dolphins' rehabilitation into the wild, just as John Lilly's dolphin companions, Joe and Rose, were successfully released back into their native ocean. And just as now in the Florida Keys there is a project to rehabilitate ex-navy and ex-captive dolphins for return to the wild.

Recently while on a humpback whale research trip to Hawaii, I had the great good fortune to kayak into a warm-water bay and find myself suddenly surrounded by a sister pod of sleek spinner dolphins.

"We're in the middle of their nursery," our kayak guide whispered as the three of us paddled slowly through deep, turquoise waters.

Six dorsal fins swam close behind me, their *twoosh, twoosh* a fast, intimate exhalation, like a musical, synchronized sigh.

Then there were more dolphin inspirations as thirty or so spinners swam close, circling us. At the sight of so many wild dolphins I leaned over in wonder and capsized. Plunged underwater, I was laughing so much I swallowed salty gulps of ocean. Then I heard them, that familiar high-pitched *click* and *whirr* like a cross between a Geiger counter and a small jet engine. I floated, holding my breath and listening and smiling as the nursery pod circled me, spinning through the waves.

Whenever I swim with dolphins, I can feel the communication. First, there is that calming quiet of my nervous system as I leave gravity above and float—warm water like an intimate second skin in perfect and complete embrace of me. Then there is the dolphin signature whistling and sonar like a much-loved song, lulling and caressing my body from the inside outward, along each limb until my fingers and toes feel radiant, electric. Ecstasy eases into every ache and hidden hurt in my body and I stretch out as if in a serene flying dream. Only, this rapture is underwater and accompanied by the clicking, kind scrutiny of an alien intelligence I can only begin to fathom.

The dolphins always surprise me with their tenderness. I tried to synchronize my breathing with the dolphins and when I lifted my face, I saw several spinners leaping up, somersaulting, then diving back into the sea, their wake splashing over my back. I attempted my human version of a signature whistle, complete with rapid-fire gurgles and bleeps. It seemed to amuse and interest the nursery pod because they all suddenly cruised closer in a dazzling display of acrobatic dolphin dance. Imagine dozens of dolphins speeding by in a blur of silver and gray skin, ultrasound, and curve of fin, streaking past, in one breath, as if one body. Inside my body their speed and sound registers like a trillion ricochets, tiny vibrations echoing off my ribs, within each lobe of my lungs, and spinning inside my labyrinthian brain like new synapses.

Then I was alone for a moment. I drifted through the depths so lost in this watery dreamtime that my mind was also adrift. It is always during these meditative underwater moments that the dolphins seem most to cherish their human companions. Suddenly I saw out of the corner of each eye three dolphins flanking me—and among them were several tiny dorsal fins—newborns guarded by their nursery pod. I was accepted inside their pod, surrounded by fast spinners who slowed to accompany my pace. They kept me in their exact center for what seemed an hour, and it was only then that I understood what it feels like to be fully adopted into the deep, welcoming physical communion of dolphins.

I am pod, I felt, with no sense of my single self; *I belong.*

Mystics may call it divine union, this melding of minds, bodies, and souls, this solitude that suddenly opens into the solace of *We are one*. If dolphins are known to be self-aware, they also show us this soul-mingling and connection which our human species only glimpses in rare spiritual insights. Perhaps this is what dolphins have spent their long evolution achieving: Instead of changing the environment around them, they have changed themselves; those big brains are attuning themselves to one another and the natural world. Dolphins bring their whole mind to bear upon the skills of communication and group survival—maybe that's what they've been doing these thirty million years longer than humans have been around: seeking to survive together as a whole. Meanwhile, we've been battling and selecting who among us will survive, never imagining that we are all humans, all one pod.

It was time to ease myself out of the middle of this nursery pod and back up into my kayak—a watery feat I accomplished with much less grace than what my dolphin companions possessed. They were executing perfect leaps and gymnastic spirals all around me. From the sea level height of my kayak I recognized with delight several mother-calf duos accompanied by what must have been aunts, sisters, and perhaps even a few brother scouts swimming together in their protective pod.

I, too, felt protected and nurtured in this dolphin nursery, made up mostly of strong females concerned with the survival of their next generation. And I wished my own human nursery-sisterhood of Paula and my nieces could be with me in these expansive, warm waters to meet this wild pod. If there is anything I hope to teach my nieces and nephews as an elder aunt, it will be this vision of animals as our brothers and sisters—all born and belonging together as family, as lifelong pod.

If listening to our female elders is what has often assured the well-being of an entire species, then perhaps we human beings can learn to listen again to animals such as the dolphins and elephants who have been on this earth so much longer than our species.

Katharine Payne ends her book, *Elephants Calling*, with a plea that every sister pod and pachyderm and human tribe might take to heart. "I try to help people understand what the world is losing," she writes. "It is losing deep voices—and some of the richest sounds that have ever been heard are in the songs of whales. It is losing great listeners—and the most intense listening I have ever observed is the listening of elephants, which unites and bonds their peaceful society. . . . If we learn to listen as often and as well as elephants do, it is possible that listening will keep the world safe."

Keeping the world safe by listening: Now that is a very feminine concept, one that every sisterhood knows to be true. In listening to the women in this book tell their sister stories, I've been moved to hear how many times those stories are about keeping one's sisters, one's family, one's tribe, and one's world safe. As always, a survival skill is in remembering, or discovering, a lost language, of elephants, of sisterhood.

5

Girls of God: Sisters as Tribe

In the Zulu language, her tribal name is *Ntombizenko*, which means "Girls of God." This name was given in benediction by her Anglican minister father, and was meant to include all her five sisters, of which she was the last. In South Africa, every black child had three names: a mandatory English name, a Zulu name, and a tribal name. So this last daughter of a family that had struggled to migrate from the rural Zululand to city life, was called Jeanne Zenko Zulu. She was the only one of the daughters raised in the lush harbor city of Durban, in a house on a small acreage that her mother's family bought them. Most other urban Zulus lived in Durban's two-room, look-alike cinderblock dwellings that apartheid dictated as the separate black sections. As the first black bishop in the South African Anglican church, Zenko's father devoted his considerable political and negotiating skills to working within the church to end apartheid and establish equality. One of the original founders of the Inkatha black freedom movement which would later clash with the African National Congress (ANC) in the struggle to establish an African power base, Bishop Alphaeus Zulu was a visionary and a heroic figure whom his older daughters feared, yet often protected from their own troubles.

"Girl trouble" among her sisters were the first conflicts Zenko re-membered. Traditionally, Zulus depended upon extended families, but the city had separated Zenko's family from their relatives. Adrift with-out aunts and other family, the five preteen and teenage Zulu sisters were free to experiment.

The oldest, Makhizi, rebelled against her father's high expectations by getting pregnant at fourteen and not finishing high school. Instead, Makhizi married and devoted herself to mothering many children. She is determinedly antipolitical. Her first child, a son, was raised by her parents and sisters alongside Zenko like a little brother.

"At every family gathering," Zenko remembered one bright fall day as she sat in her Seattle clapboard house in this country she has called home since 1970, "when my parents introduced their children, they would point to me and say, 'She's the last of our Zulu family.' But then there'd be this little boy beside me, my sister's child, with no introduction. He was just there. That's how it was in my family, we didn't talk about these things. And I, being the baby sister, didn't talk at all, because by the time I could get a sentence out, my sisters had already finished it for me. So I was very quiet, really. I learned to watch, stand back a little—it's sometimes good to be an observer."

Zenko is still quiet, still taking everything in with the thoughtful manner of a born observer. Her dark eyes are remarkable in their reticence, for while she directly meets one's gaze, this Zulu tribal daughter has a privacy about her, an inward-turning intensity that is at once dignified and detached. Her face is exquisite, with her high cheekbones and generous mouth; her smooth, unwrinkled skin is a rich, coffee color. She is turning fifty this year, but looks to be in her late thirties. Her twenty-three-year-old daughter, Jabulile, and twenty-two-year-old son, Themba, are all that betray Zenko's age. Her close-cropped curly hair is cupped by a bright red scarf with paisley yellow and orange patterns to complement her dark red sweatshirt and black pants. She is obviously an athlete, moving with grace and pur-pose and poise, a reminder that she founded the first tennis team in her all-black girls' boarding school. Zenko is also a singer and her voice is soft, with the melody and cadence of South African English. She speaks English and Zulu, but rejected the mandatory Afrikaans Dutch language—a rebellion that jeopardized her career as a nurse. "I hate that language," she said quietly, in her low, lilting voice. "It's so guttural . . . there's no music to it. You know, that's what the terrible riots of 1976 were all about. Blacks refusing to learn the Afrikaans language."

Zenko fell silent for a long while, as if to commemorate this unspeakable summer in her country's history—a summer when many black women in Soweto lost their jobs because they were searching for their murdered schoolchildren. That June, the Afrikaans government demanded that all black children be educated in the Boer language. When the blacks protested, countless of their children were "disappeared" into apartheid jails; multitudes of black boys and girls were gunned down in schoolyards. There is a phrase common in Afrikaans that amply explains why blacks might not want to learn this language: *Sit die kaffir in sy plek* ("Put the kaffir [black] in his place"). In Soweto, in the summer of 1976, that "place" was death.

Zenko Zulu has been witness, not only to the bloody, racist history of her native South Africa, but to the ironic sorrows of seeing apartheid's agonized politics played out in her immediate tribe. In Zenko's family the personal and political converge with often fatal consequences. From her more distant vantage point in America over the past decades, Zenko has been the sister to whom many of the other sisters turned for advice and for, again, that detached vision. "Sometimes my sisters tell me, 'It's easy for you to see, you're not here. You don't have to live in South Africa every day.' " She paused, and cocked her head as if listening to those sisters just out of earshot. "But it's because I'm *not* in South Africa that I can see what I see," she concluded.

What Zenko sees is a country corrupted by racism, but also confused over how to face a future in which blacks now at last take their rightful place in power and government. "I do not know what will happen," Zenko said, the week Nelson Mandela and Willem deKlerk jointly won the Nobel Peace Prize. "So much of my family is there. . . . I can only hope it will go well."

It has not gone well for one of her sisters. This was her beloved Bhikie, the second oldest sister, to whom Zenko is closest. Bhikie, in the tradition of four of this Zulu sister-tribe, is a nurse, the matron of a teaching hospital. Her high position has made Bhikie visible in her own right, beyond being the daughter of Bishop Zulu. Like her eldest sister, Makhizi, Bhikie wanted nothing of politics. Their father's

prestigious role as a black bishop in a denomination of white ministers
had left Bhikie with a desire to do her own work in medicine without
the continual intrusion of her country's political infighting. But
Bhikie's hospital was funded by the Zulu government, which was
fiercely Inkatha-controlled. And even though her father had helped
form Inkatha and was considered a revered founder, when Bhikie's
teenage kids started holding ANC meetings in her home, she found
her father's position was no protection. "One night," Zenko said, her
voice dropping to barely a whisper, "Bhikie and her family were sleeping when suddenly a bomb exploded just outside her window. All the
other windows were shattered and the house caught fire. It was a
miracle that the window next to Bhikie's bed simply fell in, without
breaking. She just missed having her face blown off." The family ran
out into the street and watched half their house burn. There was no
mistake; it was an Inkatha bombing meant to give the strong warning
against any more ANC meetings in Bhikie's home. "They waited two
weeks," Zenko said sadly. "Then Inkatha came back and burned down
the rest of the house. At her hospital, my sister was demoted, even
though she herself was not involved in either the Inkatha or ANC
politics."

Zenko fell quiet awhile, then said in a pensive voice, "You see,
Bhikie never told my father about the Inkatha bombings. 'I don't
want to trouble him,' she told me. All the sisters knew it, were talking
all around the world about it from Australia to America to South
Africa—but Father had no idea. I suppose he just thought it was a
fire."

Were the sisters protecting their father from the reality of their
lives? Why didn't Bhikie turn to her father and his powerful friends
in Inkatha to make recompense for what she had lost? Zenko considered a moment, then said, "My father was an idealist and as such was
strangely naive. He could not have imagined that the people with
whom he was fighting for black freedom might also bomb his own
daughter. And I guess my sisters were also afraid of Father, awed by
him, didn't want to distract him from his mission. You know, more
'girl trouble.' But I . . . I was closest to him simply because I'd insist
upon his attention. And I got it."

As a child, Zenko would plant herself in the front seat of the car, the church automobile finally given Bishop Zulu as befitting his position. For so many years he had taken the bus at all hours of the day to visit the sick or dying in his congregation. When he finally got his car, it was as if his youngest daughter came with it. She rode with him on his every call. "Baba" was what she called him, and she grew up to be his liaison with her sisters. There was a brother, barely ever mentioned. At sixteen, crushed by the expectation that he follow in his father's footsteps, this brother abandoned himself to alcohol. The sisters do not speak of him much, though the sisters speak to and of one another very often.

Traveling with and being surrounded by a tribe of her sisters is still second nature to Zenko. Having been raised until she was sixteen as one of six sisters, she then spent the next decade in all-girl religious boarding schools and colleges, mostly in rural areas. And, of course, when Zenko attended these schools, she was following in the footsteps of her sisters. "When I first went to boarding school, it was not so great. These schoolgirls were not like sisters. Instead it was a real pecking order. In fact, I'd say these cruel girl groups were the first training I had, apart from apartheid, of course, when I learned how not to feel or think—just to survive."

When Zenko arrived in boarding school, an economics professor who had championed one of Zenko's older sisters tried to offer the same patronage to Zenko. The novice girls were expected to carry the older girls' bags and iron their uniforms. But because of Zenko's patron, she was relieved of such chores and allowed to use an electric iron: a luxury the older girls resented. They also resented that she was a city girl of a higher class. To try and fit in, Zenko gave away all her good clothes and possessions. Then she begged the economics professor not to give her any more patronage. "After that," Zenko said, "it was better. But I did learn something from those schoolgirls. If not for those first years in boarding school, I would have been a softie." And being fragile or vulnerable is not what a black woman needs to survive in South Africa. It's interesting to see the so-called school of hard knocks translated into the language of sisterhood. We women tend to assume that sisterhoods are always loyal alliances to shelter and strengthen us; but sisterhood, like any other bond, can have its dark side. For Zenko Zulu, both the positive and negative poles of sisterhood served to strengthen her and prepare her to face injustice and intimidation—the daily face of black women raised under apartheid.

"I have learned so much in the company of women," Zenko said. "It made me very knowledgeable about females—about how to relate to my own sex on very many different, subtle levels. I learned also how to perceive certain things in people, to understand others more deeply."

In school, Zenko studied her own gender and learned the feminine survival skills of keen penetration and emotional discrimination. "You found out who your true sisters were in that hierarchy," Zenko remarked. If the all-girls' schools she attended strengthened and toughened Zenko, her own real sister-tribe soothed and nurtured her. From them Zenko learned empathy and caretaking. To this day, even though she is far away from her Zulu family and divorced, Zenko has woven around herself a tribe of close women friends who meet at least monthly. So now Zenko has two tribes of sisters—those of her Zulu blood—sisters back in South Africa, and the American sisters she shares her daily life with, supporting one another through divorces, death, child rearing, and careers.

"We all have the same kind of shoulder," is the way Zenko described these American sisters. "I do not know what I would have done without these strong women in my life now," she commented pensively.

Now is after the death of her marriage, and seeing her last child almost ready to leave home. "I am a completely different person than when I married twenty-two years ago," she reflected one cool fall day. Outside her spacious home, the leaves were a golden and green blaze, the same blond and green shades as the savannahs and verdant hills of her South African homeland. "Back in 1970 when I first met my husband, Eli, I was always so scared. In South Africa everyone is so scared you can't think. I had more reasons than most black women to be scared." Zenko paused. "Now, though, things are changing."

In the small rural hospital where Zenko was finishing her nurse's training, working in an operating room on the night shift, there was a color line no one dared cross. "You did not have any real communication with white people. The only white friend I ever had was in this little hospital when I was training as a nurse. Her name was Liz and she was the entertainment director; but every time she tried to organize sports events in the morning, no one signed up except myself and this white medical student, Eli. So Liz, Eli, and I would play tennis or whatever in the early hours of the morning and that's how we all got thrown together. Without Liz I would never have allowed myself to get anywhere near Eli. It scared the hell out of me! A white and black love in South Africa was absolutely forbidden."

Nevertheless, the two found ways to be together outside of organized staff activities. And when Zenko found herself pregnant, neither she nor Eli talked about abortion. All they could talk about was getting out of South Africa. For if they were discovered, Eli would have been thrown out of the country and Zenko into jail. Zenko's father was attending a bishop's conference in Mozambique, and he suggested that Zenko come with him, feigning a vacation. Both knew she would not be coming home. They arranged for Eli to meet them in Mozambique. But because it was a Catholic country, which required a waiting period for a marriage license, they traveled to Swaziland on her temporary visa. Because this country was a British protectorate, they could marry without punishment. However, there was lots of fighting between the ruling Portuguese and the blacks struggling for freedom; Zenko's memories of the wedding are charged with a sense of disaster and violence. Then, once married, she and Eli could not get across the border to Portugal without the help of a Portuguese bishop who spoke up for them to the authorities. Once across the border into Portugal, she could seek sanctuary and help from the American embassy and within days they were flying to America.

"I was in a state of shock," Zenko remembered. "I don't think I felt anything. On the plane Eli started shivering and couldn't stop. We still don't know whether it was malaria or if he was shivering so much because he found himself suddenly married to a Zulu." Zenko smiled, but there was much sorrow in her eyes. She was quiet a long time, then she murmured, "I don't know how to explain South Africa to you. After all these years, I still don't know how to explain South Africa . . ."

How to explain a country of such bloodshed and violence, where the contrast of black and white stands out as if those are the only two colors in the world? How to explain that between 1984 and 1992 the South African Institute of Race Relations estimates that approximately

14,000 people, mostly black, have been killed in political violence? How to explain the warrior history of the Zulus themselves, a tribe which was once the mightiest in South Africa under the brilliant and brutal rule of Shaka Zulu, warrior king; or how to explain the devouring European invasion that relegated most of these proud Zulu tribespeople to native reserves in Natal where they now languish in poverty and township violence?

And what happens to the feminine after decades of violent struggle? In Zenko Zulu's tribe, the male warrior tradition is exemplified in the iron hand of Shaka Zulu who, through imperious military stratagems, established a Zulu kingdom in the early 1800s. Ironically, it was the very marauding devastation of the Shaka Zulu victory that left many of the other tribal clans broken and unable to resist the equally deadly Boer Great Trek of the 1830s, which in turn led to the colonization and eventual conquest of the Zulus. One tale from Shaka Zulu's rule speaks volumes: In 1827, when his beloved mother, Nandi, died, Shaka declared that for a year no crops could be planted and no milk, a Zulu staple, drunk. All pregnant women were killed, along with their husbands and thousands of cows; Shaka's reasoning was that others must be forced to understand what it was to lose one's mother.

The Zulu warrior tradition is at once a source of historical pride and problems for Zulu women, even those who, like Zenko, have left behind the more traditional village tribal ways. Though the Zulu religion reveres Nomkhubulwane, the daughter of God and goddess of balance, and even though she is given great respect as the central symbol of creation, to be a Zulu woman is to be under the dominion of the man, who in turn owes his allegiance to the king of his kinship leaders. Property and status are passed down through the male line. It is also ironic that while the Zulu God creator is male with an only daughter, the Christian religion which was adopted by many Zulus has a God as Father with an only son. Both the Zulu and Christian traditions are in the warrior, patriarchal cast, but certain of their other religious beliefs are vastly different.

The Zulus see the earth as paradise and they feel their ancestors close to them—not off in some heavenly sky, but companionable, responsible for the living and their well-being. In his remarkable book, *Anthem of the Decades*, Zulu poet and scholar Mazisi Kunene comments, "The Ancestal Spirits, the gods, and all the cosmic forces must serve the interests of the living for their own peace and fulfillment. . . . the gods acknowledge the superiority of man whose experience of the earth they consider deeper than theirs." With this Zulu emphasis on the human and the earth, the colonizing Christian focus on heaven and human sin is not easily reconciled. Yet for many women, the reconciliation came from the simple pragmatic expansion of their opportunities under Christian influence. Instead of being wives and mothers as their only choice, many women could choose education and even careers—albeit limited to Zenko's and her sisters' options: nurse or teacher.

Ellen Kuzwayo, the legendary South African leader who worked all her life for both black and female freedom, wrote in her autobiography, *Call Me Woman*, that as the black sisterhood struggles for educational and professional recognition, their gains are not without "relationship problems within and without the family." In South Africa, black women for decades have been classified as "minors," granted less status than their own sons, infant or adult. Kuzwayo tells of applying for a travel visa which necessitated that her son sign for her. While at home she might have been the widowed head of the household, in the larger society it was her sons who had dominion over her comings and goings. And this male dominion is not even prized; it is casual and expected. A typical Zulu poetic insult would be, "You are a ruler who rules over women."

And what of these women, ruled over by their own tribal men, their husbands, fathers, and sons, as well as by the larger society of a racist and patriarchal South African white male elite? What will happen now that that white male elite has at last been overturned by a black majority in the South African elections? Will anything change for women? In an article, "South Africa through Women's Eyes," *Ms.* magazine reports that the National Women's Coalition is working to "jump-start the transition to democracy." It is illustrated with a photo of black women whose signs proclaim WOMEN CAN ALSO THINK—INVOLVE THEM IN NEGOTIATIONS! As this coalition of sisters works to claim equal share of the black political power, will the value of women increase? Will a tribe of sisters such as Zenko Zulu's find themselves with more prestige in the new South African society that is now being forged?

The Zulu, or for that matter the Xhosa, Bantu, or Swazi tribes who make up the black peoples of South Africa, all have a distinct sense of tribe. The Zulu sense of communality far outweighs the more Western notion of individualism. In a Zulu epic poem or in everyday speech, when one greets another, the word is *sawubona,* meaning "we see you," or "I on behalf of my family or community pay our respects to you." The much-hallowed Western sense of individuated work is simply not a part of the language or emotion of this tribal tradition.

To be part of a tribe in a white culture that celebrates the individual is to be always caught between two worlds and two responsibilities —what one owes the tribe, the family, the kinship clan, and what one owes oneself. Even the Western concept of Self, as someone like Jung defines it, is foreign to a person raised to think of himself as not ever without others as part of a shared identity.

Something of this tribal identity is at work in the current South African conflict; just as it was at work over a decade ago when Charlotte Maxeke, the first President of the National Council of African Women, proclaimed, "This work is not for yourselves—kill that spirit of 'self' and do not live above your people, but live with them. If you can rise, bring someone with you. Do away with that fearful animal of jealousy—kill that spirit, and love one another as brothers and sisters." In the very next sentence, she also admonishes, "The other animal that will tear us to pieces is tribalism; I saw the shadow of it and it should cease to be." If in one speech, the appeal to and fear of the tribal is invoked, how much more confusing is it to be a South African woman, the sixth of six sisters, a Zulu raised by an Anglican bishop father who, in turn, helped to start the very Inkatha that then threatens to kill her sister and separate her kinspeople in bloody strife? Add to this the fact that this expatriate Zulu woman is now far from both her tribes, Zulu and sisters; she is divorced and, to use a word that might traditionally bring terror to many African women, single. Writing about just this dilemma in a 1993 *New York Times Magazine* "Hers" column, a Nigerian professor, Dympna Ugwu-Oju, explains the identity conflicts for African women in the West: "An Ibo woman has very little personal identity, even if she lives in the United States and has success in her career. Our culture takes very little pride in a woman's accomplishment. At an Ibo gathering a woman is more likely to be asked whose wife or mother she is before she is asked what her name is or what she does for a living." She concludes that she is not alone with her African sisters in this dilemma. "Hundreds of thousands of women from the Third World and other traditional societies share my experience. . . . Mainstream America . . . dictates that we be assertive and independent like men. Our traditional culture, dictated by religion and years of socializatoin, demands that we be docile and content in our role as mothers and wives—careers or not."

In a way, the Third World woman's identity conflicts between tribe and individual are a large mirror for all women to face. For no matter how successful, single, or self-fulfilled women are, we still see ourselves more in terms of relationships than men do. Women live in a world of relatedness, and as such are still demeaned by a patriarchal society which values the individual, heroic, unattached male. For decades women have explored the options of becoming more masculine, as we've modeled ourselves on this tradition. But like Zenko Zulu, who has re-created the tribal world of her sisters here in a faraway country and culture, perhaps we as women have many other options within the feminine context of relatedness. If we set aside the masculine mirror and value ourselves as both individuals *and* sisters, then we can even model for men the skills of strongly identifying ourselves separately, within the larger context of the whole. Women have always defined themselves within myriad identities. As powerful and successful as women may be, there is also the juggling of other roles: mate, mother, sister, friend. The personal struggle of finding one's true self while still committing to strong relationships is an arena in which women have a long history. One of the advantages women have traditionally had over men is our sense of community. Many sisterhoods in fact serve as strong support systems for helping individual women grow and accomplish their goals. As one of my sister-friends is fond of saying, "When the sun comes out, everybody can bask in its light—so shine, sister, and you'll shine on me."

This shining of sisterhood could literally save the next generation of girls. In a world that devalues the birth of a girl child—from China to Africa to Saudi Arabia—what might happen if the sisterhood surrounding that baby girl welcomed her with high ceremony? What if the sisters formed an inner sanctum that celebrated the newborn girl's very femaleness, as if she were truly like Zenko's name, a "girl of God," or like the Zulu myth, *Nomkhubulwane,* the daughter of God? Would the world change for sisterhoods?

Now that South Africa had elected an all-races government, Zenko hopes that her countrywomen will be a greater part of the struggle toward a new global sisterhood.

"My sisters, both Zulu and American, are my true family now," Zenko commented with a firm nod and rare laughter. "I do not know what I would have done, what I would do, without them as my tribe."

Zenko Zulu has lost one of the sisters in her Zulu tribe; and it is this sister she saved to talk about until the last, as if to sum up and finally explain the South Africa she loves and has left. After all the talk of apartheid, of Afrikaans-Zulu politics, of the paradoxical bleak and hopeful future for black rule, it was with the haunting memory of her sister Sivela that Zenko ended her story.

Sylvia Sivela Zulu was an older sister born in 1931; Zenko was born thirteen years later in 1944. In Zulu *Sivela* means "we up here" and Sivela's betrayal has much to do with raising herself above her family. As she told the story, Zenko's voice was low, trembling with anger and something else: pity. Well she knew why a sister would not claim her sisters, her family, her tribe, in a country that judged a person not by character but by color. Inheriting their mother's lighter skin, Sivela could "pass" in South Africa—if she disinherited herself, hid her parentage, her extended family, her dark-skinned Zulu roots. As she explained the color-line hierarchy, Zenko sighed; and in that breath was a world of shame, rage, and a child's bewilderment. Zenko was a child when her sister Sivela first began passing as "colored." In South Africa the pecking order of class and privilege descends from white to colored to Indian to black at the bottom. "Someone can act and talk colored," Zenko explained, "it's a class thing. The right schools, the anglicized accent so that no one hears you speaking like a Zulu, but instead like a British-educated person. It's all about education and rejecting the Zulu in you so that even dark-skinned people can pass as colored instead of black by the way they behave. It's really amazing. You raise yourself up, live only in colored areas, go to colored schools, sit in colored sections of buses or theaters. My sister got married to a Malawi man, very dark black, and their two children were not as light as she was, but they assumed the colored class, cut themselves off from our Zulu family, and simply began all over again as if they could change themselves inside out."

In America one might call this denial of roots "passing," but Zenko referred to it again and again as "changing," as if a metamorphosis was complete and her sister was not simply rejecting her family, but saw herself as evolving out of it entirely. "When I was ten in the 1950s, Sivela came to visit us from Zimbabwe where she and her husband and two children had gone to better change themselves away from Zulu into colored. Sivela asked me to baby-sit her children and take them to a movie theater. When we got there I naturally assumed we would go sit in the black section; the seats were divided into white, colored, and black. But those children put up such a fuss—they did not belong with the blacks, they told me, and they were so angry. 'We're colored,' they said," Zenko murmured softly. "After that, I hardly saw my sister. In some ways she was the most loving of all the sisters. But loving from afar. She'd send my parents the kindest letters, but it was not the same as claiming us. My father, I can just hear him saying 'Father, forgive them for they know not what they do,' because that's the way he was about my sister's leaving us. And my mother, she was always close to Sivela—they both liked clothes and Sivela came when my mother was dying to stay and nurse her. But when my mother visited Sivela in Zimbabwe, they showed her around with pride—she was so light-skinned, you know." Zenko paused again as if to swallow the bitterness that rose up like bile. At last she said, "We never made up, Sivela and me. She died in 1983 and I had not seen her for so many years. Right after she came to nurse Mother, she returned to Zimbabwe and was killed in an auto accident. When they called with the news, it was Mother who heard it first. She went to bed. She never recovered."

There is not blame in Zenko's voice; there is instead that kind of bewilderment that marks all her most private reckonings with the family and country that has suffered such betrayals. When one has been betrayed by a political system, one often betrays oneself and those one loves. This is the legacy of South African apartheid: that it destroys the soul through denial of one's true Self.

"I understand what Sivela did . . . ," Zenko said softly. "But I never really forgave my sister."

How can we, any of us, no matter what country, forgive those sisters who have abandoned and betrayed the sisterhood unless we first see that it is also a betrayal of the true Self? In the anthology *South Africa in Search of a Soul: Jungian Perspectives on the Wilderness Within*, Philip

Faber writes in his essay, "Archetypal Symbolism and the Ideology of Apartheid," that apartheid was the religious response of a European patriarchal tradition, a profound fear of the feminine. "A failure of white to triumph over black therefore symbolizes a failure of differentiation of the masculine and a reversion or regression to the primordial darkness of the archetypal feminine. In a patriarchy, therefore, the 'black-feminine' must be conquered by the 'white-masculine' in order for the latter to survive."

Zenko's sister story of Sivela changing herself to become colored, or closer to white, embodies the tragic history of not only the black struggle, but also the sisterhood's struggle against the patriarchal fear of women's primal power. For when Sivela rejected her Zulu tribe, she also denied her sisters, and so lost a feminine clan within which she might have survived apartheid without changing herself into what she is not.

The model of Sivela for all women may seem far afield, but in her denial of her sisters there is a mirror for women who reject other women because they cannot find self-acceptance—as either black or female. In her remarkable book, *A Passion for Friends: Toward a Philosophy of Female Affection*, Janice G. Raymond identifies this haunted, self-rejecting woman by using Mary Daly's term, "dismemberment"; in other words, the inability or refusal to remember oneself as part of a whole. And wholeness here means integrating the true feminine, not as defined by the patriarchal, but as explored and identified *by women for women*. "The dismembering of female friendship is initially the dismembering of the woman-identified Self. This lack of Self-love is grafted onto the female Self under patriarchy. If the graft takes, women who do not love their Selves cannot love others like their Selves."

If we cannot love ourselves as female, we cannot love or revere our sisters. We ourselves unconsciously partake of the culture's sexism: what Naomi Wolf calls "gender apartheid." When women participate in discrimination against themselves and one other, it is particularly insidious and painful because its root is in self-revulsion. We turn against one another as women because we are following in a religious and political tradition that teaches that to be a woman is to be born bad, born dark, and associated with all those subterranean female attributes which must be vanquished by the light—of God the Father or the masculine ideal.

It is a commonly accepted stage of psychological development that both sexes must separate from the mother to differentiate themselves and to grow as individuals. Our masculine culture has done a very good job of separating from the feminine. What we have forgotten in all this separation is that it is equally important for our psychological growth to complete the next stage which is a *return to the feminine*. In Faber's apartheid essay, he argues that apartheid, while forged from the "first phase of individuation, the assertion of the masculine and the denial of the feminine . . . must be corrected, during the second phase, through a reintegration of the feminine." This reunion with the feminine is essential to the inner balance of both men and women. But I think for women it is even more crucial since we have been taught to despise and devalue our feminine selves and so our sisterhoods. If we deny our sisters, we lose our very birthright, our mirror, our center. This loss is akin to condemning ourselves to second-class status, like that of an inner apartheid.

Many women have related to their sisters as if we all existed in a kind of South Africa of the female psyche—where some women "pass" professionally as men and others judge their sisters as less-than. I can't count how many times I've heard women declare, without any apology, that they prefer the "more stimulating" company of men over women. It saddens me when I've heard some women turning down an invitation to a gathering that is "just a bunch of women." Don't they see the self-hatred and self-bigotry in their words? A student of mine blithely suggested in front of her all-women class that a female response to her work was not, after all, "the real world or real readers." Did she mean to imply that somehow she herself, as a woman, was not real?

We are so ill-trained to gaze steadily and without apology into the feminine mirror, to define, witness, and gauge ourselves without the approval of men. One of my friends admits that if all of her girlfriends told her she was beautiful, it would mean less than if a man gave her the compliment. In denying our sisters' authority and approval, we participate in that gender apartheid which demeans our own kind. It was not only the desertion that Zenko couldn't forgive her sister; it was the fact that Sivela never returned to claim and acknowledge her true sisterhood. By cutting herself off from her own kind, Sivela forfeited her future, her deep bond to sister and Self.

The future for Zenko Zulu, as for South Africa, seems to be a return to the Self, the black African roots of self-rule, the evolutionary step beyond the white, patriarchal dominion. Does this mean then that the feminine will be re-membered, revitalized, restored to its balancing principle?

In her recent brave book *Warrior Marks: The Sexual Blinding of Women*, and in her novel *Possessing the Secret of Joy*, Alice Walker takes an unblinking look at the ritual of clitoridectomies, as sanctioned by the African tribal males and performed by the females, mother to daughter. In the novel, it is the revered tribal matriarch, MamaLisa, who is murdered by Tashi, an Olenka tribal woman upon whom the elder performed this ancient ritual. Tashi has already lost her sister in childhood to this brutal practice; her sister bled to death while MamaLisa fed the child's clitoris to a cock rooster waiting with clenched talons. The horror of Tashi's experience of this ritual is made the more terrible by the fact that it is women who perform this genital blinding upon other women. Walker's work shows that it is not a simple war between the sexes with women throwing off the evil patriarchy to be born anew; it is also looking at the wound within, where women have harmed each other.

Perhaps this is the future of feminism: a period in which we are secure enough to look within our ranks at the many ways in which we deny and cripple and condemn each other—a wound that is particularly haunting because it feels somehow self-inflicted.

That is why Zenko's story of her sister's rejection seemed as deeply disturbing as the system of apartheid itself; one expects systems to be inhumane and rejecting, especially if one is black and female. But one never expects the enemy to be black and female, a mirror of one's deepest doubts, shadows, despairs.

In *A Passion for Friends*, Janice Raymond concludes with a strong argument for women to identify and focus on one another in order to shape a new future: "When women turn their eyes toward their Selves and other women, they put the world in perspective. The invisibility of women to each other has been the condition of women . . . and affects women's total loss of sensation for their Selves and other women. Women can choose their line of vision. Women can choose to see each other."

When a Zulu child is born, his or her umbilical cord is buried in the ground of that birthplace. Ever after, a Zulu will refer to his native ground as "the place where my umbilical cord is." This cord is not only a link between generations, it is a direct bond to the mother, the Earth. It is the feminine which grounds and holds our lifeline the world over. It is the sisterhood which must midwife and keep safe that lifeline. By choosing to return consciously to that umbilical link with the feminine, we can begin again to re-create a heaven on earth and bring back the long-forgotten daughter of God, a daughter who may well have a sister, a whole tribe of sisters.

Zenko Zulu has chosen to see her tribe of sisters as more valuable than the broken mirror held up to her by a racist country. By seeing each other, the Zulu sisters have done more than survive the tyranny of apartheid, they have held each other safe in strong, dark arms— arms that will also hold and shape the more feminine future, the girls of God.

But what about the past, when those girls of God were the women priestesses of a female deity? What happens when we return to claim our sense of the sacred feminine, the lost language and rituals of our ancient sister societies?

6

Sister Societies

Ever since I was a child I've had a recurring daydream: Clad in a white cloth robe with a wide hood over my head, I'm led down seven stairs into the warm, intimate waters of an underground hot spring. Around me, waist-deep in the azure pool, are seven other women, also in white robes. Their faces are hidden in the recesses of their hoods and they are chanting, their lilting voices low in a language only part of me still recognizes—but the singing is tender and knowing like a lullaby. It doesn't matter that it's a lost language of women, I still understand the meaning—that I am here for a purifying and spiritual ceremony, that I've walked down these seven steps many times before and always with this same sense of awe and grateful surrender. I know what's coming and I have longed for it; my body is so weary and burdened with the many cares of caretaking others—somehow I sense I've been a healer or in a grave position of responsibility which has taken its physical toll. Though I am not old, my back is bent; though I have power, I am keenly aware of my need for nurturance. Walking barefoot down these underground steps and shedding my soft robe I know I am also shedding my outward trappings of splendor and position; instead, I am naked and returning to the very beginning. Here in the island womb of the earth herself, the Mother, I am reenacting a ritual of rebirth that is also a holy preparation for my eventual death.

I hold my arms out at my side and fall back into the outstretched arms of the seven women whose faces I will never see, whose bodies are hidden beneath white robes that float about their legs in billows like pale underwater clouds. I recognize some of my sisters by their smells: an elder has a musty sandalwood scent that has sunk deep into her ancient skin from her years shrouded in incense smoke encircling the ceremonial altars; several of the priestesses smell so familiar and fresh, their fragrant pine perfume of frankincense mixed with the healing, sulphurous steam off these hot springs. They bathe me, these sisterly ministers, their strong hands and arms in sensual support of my whole body as I float among them. Singing, they soothe my aching shoulders, massaging the sore slopes of my back, tracing the tired tendons along my legs, stroking my neck so that I feel suddenly taller, my spine spacious and supple. I realize these women have known me all my life; these are the arms that have embraced, the hands that have memorized my frailties. These are my sacred sisters, these old voices and very young girls, these knowing, mature women who tend to me with patience and compassion—and something else: reverence. I close my eyes and give over completely to this sister society and it is only then, when I am the most open, when the vision is the most real, that I realize this is a religious ceremony from no religion I recognize now on earth—that this is a memory from another time and place.

Always at this moment I am overwhelmed with sorrow and begin to weep. *We are losing our ways,* one of the women whispers to me as they gently rock my body. Now the singing sounds just like keening. I realize that we are underground because there is nowhere left aboveground that is safe for this ritual, that we are in danger even now as we practice our ritual cleansing. *Remember this about us,* one of the eldest women says; her voice is cracked and familiar; in my vision I know and trust her well. I hold this picture of the seven steps, the robes and warm pool, the hidden, holy women holding and healing me. I tell myself never to forget this no matter where I end up, what lifetimes I endure. *Remember this.*

This is all I remember. Everything else about what this ritual might have been or when and why and where it took place, I've come to

through research, talking with other women, and through my own meditations. Perhaps this was some past life or collective memory of the
Eleusinian Mysteries, the ancient sacred rites which endured for almost
two thousand years from their earliest recorded ceremonies in Greece
in 1300 B.C. up to their last celebration in the fourth century A.D.
In these sacred ceremonies held every September, people were selected
to participate in the holy Mysteries, presided over by rigorously trained
priests and priestesses; everyone who spoke Greek and had not committed murder might present him or herself. These chosen initiates
reverently entered the caves at Eleusis, expecting to be utterly transformed. As described in Asia Shepsut's recent scholarly *Journey of the
Priestess*, the sacred purpose of the Mysteries was to "give firm reassur-
ance of future happiness in the life beyond the body, something that
no other Greek cult offered." Though these Eleusinian Mysteries lasted
for centuries, little is known of what actually happened during the
secret rites because the initiates were sworn to silence on pain of death,
if they revealed either their visions or what exactly they had endured.
There are many scholarly speculations as to what actually happened
during the ceremonies held to celebrate the mother-daughter mythic
reunion of Demeter and Persephone (or Kore).

How ironic that this ancient Greek myth of feminine reunion, of
the re-membering of the female Self (after long histories of deliberate
dismemberment), was the very myth which once transfixed our ancient
ancestors. It is eerily prescient: Persephone's descent into the underworld, and the subsequent loss of the feminine balance in the natural
world is an apt description of where we find ourselves today. In the
twentieth century, after two thousand years of patriarchal religions,
much of our ancient legacy of feminine religious rites or sacred celebrations of nature have been denied, driven out or underground. And
yet in recent decades there has been a resurgence of fascination in
feminine religious traditions, distinct from the major, organized world
religions. A plethora of books celebrating female rituals and sacred
traditions is now restoring a piece of female history—everything from
Merlin Stone's classic *When God Was a Woman* to the respected archeological research of the late Marija Gimbutas in her groundbreaking *Language of the Goddess*. Indeed, there is such a resurgence of
scholarship and interest in sacred feminine traditions that even among
my friends who have pursued their feminine spirituality within more

mainstream Catholic or Jewish or Protestant faiths, it is possible to find ourselves discussing the Marian cult of the Black Madonna, or Lilith, the bibilical first wife of Adam, or Sophia, the wise Gnostic Great Mother. Among my women friends who are finding spiritual nurturance away from the organized religions, the lively discussions might range from Yemaya, the Afro-Caribbean Yoruba Queen Mother, to the Tibetan Green Tara and Hindu dark goddess Kali, to the Chinese Buddhist goddess of compassion, Kuan Yin, to the Wicca nature worship of the Great Goddess, to the Celtic fertility goddess Cerredwin, to the Native American Hopi myth of Spider Grandmother.

My first memory of telling anyone about my vision of the underground women's ritual was when I was ten and staying the summer with my grandparents on their farm in the Ozarks. My stepgrandmother, Vergie, herself somewhat of a healer and wise woman, listened closely to my tentative description of the secret society of seven women bathing me in warm underground pools. She hinted to me that this might not be just a childish fantasy.

"Women always came together, either for planting or birthing or healing. They's all sorts of secret societies . . . you just don't never tell nobody." She paused and drew me into her own farmhouse kitchen where she heated well water in huge pots to give her grandchildren baths.

I sat naked in a steaming tin tub and my grandmother poured perfectly heated warm water over my head like a baptism. This was the grandmother who was not my blood, but whom I loved the best. Some folks whispered that Vergie was part-black because she was so dark and no one knew her origins—and because she knew things that were forbidden most women—like herbs and death chores and other healing rituals that my fundamentalist family lumped under the title "hoodoo." Vergie was so flamboyant, such a good storyteller, especially when she gave us those long, luxurious baths. Vergie had earned her beauty license after much hard work and had opened her own shop. She was famous for her permanents and her good gossip. But her other sacred function was to "beautify" her ladies for eternity—she moonlighted as the morgue's beautician. Any client could count on Vergie to beautify them in death as in life.

Whether my grandmother was primping my hair "better than any Breck gal," or telling me ghost stories while she bathed me in her hot tub, or regaling her ladies with the latest town horror story of sickness or betrayal, Vergie was the wise woman of my wandering childhood. That summer when I timidly told her about my recurring vision, she stopped my bath and came around to stare at me thoughtfully, soapy sponge in hand.

"You're not talking about no church ladies or missionary unions," she told me, but in a very soft voice as if no one must overhear us. "You're talking 'bout deep secrets, women's knowing, that we hardly even remember ourselves. But you know, there's something left of us. In my shop the ladies tell me their dreams, some of them getting ready to die and they have these visions. They see other women gathering round, in white robes. They ain't angels, honey, looking sickly and winged, they's real women with wide hips and babies on them, and herbs and singing, just like any woman you'd see on earth who knows how to take care of herself and them she loves. But my ladies, they see these women gathering to welcome them. Where are they, heaven, you think? No, I don't think it's in the sky up there. I think it's in some other place right alongside us here on earth, these secret sisters who watch over and love us, especially womenfolk who got so much to get through like childbirthing and taking care of the dead —that's a chore always falls to women—bringing them in and seeing them out."

Vergie confided in me that once or twice she'd actually sensed these secret sisters just out of sight over her shoulder or lingering near a corpse she was washing and preparing for her funeral. "Strange things happen in that morgue where everyone thinks it's just dead people . . . all sorts of spirits working alongside me. . . . I'm doing hair, they're seeing to souls, I guess. We all got our beautification jobs to do."

When other girls my age were talking about angels or Mother Mary, I kept my own counsel as Vergie had told me and thought about the secret sisters living alongside this world, doing normal things like bathing and childbearing and healing—not winging around like heroes with important messages from God. Only one other time in my entire childhood did I confide my vision to anyone and that was to a beloved Sunday school teacher who was slightly shocked at the depth of my description; tenderly she told me that maybe these must be my guardian angels and I was lucky enough to have a whole girl gang of them.

"But they lived once, and . . . and I was with them in that secret cave," I insisted only to see my favorite teacher's face fall into the frown of fundamentalist fear.

"We don't believe in reincarnation," she said, but not unkindly. She saw my despair and shame and added in a low voice as if she were saying something wildly subversive, "Not in this part of the world. Maybe when you're older and have traveled you can ask some other people and they'll tell you a different story." I was about to leave my Sunday school teacher with an apology when she impulsively took my arm and whispered, "You know, I think my mother saw them once, those secret sisters of yours. . . . it was right before she died and she kept staring out the hospital window at just a brick wall and saying, 'Oh, how beautiful . . . my sisters, all my sisters are here with me. Now I can go.' " My Sunday school teacher's face was flushed, very near mine. I could feel her hot skin and smell the sweet scent of Pond's cleansing cream like my mother used. "Don't tell anyone about this, promise!" she said and let me go, shaking herself like a wet dog. She was obviously angry with herself for having confided in me, but kind enough not to hold me responsible. Still, after that talk there was never the same delight in her voice when she called on me in Sunday school class and soon I began to stop talking or answering questions at all, even when I knew the answers. About that time, as if sensing my hidden heresy, my mother had enrolled me in a Bible Study competition in which competitors memorized hundreds of Bible passages. Soon I was on my way to the state championships. At the competitions, called Sword Drills, we'd all stand in a line like soldiers, our Bibles by our sides. The inquisitor would command, "Attention! Draw swords!" As we ceremonially raised our Bibles he'd recite a verse without reference, then shout, "Go!" We'd have to remember the exact chapter and verse to fit the quotation, then flick expertly through our Bibles to jab a finger at the reference. When we found it, we'd step out and militaristically present our "swords" to a judge to show we'd found the correct citation.

In all my Bible study I found no references to a secret society of sisters, or any reverence for any of their rituals. There was nothing but disdain for women—from Jezebel to Delilah, from Lot's wife to evil Eve. There was no woman teacher to tell me what I've now researched—that Jezebel was originally a Canaanite-Phoenician high priestess of the divine goddess Astarte (or Asherah), that the priesthood which had begun earlier in Mesopotamia, continued to flourish in Canaan from 2000 B.C., that throughout the second millennium B.C. there were both women-led and men-led religions existing simultaneously before the eventual destruction of the feminine traditions by the patriarchal, tribal Hebrew and later Christian-dominant faiths.

As I stood on those Southern Baptist stages doing my childhood Sword Drills I felt myself walking through the warrior motions of sacred word-as-weapon, and I felt more lost than any sinner woefully described in my pastor's terrifying sermons. But even within the patriarchal bastion of our Baptist church, there were women's societies that flourished like weeds struggling through cement. My mother was an active and, even though she would never admit it, feminist, leader of her Women's Missionary Union. She crusaded for everything from more power for churchwomen to foreign missions. A warrior in her own way and a true believer, she would banish her children for spiritual crimes that ranged from smoking cigarettes to "dressing like hippies," to "backsliding from regular church attendance." But in her own unconscious way, she instilled in her three daughters a subversive, sly, and secretive sense of sisterhood—always working from within to undermine the patriarchy of the church.

Between my mother's rebellious orthodoxy and my step-grand-mother's rural wise-woman tradition, I learned to keep my own spiritual counsel even in the midst of those who might persecute or exile me—the "fellowship of the believers." But it was a fellowship, not a sisterhood. And the moment I entered grade school, I began to avidly study world religions, pretending it was only geography. I finally found hints of that "different story," my Sunday school teacher had reckoned I'd someday stumble upon. I didn't know what that different story was, exactly, but I understood already I had a missing piece of it in my secret heart.

When I was baptized in the Southern Baptist Church at the age of seven I fully expected that somehow my secret-sisters' vision might come true, even though I knew full well that I would be slam-dunked in a tiny baptistry in a sanctuary, not underground in the holy caves. I knew the water would be from a faucet and a minister in rubber hip boots would in one moment lean me backwards, pinching my nose, and declare, "I now baptize you in the name of the Father, the Son, and the Holy Ghost," before jerking me back up to take a breath. There would be the baptism of the brotherhood—no mention of sisters. In a ceremony reminiscent of the slap on the bottom and first breath surrounded by bright lights and staring faces, my baptizing ceremony was more like an efficient chore. And yet, right before I glided into the glass baptistry into the tall minister's grip, I waited my turn in a dressing room filled with children, a few elderly women, and some teenage girls, primping their makeup even though they knew it wasn't allowed and that mascara would run down their repentant, saved faces. There was just that moment when we pulled on our simple, white cotton shifts, when I felt it again—that mystery and awe of my childhood vision. What I felt is that we all fully expected to be transformed right before our own and others' very eyes, that we would emerge from the water washed clean and made holy.

Maybe this was what the Eleusinian Mysteries initiates felt purifying themselves for the rites that would bestow upon the initiated the gift of an assured afterlife vision. As Sophocles states of the Mysteries: "Thrice happy are those of mortals, who having seen those rites depart for Hades; for to them alone is granted to have a true life there." Before partaking in these high holy underground initiations, the initiates fasted and prayed before their final ceremony in the Cave of Eleusis. Some scholars theorize that the memory of divine possession and the visions initiates carried with them after the Mysteries were in fact drug-induced by a ceremonial potion given them on this last night in the cave. In their book *The Road to Eleusis: Unveiling the Secret of the Mysteries*, authors Gordon R. Wasson, Carl A. P. Ruck, and Albert Hofmann (who discovered LSD), present research that a hallucinogen not unlike our modern LSD was given initiates to induce their afterlife vision.

In my college years at the University of California during the drug-drenched sixties, I was an anomaly in that I never dropped acid, not because I didn't have any curiosity but because every time I was on the verge of taking that tiny transformative tab onto my tongue, an instinct made me spit it out again. It was at that moment I would clearly remember my vision of the underground cave and attendant priestesses. It was almost as if a familiar voice whispered to me that I must not enter that world without being properly initiated, that this was a holy journey and I was woefully without my sisterhood or any mystery rites to guide and illumine me. To take acid without the attendant priestesses would thus be a sacrilege. I felt the same way about any chemical or synthetic drug, and during all those druggie days of California dreaming I found to my disappointment that dope, hashish, and opium made me fall into unconscious, flat sleep, that only peyote and mushrooms had any visionary effect on me—and even then it was short-lived. So I followed the advice of one of my college friends and served as the "designated driver" for all my peers taking drug trips.

This was when my girlfriends and I as freshmen in a drug-obsessed coed dorm first began our Lullaby Service to sing down dormmates on bad trips. As I look back on it now, I wonder whether we were unconsciously re-creating a priestess-like ceremony for those enduring the horrors and gifts of a drug-induced initiation, without trained guides to take them through the underworld. In our Lullaby Service, was I reenacting a lost sister society's rituals?

Two decades later I met the author Deena Metzger, who has also come upon ancient temple traditions of the sacred prostitutes after she had written *The Woman Who Slept with Men to Take the War Out of Them.* Deena has led groups to Greece to reenact the Eleusinian Mysteries and she has studied the Mysteries both as scholar and storyteller. Recently I told Deena about my childhood visions of the seven women in the underground pool, asking her if she thought this was some collective or personal memory of the Eleusinian Mysteries.

To my surprise she said, "It's not the Mysteries; not with that underwater cave. I think it belongs to something that I would never in a million years have associated with you! Listen . . ." she said excitedly, "I think you're remembering a secret *mikvah,* those Jewish women's bathing and cleansing rituals which orthodox Hassidic women still practice to this day. Because your memory has those elements of hidden faces and secret, dangerous rites, I think it's about A.D. 1500 in New Mexico when the Secret Jews or *conversos*—also derogatively called *moranos*—probably took their cleansing rites underground to escape terrible persecution." Deena paused and caught her breath; in that breath I heard her own outrage over the long Jewish history of execution and exile that is in her blood. Added to this personal heritage, Deena brings to her own work a strong mystical

Jewish female tradition that parallels an emerging movement in Kabbalistic sacred studies.

"You see," she continued firmly, "in 1542 the Jews in Spain were not allowed to practice their faith. Both Jews and Moors were kicked out of Spain by the Inquisition which also confiscated all the Jewish finances—in fact, Columbus's expedition to the New World was in part funded with what Ferdinand and Isabel stole from the Spanish Jews. Some say that Columbus himself was either Jewish or half-Jewish. During the Spanish Inquisition, Jews were doomed to a double fate: They were persecuted if they admitted their faith, but if they converted, the Inquisitors still believed they practiced secretly. Many of the Spanish Jews fled to Mexico until the Inquisition caught up with them there, too. So they fled again to New Mexico, where they settled in and adopted Christian practices. But many did continue to secretly practice their Jewish traditions." Deena stopped and let out a sad sigh. "Over generations, of course, those Jewish traditions were integrated into Catholicism without their proper meanings because it was all so dangerous and secretive; so children grew up carrying on traditions they didn't understand." Deena laughed. "Have you ever heard of Saint Esther? She's an Old Testament, Jewish queen who, with Mordecai, helped free the Jews. Recognition of Saint Esther among New Mexico Catholics is in fact the remnant of their Jewish heritage, which they may not even dimly remember."

I suddenly remembered from my own reading that *morano* was a pejorative word for "pig," which reminded me that during the Eleusinian Mysteries, there were pigs sacrificed instead of humans. The later Old Testament dictum against eating pork as "unclean" was a code referring to the uncleanliness of pagan or goddess-centered religions. But we often forget in our more rigid sense of the bibical past that there were centuries during which the monotheistic Yahweh of the Bible was not yet the dominant faith—in fact, it was one of many faiths, including many polytheistic traditions, struggling for widespread acceptance.

I asked Deena, "What about those white, hooded robes? You think they're not Greek, but Arab or Moorish Jews?"

"Oh, yes," Deena took up again. "The Arab-Moorish influence in Spain was very strong and those white robes are like djellabahs—perfect for hiding faces and bodies. And why were the women underground, hiding their faces even from one another? Because it was so dangerous! Perhaps what they were doing was continuing a Jewish ritual for which they'd seen their family and friends murdered."

"Maybe that's why there was so much grief and secrecy," I said slowly. "Why I always feel this deep pain and loss . . . why I swore to myself to remember no matter what!"

Deena was quiet a moment, then her voice was soothing. "Listen, let me tell you about a *mikvah*. A Jewish woman during her period will go into a sacred bath to be purified. There is also a *mikvah* before any sacred ritual, say a wedding. The woman is completely immersed underwater three times to make sure of her purity. She does this in solitude, as well as in the company of other women. There is such a great feeling of relief! A *mikvah* eases sorrows and cares . . . it cleanses deep. And performed by other women, it is very healing, intimate, sacred, and knowing . . ."

As I listened it felt as if her words washed over me, the way Vergie long ago poured steaming well water over my small head and then put her big, trained hands on my skull and massaged every hollow.

"Oh, don't we wish we still had those women's bathing rituals . . . one of the few times I envy the orthodoxy!" Deena laughed. "Did you know that many Hassidic women at the *mikvah* ritual before their wedding day will put on the white bridal gown that will also one day be their shroud?"

"Like another kind of sacred marriage," I suggested.

"Yes," Deena said. "Now, let me tell you about the number seven that's so much in your vision. Seven steps, seven women."

Deena explained that seven is the most mystical number in many traditions, but for the Jews it has particular significance because it corresponds to the seven days of creation. Every Sabbath, it is the women who bring down Yahweh. It's a women's tradition to light the candles on Friday night and literally bring down the female aspect of God, the *shechinah,* or that aspect of God that is present in the world. She descends into the world on the Sabbath. At sundown the woman prepares the table with a white cloth, wine, two candles to represent both this world and the sacred world. The woman puts a cloth over her head and lights the candles; then she moves her hands over the lighted candles three times, gathering the light onto her face. She holds the light as she places her hands over her illumined eyes.

It is at this moment that the Vestige of the Goddess, the female aspect of God, descends; for the next twenty-four hours there is no work, only prayer, family, story, celebration, and study. The divine has descended through the woman.

I thanked Deena deeply for her interpretation of my childhood vision. But there was still something missing. It could in fact have been a *mikvah,* but there was an element missing in her version that she was the first to admit. What was missing is what is still missing in all our feminine traditions, half-remembered, performed without full understanding. What's missing is the sense of well-trained priestesshood and authority. In my vision there was a clear and grave sense of responsibility, not guilt or atonement, which belongs so much to the monotheistic religions that conquered the native or pagan traditions. In my dream of the secret sister society, along with the fear of consequences, there is also a deep celebration, even joy in our full, female knowledge. What we don't want to lose is this knowing, this feminine *gnosis* that comes not only from tradition, but from pride and conscious power.

Still seeking other interpretations for my vision, I turned to the painter Christine Lamb. She had just finished illustrating a children's book, *Tale of Two Rice Birds,* which is a compassionate retelling of an old Thai folktale of reincarnation. Christine has long studied diverse artist traditions, from Japanese *sumi-e* painting to intricate Russian orthodox gilded icons of Byzantine archangels. Her nature paintings have been compared to the delicate, gilded temple paintings found in archeological digs from ancient Mayan pyramids to Egyptian murals.

"Oh, it's Crete, Minoan Crete!" Christine pronounced immediately upon my telling her the childhood vision. "Don't you just love those Minoan Crete goddess statues of the women priestesses holding high their hands and snakes encircling their wrists and arms and waists? I'll just bet you and I were in Crete together," Christine continued. We were walking at low tide along Alki Beach, which stretches around a wide point and into Seattle's Elliott Bay. The rare, white sandy beach was exposed because it was a very low summer tide, and we started our walk only to find upon our return that we were wading thigh-deep in warm seawater as we talked. "Minoan Crete was an artist's dream," Christine said. "The culture was so feminine and playful, all those nature paintings on clay sarcophagi of dolphins and snakes.

The creative feminine principle—that's what it was all about! Even the temple priests wore women's dresses . . ."

"Still do," I said, and laughed, "if you include the Pope."

We talked on about the Catholic Church's long centuries of holy war against women, reducing the pagan priestesshood to what Christine calls those "sad-eyed sisters"—the nuns. It reminded me of one of my students, an ex-nun, who told me the shocking story of her German order in which the women had to lower their eyes when passing or sitting across from each other. This turning away from one another was called "The Custody of the Eyes," and was intended to ward off any developing intimacy among the sisters. When I researched the significance of the women's eyes I was startled to find that among the ancient Canaanite-Phoenician priestesses (such as Jezebel), the sacred priestesses would sit at a window and beckon with their eyes to invite the initiates in, to partake of the sacred marriage. As Shepsut comments in her *Journey of the Priestess*, these Astarte cult temple priestesses gave a "special look," a direct and dark-eyed stare which was known as the "look of the priestess." Shepsut adds that this look, when separated from its spiritual origins, became degraded and dissolute, both when "the priestesses brought scorn upon themselves," by inviting only "personal sexual experience," and later by the onslaught of the new religion of Hebrew monotheistic Yahweh who declared in Exodus 19:6, "And ye shall be unto me a kingdom of priests."

In thinking about the many ways in which the sisterhood has found itself stripped of power by the brotherhood, I was struck by the male effort to control everything from a woman's womb to her eyes.

In the old temple priestess days, women certainly belonged to themselves. As earthly embodiments of the Goddess, their physical grace and beauty was a reflection of the Great Mother. Many of the women were not physical virgins—they led and choreographed and gladly performed the sacred marriage to assure fertility—and yet they were often called "virgin," which means "unto herself." This self-possession is what struck me most about all the research I've done into different priestess traditions; it is also true of any culture which encourages a feminine deity, such as that which Christine spoke about in Crete.

"Tell me something," she had said impulsively as we both waded in seawater up to our hips; we barely avoided a floating jellyfish, its gelatinous white mass bobbing about our waists. "When you close your eyes and really remember your childhood vision . . . do it now. Go back to the cave and really look around, not with the eyes of a writer, but like an artist. What's on the walls, any bracelets or other jewelry on the women? If you go back in your mind to what exists just outside your field of vision, the threshold you just crossed, is it a temple or a cave . . . any murals or ceremonial objects?"

It had never occurred to me to re-enter the vision and see it anew, re-imagine it all. We stopped and stood in Puget Sound as the tide tipped us forward and back, our bare feet sinking into sand that fell away as if dropping off a ledge. I swayed easily and remembered: There were torches glowing in the curves of the cave; it was a cave because I could see stalagmites and luminous, mineral walls. Were there murals? No, not in this hot springs cave, but on the way to the ceremony I had passed through a long hallway with bright turquoise paintings of the sea and dolphins, highly stylized, and gilded snakes. Snakes everywhere, and some of them were real. Some of them were in fact looped elegantly around the waists of several of the women in those white robes. Such beautiful bright skin and designs on those snakes who were calm and majestic in their embrace of these priestesses.

The snakes are laid very tenderly on the seven steps as the women step into the pool to receive me. I walk out of my white robe and into the water, but I recognize suddenly a dear friend of mine, another priestess of my rank, and we exchange smiles. She holds my right side and as I look down the length of my body I realize I am much smaller than I am in this life. I am small-boned and very dark-skinned, with long, tightly curled or kinked hair. My body is about the same age as I am now, mid-forties, and as I gaze down over my breasts I realize that unlike in this life, I have been pregnant—there are stretch marks on my stomach and thighs. Then I am startled and smile—for at the very tip of my legs, on each delicate ankle, are brilliant red and black and white serpent tattoos. They coil up my calves in ceremonial splendor. In the water, they sting slightly which means they are new tattoos and as such represent some rite of passage I've just completed.

I look up at the hooded women's faces and can make out only the face of my priestess friend who I realize envies me these serpent tattoos. I am initiated before her and she will follow my path. In her eyes I see the reflection of my face and I realize that my expression is proud and grateful and in that moment when I see the guardian snakes on my ankles and feel the women's strong arms holding me aloft in the warm water—I realize that I am afraid of nothing. I have already gone through the underworld and endured the visions, the potion, the initiation. Now I can rest in the arms of my sisters.

"Well, I guess that explains why your house is full of stuffed snakes and why you've always wanted a cobra tattooed on your ankle!" Christine laughed and shook her head. "I was right to give you my snake painting for your snake altar. It also explains all your Hopi Indian snake-dance photos and your first book."

I nodded slowly, taking it all in, remembering how at a loss I was when finishing my first novel with a snake-handling scene from a Deep South fellowship of true believers. Suddenly, the whole ending changed and I found myself writing a sermon about the Fall in the Garden of Eden from the serpent's point of view. At the time, in 1976, I had no idea what I was doing—another unconscious groping for something dimly remembered. It was only in 1989 when I began to research the old goddess religions that I came across a book, *The Serpent and the Goddess: Women, Religion, and Power in Celtic Ireland*, by Mary Codren, that claimed that the name Eve, *hawwah,* means "mother of all the living," but *hawwah* also means "serpent" in many Semitic languages. Codren comments, "The symbol of the Serpent was the one most widely used to represent or adorn the Goddess of the ancient Near East or to depict, or mediate, the relationship between goddesses and human culture." As a symbol of feminine power, knowledge, of birth and rebirth, the Serpent also suggested the intermingling of good and evil, the reconciliation of opposites. Codren goes on to remark, "The Serpent religions had portrayed their gods as both good and evil, symbolizing the essential ambiguity and tragedy of existence. But the God of the Israelites, to be effective, could not be both good and evil."

When the world changed from the old goddess/pagan/earth and feminine-centered faith to the male warrior sky-god religion of Yahweh, the serpent, like the feminine principle, was forced underground. In the Book of Genesis, the serpent who was once that "beautiful and subtle creature," is doomed to crawl the earth on its belly, to be crushed underfoot, conquered. As Codren explains it, "The change from polytheism to monotheism was to have far-reaching implications. Polytheism was a direct threat to the religious and social organization of Israel, and the Serpent personified that threat in the Genesis story. That Adam and Eve took the fruit, therefore, symbolized not only a petty act of disobedience but a possible sign that they preferred or were going back to the religion of the Serpent."

"You know," Christine continued, musingly, "I used to love snakes as a kid, made these little cardboard-box beds for them, kept them cozy. In Catholic school the nuns always talked about how Saint Patrick ran all the snakes out of Ireland. In the hallways I saw statues of Mary and Saint Theresa standing on top of snakes. I always felt so bad for those poor snakes being stomped on by the saints. Much later I found out that Saint Patrick actually went after the Celtic and Druid priestesses, especially wise women and healers—those people were what the snakes symbolized."

We were wading in toward shore now, the tide so high most everyone else had scampered up the beach; as we pulled ourselves through the green, cool water.

"I've got an idea," Christine volunteered as we brushed the sand off each other and headed for high ground. "Maybe your dream is just an amalgamation of memories, like a mosaic, some collective vision you're just tapping into. Maybe memories of secret sisterhoods are deeply embedded in all women and we're just waking up to them." She laughed. "We've got those secret ways inside us, just all jumbled up . . . like finding pottery shards at a dig. Pottery from hundreds of different traditions, but we're just trying to piece one pot back together from all the broken parts."

All the broken parts, I thought, when I called a filmmaker friend, Clara. "Have you ever considered that your vision is about the oracle at Delphi with that famous dictum 'Know thyself'?" she asked. She herself comes from a long line of strong farm women whose histories are lost, overlooked in favor of the men's frontier heroics. "With all the snakes in your vision it could also be the priestesses at Delphi who descended into their underground sanctuaries and acted as seers. Don't you remember, they called the High Priestess the Pythia—you know, named after the python snake, which was also that mythic dragon Pytho. Didn't Apollo kill Pytho, the sun god conquering the earth goddess? Like the way the priesthood wiped out the priestesses?

Maybe that's why in your dream-vision you're all so scared—you know you're doomed, dying out."

I researched the Delphic Oracle and in a fascinating book, *Priestesses*, by Norma L. Goodrich, about the famous Greek Oracles which flourished from 700 B.C. to about A.D. 300. Of the more than 260 practicing Oracles in ancient Greece, the Delphic Oracle was the most sacred. Presided over by a Pythia, a high priestess trained in the arts of prophecy, mathematics, poetry, music, and all knowledge of the invisible, mystic worlds, the Delphic Oracle held the ancient mind in thrall. It was here in Delphi that the Pythia would descend into her holy underground sanctuary deep in the jagged sea cliffs of Parnassus, soaring high above the Gulf of Corinth. In her sanctuary, the Pythia would endure visions from the other worlds and bring her truths back for any brave enough to seek her sacred counsel. Agamemnon was said to have asked her advice, as did Sophocles, Plutarch, and Plato before he wrote *The Republic*. Odysseus consulted at Delphi before the Trojan War. At Delphi, Homer is believed to have written his epics, and Pindar composed poetry there. Pythagoras, the famous Greek philosopher-mathematician, claimed he was taught ethics by a Delphic priestess, Themistoclea, and Socrates' mentor was Diotema, a priestess of Mantinea.

It is difficult today to imagine an ancient world in which women played so grave and profound a part in sacred teachings, to realize that in fact, the women *were* the religious leaders. But as Goodrich explains, the Greeks revered their Pythia priestess: "For more than two thousand years, this priestess was the highest religious authority in the world, and this [was] in Greece where classical scholars insist women were objects of general contempt. The Delphic Oracles, or priestesses, must have been exceptions to this generality." Were they really exceptions? With all the feminist scholarship under way nowadays, more and more is being revealed about powerful women in antiquity whose stories are simply not yet told. But what is true and documented is that the priestess tradition, even at Delphi, was systematically erased and demonized when the monotheistic religions conquered them to establish the patriarchy we've endured for the past two thousand years. As for the Delphic Oracle, its decline was a long, agonizing one—plundered by Philip II of Macedon in 359–336 B.C. and successfully sacked by Gaul and barbarian invaders in 279 B.C.

and 83 B.C., its art treasures looted by Roman emperors Sulla and Nero in A.D. 54–58. Finally, chronicles Goodrich, "The Emperor Justinian, who himself could neither read nor write *closed the oracle and the schools* of Philosophy in Greece in A.D. 529, after which indescribably tragic date *there were no more educated women in Greece for well over a thousand years . . . no more priestesses.*"

No more priestesses. On one hand this is a phrase that could be uttered by women in sorrow and with a keen sense of loss—like that grief I felt in my vision, even as I performed the celebratory ceremony. On the other hand, "No more priestesses!" could be fervently shouted by an early Church inquisitor at a witch-hunt trial or even still today by a fundamentalist outside an abortion clinic as he carries a sign like the one pictured in a recent *New York Times* photo, "Femi-Nazis Everywhere!"

What became of the sacred priestess traditions? Did they go underground and survive persecution in some form only dimly remembered, the way those secret Jews who converted to the dominant religion still kept some remnant of their original beliefs, however confused or unconscious? In the past several decades, more scholarship has emerged to document the widespread destruction of sister societies, whether they were sacred or social. Along with the worldwide political systems that denied women property, the vote, or any power of ownership, there was also the elimination of any competition from women in the fields of healing and religion. The early church, that brotherhood of priests proclaimed in Exodus, introduced a God who would have no other gods before Him. This certainly meant no goddesses. And no more priestesses. The early pagan deities of nature were proclaimed as devils or demons, the sibling rivalry of the Greek pantheon of gods and goddesses was destroyed by a Roman church that adopted Christianity as the state religion, and the flourishing folk traditions of prophecy and rituals around birth, death, and illness were brutally destroyed by the dark age of the Inquisition and witch-hunts in Old Europe.

In her book *Witchcraze: A New History of the European Witch Hunts: Our Legacy of Violence Against Women*, author Anne Llewellyn Barstow documents the terror of three centuries of a calculated holocaust against women in which more than 100,000 midwives, healers, diviners, seers, wizards, dowsers, astrologers, exorcists, spell-casters, counselors, and herbalists were annihilated. The world of the sixteenth century, she explains, was much more a world of women than we know today. Only the wealthy could seek out the services of the new professionals called doctors (all male); the mainstream sought help from trained women who knew the mysteries of birth, death, and the supernatural. As such, these women were direct competition and a threat to the priests and male doctors. In fact, women had a "special edge over the clergy: as the authorities on matters of sex, they asserted what control was possible over fertility, conception, successful pregnancy, and safe childbirth." As experts, these women held "a power that the churches were determined to wrest from them."

And they did, so successfully in fact, that even now, four centuries later, there is still a struggle between the powerful lobby of the American Medical Association and the resurgence of the midwife tradition. Women priests are still furiously excluded from the Catholic Church, though a few Episcopal and Anglican women serve as priests, and there have been only a handful of rogue Christian female ministers, mostly healers and charismatics, who have found followings. In the last years, a few rare female rabbis now find synagogues open to them. The Mormon Church prohibits women from giving the sacred blessing and only men can be priests. Muslims rigorously refuse any female authority within their religion and in places like Saudi Arabia the man still has the right to kill or punish his wives or sisters. Even among the Eastern traditions of Hinduism and Buddhism, which celebrate female divinities, mortal women have hardly fared better; there are painfully few yoga masters who are women, and no history of any Tibetan Dalai Lama being a woman.

Here at the end of the twentieth century, the brotherhood is still very much in control, though many inroads are being made and a new millennium promises to bring revolutionary changes. Who knows what the sacred traditions will look like in the twenty-first century? Will we return to brotherhood traditions living side by side with reestablished sisterhoods? Will the brotherhoods realize their deep loss and need for the feminine? Will women one day, without fear and with graceful authority, re-create visions such as the one I've carried within me since childhood?

"Well, maybe it wasn't Delphi," Clara continued in our search to define the tradition I remembered in my vision. "Did you know that they never allowed women to seek the counsel of the High Priestess, the Pythia?"

"Yes, I read about that," I said sadly. "I wonder how it felt for those priestesses to offer their visions and teachings only to men. Did that isolate them from each other somehow, if their feminine contact was only with each other and not with ordinary women from all social classes? And without the support of a society which valued all women, did those priestesses turn to each other both with respect, but also . . ." I hesitated, but Clara urged me on. "Well . . . I can hardly say it, with contempt? Did they take that all-pervasive misogyny in the ancient society and turn it against themselves?"

"And what happens," Clara asked softly, "when now we look in the mirror of one another's eyes, those who have begun to heal all that internalized self-hatred from the patriarchy? What happens when we steal a glance at our sister who looks back at us, as that priestess did in your vision, and reflects back to us an image of beauty and holiness?"

"The world changes," I whispered, as if afraid we would be overheard. "The whole world changes."

A rediscovered language of sacred sisterhood can change the world. One way to begin this work is to reestablish and claim the lost, feminine traditions of spiritual practice: to know ourselves, and mirror each other, without blaming our brothers. In fact, the brotherhood should no longer be our standard or focus. In the way that the women's movement began with rightful outrage, it is now moving into a more visionary period in which women re-imagine the feminine as distinct and powerful in itself. We know who we are not; we are not men. Then how can we know ourselves now as women? Nearing the new millennium, let's imagine that women are at last admitted entrance to seek counsel from a Delphic Oracle that still exists collectively within every one of us—and teaches "Know thyself."

In my own search for a spiritual sisterhood with which to expand upon that of my blood sisters and chosen sister friends, I've discovered a common theme: Sacred feminine traditions, whether they're pagan Wicca, mystical Kabbalistic Jewish, Native American women's societies, or goddess-based, are all fiercely committed to grass-roots groups. They eschew the hierarchies and evangelical zeal that form the power base of many organized religions. As Asia Shepsut comments in *Journey of the Priestess*, the priestess traditions such as those found in Cretan shrines were not grandiose, but intimate: "In contrast to Mesopotamia or Egypt (or present-day religions) they had no monumental temples, and their cult images were on a small scale." This small scale seems an enduring characteristic of the sacred feminine, which turns inward and away from the monolithic and highly structured religious path of the orthodox religions. It also avoids the warrior traditions of fundamentalist faiths which might kill to claim a soul for their cause. In the famous words of the Greek poet Sappho, whose native island of Lesbos was the site of Demeter-Persephone sanctuaries and a flourishing priestess tradition, "Some say cavalry and others claim infantry or a fleet of long oars is the supreme sight on the black earth. I say it is the one you love."

When the story line of war replaced the drama of love, when the warrior-priests conquered the priestess traditions, our world religions began to revere death over life, the masculine, conquering king-hero over the underworld-queen's inward journey. But were there other reasons the priestess tradition failed? I do not want to be a pagan-priestess fundamentalist and proclaim that the Judeo-Christian patriarchal tradition is all bad and the sacred, polytheistic priestess traditions are all good. I've often wondered if the fall of the priestesshood came from within, as well as from without. The secretive and dangerous sense of my own childhood vision, the way I had to hide it and keep my own counsel while being raised by a Southern Baptist brotherhood tradition, has taught me much about the collective repression and calculated misogyny of the patriarchy. But I will not heal myself through reverse prejudice or switching from one polarity to the other. Perhaps I can learn from that biblical story of Jezebel, priestess of Astarte, and Elijah, Jehovah's prophet. According to Professor Phyllis Trible in *Out of the Garden: Women Writers on the Bible*, both priestess and prophet are "mirror images" who are "inextricably hinged through the convergence of opposites." Here, too, is the place where polarities meet, where pagan priestess and prophet of Yahweh become a paradoxical "odd couple." Trible concludes, "In Elijah, Jezebel resides; in Jezebel, Elijah resides."

We are all odd couples within—extremists struggling and seeking some balance, that middle path which is spacious enough to contain and even celebrate the opposite poles which would pull us apart.

If as modern women we reclaim our priestess traditions, we will also have to look unflinchingly at the inner betrayals and politics within our sisterhoods. Jezebel and Elijah both called down terrible violence upon each other in the names of their deities. Jezebel and Elijah were also both intent on dominion over the other—a holy war. Were the sisterhoods, like the brotherhoods, also prey to narrow-mindedness? Did the secretive and inward-turning priestess traditions forget the gifts of the expansive, outer-directed masculine sun gods? While the brotherhood excluded and condemned in its witch-hunts and fanatic control of women's bodies, did the sisterhood exclude and condemn some part of the masculine that it needed to integrate in order to survive? Whenever the leadership of a faith is exclusively female or male, we lose some balance within ourselves, the sense of wholeness that was long ago symbolized by the sacred marriage of masculine and feminine.

In the modern world of polarities, asking questions such as these may not be popular with either men or women, religious or secular —but they must be asked because it is not blame I am looking for, it is balance. And it seems to me that the brotherhoods and sisterhoods need each other to find their mirror and mates—and to reconcile the opposites that have been too long segregated. Somewhere in the middle exists a sacred tradition in which both men-led and women-led faiths coexist; perhaps even in the future there may be two male ministers such as the openly gay theologians now serving Seattle's Church of Christ, two female priests (priestesses) leading an Episcopal congregation, or male-and-female partners serving as rabbis. Perhaps even one day, wonder of wonders, there might be a female Pope, as the Catholic scholar and theologian Uta Ranke-Heinemann has envisioned.

I may never really know what exact sister-society tradition I so fiercely remembered and held secret during my childhood, and have been researching and trying to reclaim ever since. I have attempted to find spiritual solace and community in small groups of women, each of whom is pursuing her own sacred tradition. In my drumming circle, at my yoga studio, which is also a holistic childbirth center, among my literary and bodyworker friends, even in my book club, I have enjoyed some of the most spiritually nurturing rituals and practices of any lifetime. As much as I mourn the loss of the official priestess tradition, perhaps it is exactly that sense of grief that has made me search out my own path. One of my elderly friends, a religious scholar, once soothed me by saying, "Motherless children are most loved by the Great Mother." I might add that perhaps we sisterless or priestessless women of the twentieth century are also the most dear to the divine feminine—being as we are so keenly aware of what we have lost. Such longing can also create a passionate search to restore ourselves to wholeness, to know ourselves as women and sisters, to grow old, taking the sacred journey of sisterhood together.

Growing old together and consciously re-creating sisterhood traditions that involve companionship, spiritual ritual, and support is exactly what many women have been doing in the burgeoning, grass-roots movement called Crones. These Crone societies of women aged fifty to ninety have sprung up all over the country. This wise and remarkable sister society of our elders is a sharp contrast to the "Golden Girls" media stereotypes. On a recent visit to a Crone meeting, I found a lively, admirable, and enlightened group—especially in their blend of compassion and black humor. The Crone image is based on the Triple Goddess symbols of maiden/mother/crone. As defined by Jungian analyst and author Marion Woodman, this Hecate, or third part of the trilogy, is "goddess of the crossroads . . . the personal road and the transpersonal, the transitory and the eternal." She goes on to say, "I see the Crone without desire for power; without desire, that is, to control others. She is an empowered feminine. She has no desire to control because she has nothing to lose. Who she is, is, and you cannot take it away from her." The Crone is a wise woman, says Woodman, because she is both discriminating and also loving; she is detached with her transpersonal view, but she can also express her grief—after all, at her age, a Crone has accumulated many sorrows; but she tends to see herself as part of a divine comedy, because her age gives her a time span in which she has witnessed many cycles.

When I was invited to witness a Seattle Crone gathering I was delighted to be welcomed by ten or so women who defied any common denominator, except that all were over fifty. There was Abigail, wearing a hot-pink velour top with her African carved wooden animal necklace, next to a stylishly tailored art student, Jean, who laughed with Peggy, a retired English teacher and journalist who spent years in Hawaii studying dolphins. There were women who at sixty had returned to school or begun a business; there were grandmothers who rigorously refused to discuss grandchildren or show family photos, saying, "You notice we have no refreshments. We aren't going to sit around swapping recipes or stories of our kids. We're here to talk about ourselves, our lives and ideas. It's our turn."

The women in this subversive, fascinating sister society of elders gave one another such deep attention that I was startled at the intensity and passion of their discourse. It ranged from politics to meditation, from housing alternatives for older women, to poetry. One of the women remarked, "Women are wonderful company. Not a lot of men my age now measure up to that."

"That" is the standard by which Crones take one another's measure. It is a standard that is both spoken and celebrated. "I want to be with women in power, women who know themselves," Peggy explained to me as the other women nodded empathically. "There is, at our ages, more time to know who we are. You see, we've got time to be more aware, the larger capacity to feel everything from ecstasy to the deepest grief. We've got the depth and time, even the bodies now, to contain it. We see the end approaching . . . like that law of *physics*—as you approach a wall, things seem to go faster. That's how it is facing death. We know things are speeding up and we have to understand and face them as they come." She paused thoughtfully. "Yet there is this delicious sense of spaciousness, too, of really having all the time in the world to talk about ideas! I don't want any one-on-one nurturing where I'm the main caretaker. I want community, tribe."

"Remember how our mothers gathered on front porches?" another Crone took up. "There was that old-lady time of rocking and knowing the world and each other. How many younger women ever have that experience?"

"Yeah," another Crone countered. "All you younger women do is network, do lunch—that's a very businesslike and masculine approach to relationships."

When I explained that some of us purposely seek spiritual or sisterly communities, some of the Crones agreed that sisterhood was much more than a political agenda—that it was, in fact, a way of being in the world with one another. Of the ten Crones gathered that night, only three had sisters.

"Oh, I always wanted a sister!" one of them mused. "You know, women from my generation. . . . I'm in my late sixties, we didn't have your sixties feminism to say it's okay to value the company of women. Our notion of sisterhood was limited to biological or extended family. Between our men and our children, we had so many demands made on us. Now, the husbands are dead, the children are grown up —and we finally have time to make a sisterhood."

"Right," agreed another Crone. "We certainly never dreamed that in midlife we were creating a baby boom! But the upshot is that the post-sixties idea of women in relationship with one another is not only relatively new, it is a real opportunity for us all." She stopped, then gazed around at her peers, adding, "It has saved my life to be with women my age . . . not only my health, but my spirit. We read together, we've taught each other yoga and how to meditate. There're so few role models for us, but by the time your generation is our age, there'll be a gazillion of you!"

"So, listen up," Peggy said and laughed. "Maybe we can teach you a thing or two."

I did listen up and I did learn much about the exhilarating and soulful nature of elders in communion, in community. What struck me most was the laughter coming so close as it did to grief—the emotional range of the older women reminded me of that flexible continuum of emotions usually allowed only in childhood. These women had that expansiveness, but also they were keenly aware of their limitations.

Jean, the journalist, commented, "I had children in my house for thirty years, from the time I was twenty-five until I was sixty! Now I don't baby-sit and when my children expect me to do physical things my body can't handle or demand emotional support I might need for myself, I tell them *Enough!* I want to be alone—or else with my sisters. Crone meetings are one of the few times I give up my cherished solitude."

"My husband loves it when I go to Crone meetings," Doreen added. "It gives him more time with his computer."

"And my husband always sneaks around and tries to get me to go to dinner with him the same night as Crones. In the old days I would follow his wishes, but now I remind him it's *my* night with the girls!"

When I make the idealistic suggestion that their elder sister society might want to initiate the younger women, much the way the ancient sister societies taught rites of death and rebirth, several of the women set me straight.

"We're tired of caretaking!" one Crone smiled, but her expression was dead serious. "We've taken care of children, then our own parents, then our husbands . . . now it's time for *us!*"

"Yeah," another Crone joined in. "Don't take this personally, but at some of our Crone retreats and picnics there are these younger women, about your age, hanging around . . . like . . . well, like groupies!" The women all howled, glancing my way with no attempt at discretion. "We call them Cronelings," the older woman continued with gleeful contempt. "Don't think us wicked old women, but I'm sorry, women who haven't been through the change, they just don't know enough . . ."

"Right," Peggy joked. "Do you know that we have hired a private eye to investigate physicians' records to make sure that every Crone is postmenopausal?"

"No premenopausal women can be Croned," teased another. "At my croning ceremony, it was so moving, so spirit-filled. . . . I felt—" Suddenly the woman stopped, glanced around the room at her elder sisters, and simply fell silent. She smiled at me and nodded. "Sorry," she said, "secret."

"Like most mystery rites," I nodded. I was torn between chagrin and pleasure. It was good to be set straight, to be put in my place between these elders who by their own description subtitled their Crone sister society "Women growing older with power, passion, and purpose." I thought of the other elder women's organizations popping up all over the country, such as the Oregon-based BLOWS (Bag Ladies of the World), and the more radical communities such as Wicked Aunties, Fast Women, and Bull Leapers. I remembered that part of the sacred play and ritual of ancient Crete were the male and female bull leapers who celebrated their mystery rites by leaping over the backs of bulls to honor the Great Goddess.

This honoring of elder women is a trend which I hope will only continue in our society—a culture which by the year 2000 will embrace 42 percent of a female population over fifty. Add to that statistic the fact that women between the ages of forty and sixty are the fastest-growing population in America and you have the ingredients, not for a recipe, but for a revolution.

Perhaps this is exactly what I was witnessing at that Crone meeting. But if it is a revolution, it is beginning, as post-fifty Gloria Steinem declares, as a revolution from within. "I had to shed a lot of things to get here . . ." Peggy concluded, speaking for many of the elders in the Crones. "We're a sassy lot, but we've got a lot on our minds." Then, after an announcement that there would be a meditation meeting at Peggy's home, the Crone gathering turned inward and away from any outsider, any observer. They spoke their private language of age and lost illusions, of humor and dismay. And I left them to their profound work.

It is work I hope to take part in when I reach the Crone stage of my life; and I hope that when I am that age I have the grace and self-possession of the women I had the pleasure of sitting with that night. Surrounded by my female elders, I felt an echo of that long-ago childhood vision in which I endured an initiation rite of death and rebirth, supported in my sisters' arms.

Some of what is lost can be found again, I reminded myself that night—whether it's a lost language, a tradition, a tribe, or a sister. And our elders teach us that even as we lose some things, such as our youth, our physical beauty, even our mates, we also find gifts along the way. One of those gifts is self-knowledge, as the Delphic Oracle counsels.

As I gazed at these aging Crone faces, I thought how natural it was to find this enduring and wise elder-sister society. It was as natural as biology—the way elder female dolphins or elephants assure that a whole pod or herd endures. This Crone gathering also felt as natural to me as any blood-sister tribe or ceremony. For here was spiritual service, but there were no sinners, no saved. There was only the mystery of steadily facing death together. Certainly that final mysterious rite is natural to the sisterhood—as my grandmother Vergie said, "bringing them in and seeing them out." It's women's work. It's soul work.

At the end of the CRONEversation, silver-haired Abigail leaned conspiratorially near me and whispered, "Know why I like Crones better than any bunch of old churchwomen? Church ladies will say, 'Oh, dear, that's not nice, is it?' "

"Goddamn goody-goodies!" another Crone cackled, and everyone joined in clapping their agreement.

"But this is not about being good or nice." Abigail gave me a deep look—exactly the way Vergie used to inform me that I must learn to keep my own feminine counsel. "This is about being at the end—and what's good about it is the company we Crones keep."

I've promised myself, when I cross the Crone threshold of fifty, I will get that tattoo—a sacred serpent gracefully embracing my ankle. Maybe I will never really trace my childhood vision of secret sister societies. But I do know this: Before I die, I will consciously reenact that underground hot springs ritual, choosing seven women from among my dearest sisters. I'll choose Crones and nieces, blood sisters and those who have proven true over our long lives together. We will call upon all the sacred sisterhoods to witness this return to our birthright, even as I prepare myself to cross the threshold of death. There will be singing and bathing and praying; we'll wear white robes and at some point in the ceremony I'll ask to look up, held in the embrace of strong, feminine arms and the hoods will be pulled back to reveal those who carry me over. What I witness will be familiar and also a revelation. What I'll see will be as ancient as death, and as much a wonder as any childhood vision. *Remember this,* I'll tell myself, looking up into the women's faces who have loved and known me all my life. Then, I can go on to whatever worlds await me, because I will have at last been initiated into mysteries that belong to me. And, if I am lucky, there will be a woman, much like my grandmother Vergie, who will perform the death chores over my brave, empty body, all the while aware of that sacred sisterhood, invisible, but waiting alongside to receive my soul, my "beautification practice."

Part Three

Sisters Lost
and Found

7

Sisters Lost and Found

I was on my way to the private funeral rites of a beloved friend—
when I ran into that very friend. Let me explain. That autumn day
in 1993, I was holding a symbolic funeral rite for my sister-friend
Beatrice, not to mourn her death, but to memorialize the death of our
friendship. I wanted to find a way to acknowledge our loss of each
other and to let go of my expectations that this lost sister would ever
return to me. That is why I was so stunned after not having seen
Beatrice for more than a year—not having spoken to her or received
any response to my several notes—to literally run in to her in a Seattle
coffeehouse on the very day of my imagined funeral for her.

The year 1992 was a bad year for what I call my chosen sisterhood;
these are the women friends who have become surrogate sisters for
me, since my own biological sisters live on the East Coast. I have
always been blessed with an intimate tribe of women friends who, as
Zenko has said of her American chosen sisters, "all have the same
shoulder," to support each other. But that year my whole world of
sister-friends turned upside down. Ironically enough, the sisters I lost
and found that year were the two friends who most reminded me of
my own blood sisters, Paula and Marla.

In Beatrice, I often found myself caught between the same bewildering extremes of loving kindness and contrariness that I experience with my little sister Marla. On one hand, Beatrice was a constant comfort, listening and nurturing, always attentive to my every sorrow, a midwife to my work, and a sweet advocate who stood beside me when I faced adversity. But there was always between Beatrice and myself a tension. We were both caretakers and as such sometimes rebelled against all the nurturing required of us. In our more mutinous phases, we would also sometimes withdraw from each other, as if resenting the expectation of our sisterhood: that we must always give to each other unstintingly. Sometimes we let each other down on purpose, if only to prove that we could still be sisters, be loved, if we didn't perform all those loving acts of kindness. Beatrice was also more spiritually narrow and inflexible than many of my friends. Long a student of Eastern religions, she was sometimes oddly otherworldly, even ethereal, while at the same time downright judgmental about others' excesses. At her core, Beatrice was an ascetic whose strong sensual skills frightened her. When Beatrice was frightened, she had what she herself called "shadow attacks," and she stonewalled everyone around her, from family to friends.

In this way, Beatrice was very much like my sister Marla. As children, my sister Paula and I secretly believed Marla was an earth angel because of her extraordinary sensitivity and sweetness; but when Marla was riled or her rigid moral universe threatened, she could shock her older sisters with her obstinacy and outrage. That's when she'd dig in her heels and stubbornly stonewall us into submission. It surprised none of us that Marla would grow up to be a staunch conservative and passionate soldier of the Christian Coalition. Now we call our little sister our "Avenging Angel." Marla still has that sisterly sweetness, though, which can melt as well as manipulate her elder sisters. She is also quite charming, beautiful, and has a playful sense of humor as well as deep melancholy. As an intensive care nurse married to an ER doctor and the mother of three boys, my little sister is also a healer in her own way. Certainly I have called upon her medical expertise and understanding. Marla is more patient than Paula. She will go to great lengths to explain an illness or diagnosis, whereas Paula is authoritative and gives strong advice. Woe to those who are fool enough not to take it! In the way that Paula is strong-willed and sometimes controlling of those she loves (all, of course, for their own good!), Marla retreats at times into her own shell, if she does not get her way. As the eldest sister, I vacillate between this authority and withdrawal. Paula often teases me that I should wear a little sign with a sliding door to indicate that I'm "in" or "out." In this way, I suppose I am also like Beatrice, the caretaker-rebel who can go from the extremes of deep, even sensual nurturing to a disappearing act.

Certainly choosing to live across the continent from my family and sisters qualifies me as being "out" much of the time in family affairs. But it doesn't stop me from re-creating, consciously or unconsciously, my own three-sister triangle here on the West Coast.

If I found in my friend Beatrice an echo of my little sister Marla's kindness and melancholy, then I found in my friend Rebecca, or "Ra," as I teasingly call her, a strong resemblance to my sister Paula. Both Rebecca and Paula are staunchly loyal, willful, and generous in their sisterhoods. Both women have strong opinions about how I should live my life and never hesitate to hold up that sister-mirror to me. Sometimes their mirror is startlingly critical, as well as devoted. I trust both Paula and Rebecca with my life. In their own ways, each of these sisters has also helped me attend to my physical body as well as my soul. When I might float or wander off in spirit realms, Paula will remind me that it's time to buy new makeup. And if Rebecca, who, as my first yoga teacher, senses that I'm not grounded, she'll literally lay skilled hands on me and readjust my spine or tell me I've been slouching too much at the computer. Rebecca often tells me that when she first met me her instinct was to make me some hot soup, "from scratch," from her bountiful kitchen. And whenever I visit my sister Paula she insists on adding to my wardrobe and taking me to high society balls. Paula is particularly appalled by my lack of high heels; one Christmas she marched me down to an Italian shoe shop and bought me designer shoes of such soft leather I was convinced they should be worn only on the hands, not the feet. Both Rebecca and Paula have a sure sense of the material world. I've dubbed Rebecca "Ms. Consumer Reports," because while she researches the best buys, often I find myself simply following after her and buying the same brightly striped Navajo couch, sheets, or natural fiber rugs. Paula is the sister who has taken it upon herself to teach me about money. When I sold my first book, she sent me a one-hundred-dollar bill and insisted that I spend it all in one day only on presents for myself and my friends. "You should know what it feels like to have everything you need," Paula informed me. "So when you do have money someday, you won't just blow it."

For almost a decade my re-created sister triangle here in Seattle was at the center of my larger sister society. When this triangle fell apart several years ago, it was as terrible to me as if I'd lost one of my own blood sisters. And that is why I needed to imagine a funeral rite to mourn my lost "little sister" Beatrice.

The symbolic funeral was almost the exact anniversary of our falling out a year before on election night, 1992. Beatrice had been my bosom friend for more than six years. We first met while she was struggling with a troubled marriage, just discovering her own life after raising two sons. Beatrice, an accomplished dancer, and I encountered each other in 1986 at an evening yoga class. I was just beginning my apprenticeship study of a Chinese bodywork called *jin shin jytsu*, a form of acupressure. We were well matched in our fascination with massage techniques and hatha-yoga, but Beatrice was definitely the more advanced. She was an inspired massage therapist and made a very good living with her practice, whereas I always kept my bodywork study secondary to my work as a writer. Still, Beatrice felt she had met a peer in me because both of us preferred to work with subtle forms of bodywork, more feminine styles of acupressure, cranial, sacral, or other light-touch techniques. Rebecca completed our triad of yoga and bodywork study; she was considered a master of the deep-tissue massage style. Rebecca has studied metaphysics and traveled all over the Third World by herself. Her Italian dark skin and striking green eyes let her pass as a native in many cultures. Add to that the small diamond that adorns her nose and you have a woman who is often mistaken for East Indian or Afghanistani.

Where Rebecca was dark and adventuresome, Beatrice had ringlets of pale blond hair and an air of vulnerability. She did not like to travel alone; in fact, Beatrice liked forming partnerships. She was often in business with her husband; she kept close tabs on her sons, and she always envisioned a colleague or partnership for every project she took on—whether it was a workshop or a massage class. Beatrice had known Rebecca for at least a decade in the massage/yoga community before I came along. At first I expected that we three would pal around together—that I could almost literally re-create my own family's three-sister triangle. But unlike my own two sisters who have a close, albeit competitive, relationship with each other aside from me, Beatrice and Rebecca chafed uncomfortably in each other's company.

What I realized several years into this threesome is that I had in fact re-created my own biological sisterhood: Beatrice and Rebecca were rivals in their own lives. Indeed, their lives paralleled each other's, just the way my own sisters have been rivals from childhood. So here I was again, cross-country from my own blood sisters, and yet engaged in watching this sibling rivalry. It fascinated me, as it did when I was a child and watched my sisters create similar lives, competing right down to the details of dates and dresses. I'm sure this rivalry intrigues me because I've not had much opportunity to engage in it myself—not because I'm immune to competition, but simply because it was not my childhood role; so I'm not set up for it or skilled at it. I am, however, involved, in that I watch from the sidelines like a girl raptly eyeing the arch of a jump rope held between two other girls and waiting my chance to enter the game.

So there I was between two chosen sisters who reminded me very much of my own blood sisters, minus their intimacy. And our weekly sister society looked like this: On Tuesday night, after my yoga class shared with Beatrice, I'd have dinner and sometimes a hot tub with her. On Wednesday night I'd scoot up to Rebecca's house for what we called our holy rite of "Veg Night." We'd eat take-out Thai food and sit in Rebecca's "Womb Room" with the big-screened TV and VCR she'd gotten from her recent divorce. We'd laugh and gossip and carry on until it was movie time. Both being film buffs of classic mysteries, we'd settle in with our desserts and try to outguess each other through every twist and delightful turn of the plots. Sometimes, mid-murder, Rebecca would leap up and announce, "I've got to make brownies or else I can't solve this one!" I called her the Goddess of Goodies, for such all-time favorites as double-fudge killer brownies, to-die-for apple pie, and delicious rhubarb crisp. Sometimes we'd forsake the murder mysteries and instead delve into Rebecca's many travel stories or her latest metaphysical journey. Between us was a playfulness and curiosity that often sent us out into the world on vacations together, from hiking Havasu Canyon to hot springs in Mendocino.

Whereas my sister bond with Rebecca often sent the two of us reeling outward into the world, my friendship with Beatrice was inward-turning. Together we sought tranquility, both psychic and emotional. Sometimes we jokingly called ourselves "The Sensitive Sisters," because much of our talk revolved around our relationships, our troubled childhoods, and our fascination with various alternative-healing practices.

If there was one common thread that bound all three of us it would be just that—healing, particularly the feminine forms of it that have often been banished or denied mainstream medical respect. I met both Beatrice and Rebecca at about the same time, after I myself had just survived a life-threatening neurological illness that defied my Western medical doctors but had found a cure in Chinese medicine. Always the student, I entered the fascinating field of alternative medicine, which has ten years later become almost mainstream. In my own study and practice, I turned toward new friends such as Rebecca and Beatrice as a novice might enter a sister society of female healers—entering their world with gratitude and deep curiosity.

During years of friendship, both Rebecca and Beatrice accepted me as an equal in my own healing-arts studies and by the time Beatrice and I broke off our sisterhood, we had seen each other through many crises, both physical and emotional. Each of us helped the other end long-term primary partnerships, our friendships like ballast in bad weather. I nursed Beatrice after her terrible car accident and she nurtured me through several health crises. When Rebecca planned her surgery, she sneaked me into the post-op to do *jin shin* and help her recover from the anesthetic; she often kept my lumbar spine aligned on the straight and not narrow.

Sometimes I wonder if I would still be alive today if it were not for these two dear friends. To know now that one of them, Beatrice, is a lost sister, grieves me; I will always mourn her loss. The irony in all of this is that when Beatrice and I had our falling out, she had called me to commiserate over a rift between myself and Rebecca.

True to her free-spirit character, Rebecca had upped and decided to cancel our Veg Nights because she wanted to be more "spontaneous" in her life. She was deeply engaged in more travel plans, her new live-in boyfriend was working on his Ph.D. and needed quiet, and Rebecca had decided the demands of her own work schedule made our weekly Wednesdays seem too constricting. "I'm tearing apart all of my daily structures," she announced with typical bombast in the fall of 1992. "I'm revising myself!"

I was hurt at her revising our weekly rendezvous. As for me, wandering in other worlds all day as a writer, I depend on the comfort of structure and ease for my evenings. Of course, I had other friends who were pleased that my Wednesdays were now open for those "spontaneous" social pleasures that Rebecca so extolled; but for me, not having to plan my weekly meetings with friends and my partner was part of the pleasure.

Many of my own private sister society of friends are self-employed. We spend so much of our time scheduling busy work lives that when the evenings come and I meet with, say, my writer pal Susan Biskeborn on what we call "Holy Tuesdays," to exchange chapter critiques and dinner, or with my editor and friend Peggy Taylor for rousing weekly intellectual confabs—we are seeking that particular feminine comfort of habit and intimacy. Doris Lessing once wrote that "habit was half of love," and my weekly sister societies have given me this deep, connecting bond.

So I'll admit Rebecca's announcement about spontaneous scheduling was met with dismay and displeasure on my part. I insisted that there was something insidious going on and covered my simple, hurt feelings with criticism of her—something sisters do a lot with each other. I can well remember my sister Paula trying to tell me how much I'd hurt her in high school when I ignored her for a clique of girlfriends my own age. Instead of telling me she was hurt, she decided never to speak to me again. Our silence lasted about three weeks—and that's hard to do when you share a bathroom. In my adult life I'd never had a rupture between my sisters and myself that stopped the dialogue; sometimes we yell and sometimes we fight dirty. But we've never stopped talking to one another for very long.

So when I found that after Rebecca canceled our Wednesday nights, we were also not speaking to each other, I was horrified. And that was where Beatrice came in. I half expected that she might even be a go-between after several months of silence had passed between myself and Rebecca. I found another comforting Veg Night structure with my painter friend Christine, but I was still miffed at Rebecca. I've learned that one cannot replace a friend, ever. So while I was happy to have more time with Christine, I mourned Rebecca and I was bewildered as to how to end our silence.

After several months it was downright awkward and it loomed between us meaningfully, if not menacingly. I talked often to Beatrice about my sadness over losing Rebecca, and Beatrice was, as always, very attentive and kind. We had sacrificed our hot tubs for politics, post-yoga class. It was the throes of the fall 1992 presidential campaign and we were following all the pre-election brouhaha with delight. It was like watching a political passion play and we couldn't get enough of it. In this way, Beatrice reminded me of my own family, which is devoted to politics and can't have a single dinner without discussing the great events of the day. Beatrice and I even considered traveling to Washington, D.C., for an Inaugural Ball to which my parents were invited.

We'd decided to spend election night glued to the returns and we spent as much time preparing for that great event as if we were teenagers plotting a prom. By that time we were so far sunk in politics that we'd decided to get a toy plastic gun that shot Ping-Pong balls so we could blast the TV screen if we heard election results we didn't like. We'd also planned a potluck and even had bought a bottle of champagne. Since neither of us drink much and can't hold our liquor, election night was anticipated as eagerly as any bacchanalia.

It's interesting looking back two years later to realize the sequence of events around this lost sisterhood. There I was, out of contact with one sister, Rebecca, and seeking succor from another. This is a typical pattern with my own biological sisters and it was playing out here again, the subtle shifting alliances between the players in a sister triangle. It was not about us-against-her; it was about comforting one another when there was deep misunderstanding between two of us.

I'll never forget my shock then, when my re-created, chosen sister triangle radically departed from my own childhood model and entered new, terrifying territory. Territory I still have yet to understand and whose broken treaties I have not yet mended. How ironic that these were the two sisters who considered themselves healers.

Two nights before the election, I got a call from Beatrice. She was checking in to see how I was doing with my terrible head cold and asked if I'd heard anything yet from Rebecca.

"No," I said sadly. "Still silence." I paused and said grudgingly, "I suppose I should be the one to call Rebecca."

"Maybe," Beatrice replied. "Maybe so."

I sensed something strange in her voice, a reserve and nervousness that was not characteristic of this woman who made a living with her soothing voice and hands. But I ignored it and continued, "I just can't understand this terrible rift. If you'd told me that one day I wouldn't be speaking to my friend Rebecca I'd say, oh, no, that would never happen, not with *her*. It would be as absurd as . . . well, not speaking with *you*."

I was referring to the temporary lapse Beatrice and I had endured several years back when her house had been broken into and I'd offered to help and she'd said no. We'd had an angry fight, a week or so of silence, and then talked it out and carried on as before.

"Well, we got through that okay," Beatrice laughed.

But there was still an edge of nervousness in her tone. "Listen," I said, "I can't imagine having a falling-out with you like this. I'm sure we'd break the stupid silence and make up."

"I'm sure we would," Beatrice said softly. Then she paused and her voice was urgent, so radically different I at last let go of my preoccupation with one lost sister and gave her my deepest attention. "I want you to promise me that we'll always talk, you and I, that we'll never murder each other in our minds, or punish each other with this kind of bitter silence."

Without even thinking I assured her. "Of course I promise. What, do you think I'm crazy? Do you think I want to lose *another* friend?"

"No," she said and even on the phone I could sense her tensing as she continued. "But I do have something to tell you that you won't like one bit."

I felt an alarm that at the moment I thought was silly, but two years later I realize it was a premonition. "Tell me quick and get it over with, will you?"

"I can't make our election night bash," she said firmly. "I've made other plans."

I waited for her excuse and explanation and then realized, with a rising anger and hurt, that Beatrice had no intention of explaining herself. In the pit of my stomach I felt a hot bolt of fury, the same quickened, lava-like, explosive outrage that one feels with real family—those intimates who can so infuriate and wound us that our response is quicksilver and often without check. "What?" I demanded. "You're cancelling our election night together? And after all our big plans?" I lowered my voice, meaning to menace and prod her. "You better have a good excuse!"

"I don't need an excuse!" Beatrice shot back, her voice shaking.

"Yes, you do," I countered, fighting back the irritating tears that threatened to overtake me mid-fight. I was utterly furious with this sister who seemed so ornery, so disloyal, when I had really counted upon her.

In my oldest sister *modus operandi,* I saw Beatrice's obstinacy as more than one of her little-sister-like mutinous stands with me. Perhaps she meant her stonewalling to be another test of our friendship. But coming as it did on the heels of my "other sister" Rebecca's desertion, I felt Beatrice's abandonment more keenly. I felt deeply betrayed and I said so.

Beatrice met my words with an even deeper stubbornness. She lowered her voice and murmured, "I'd rather not say why I can't make election night." Her tone was not at all contrite.

"Why not? If you give me a simple excuse, then I can accept it gracefully," I said, not very gracefully. "Just tell me why."

It seemed as if she was just about to give me an explanation when suddenly I felt her obstinacy rise up. It was a characteristic trait I'd often seen in Beatrice's dealing with her husband or sons. Beatrice called this stubbornness a survival skill. As a friend, I had been spared this recalcitrance more often than her family. And when I was not on the receiving end of Beatrice's defense tactics, I could always dismiss her withholding as Beatrice's need to set firm boundaries in a family that often demanded too much of her. "I'm just *not* going to tell you," she said now, with the tone that in the sixties we used to call "assertiveness training."

I found myself laughing, both to find her stubbornness so roundly turned on me and because I knew she'd decided to make this stand as if it were her last. I never imagined it would be.

"Don't you dare laugh at me," Beatrice said and this time her low voice held no secret of her anger. "That's my decision and you'll have to respect it."

I realized then in a brief but not completely coherent flash that this was all about power. Beatrice and I had always been so aligned as allies against other powerful forces—our parents, our mates, the rigors of our work—that we'd not had to fully face our own power struggles. I saw, too, in that moment, that my feud with my friend Rebecca was also about power: which of us would dictate our schedule, and which of us would change it. Even though I could see that both struggles were about power, even though I knew that women often battle for power and control most fiercely in the personal arena, I had no idea how to handle this unexpected development in my chosen sisterhood.

If it had been a struggle with my own sisters, we would have had a lifelong blood bond and history of talking through troubles to fall back on. But because these two women were not my biological sisters, I was lost as to how to proceed. As usual, when I feel lost or in unfamiliar territory, I try to take the lead.

"I don't accept your decision," I said angrily. "What I do accept is that I can't count on you anymore . . . on you *or* Rebecca, for that matter. So I'm just going to hang up now and be furious with you both." I decided not to slam down the phone because in my family no matter what horrible things we say to one another in the softest voices, we never hang up. We always stay on the line.

When Beatrice said nothing, I found myself weeping. I wanted to get off the phone, hurt and embarrassed by my own disappointment. "I'll call when I'm not so angry and hurt," I managed to say. "I promise."

I broke my promise; and so did Beatrice. I didn't call her until the next spring, six months after election night. I changed yoga studios so as not to run into her. And every week that passed I promised myself that I'd make the call. But as weeks and months passed, I became in my own way just as recalcitrant and withdrawn as I imagined Beatrice to be. Ironically enough, very shortly after my falling out with Beatrice I did call Rebecca.

Rebecca and I made up and agreed to reconstruct our friendship, minus the Wednesday Veg Nights. Our reunion was not blissful, but it was heartfelt and we both agreed to give each other room while she played with a spontaneous schedule and I continued my comforting structure. As always, Rebecca took off traveling and when she'd return she'd tell me of her metaphysical adventures; slowly we began to resurrect our friendship and today the bond is again strong and delightful. It is, however, different. We have a flexible schedule and sometimes take small trips together. We have deepened the sisterly quality of our friendship by spending holidays celebrating with each other and our partners. In fact, a group of us gathered at Rebecca's house to bring in 1995 by playing a parlor game of murder mystery. Rebecca's and my intimacy has returned and matured; but my silence with Beatrice continues to this day, five years later.

That funeral I planned for Beatrice was after the first year of our sister-silence. Before this extreme act of a symbolic funeral, I'd tried to reach out to my old friend by sending her a birthday card and making several phone calls to reestablish contact. But each offer was met with more silence until I simply fell into the habit of it myself.

So in November 1993, I visited my favorite massage supply store and purchased my funeral objects: a sea-scented candle, some incense called "Ocean," a handful of pale purple lavender. My plan was to have a silent memorial in my writing studio with incense, candle, and the soothing murmurings of the "Gregorian Chants to Mary" tape Beatrice had once made for me. Then I would bring bread and flowers down to my backyard beach and sadly cast the crusts to the gulls, the flowers to the spirit of the water goddess, Yemaya. Beatrice and I had once performed just such a ceremony to commemorate certain private events in our lives. Throughout our almost seven-year friendship, we'd always been drawn together to the water for celebration, comfort, and ceremony.

As I left the massage supply store with the paper sack of funeral objects clutched in my hand, my head was bowed. I entered my last stop, a coffeehouse, where I planned to purchase day-old bread for the birds. With my head down, I must have looked like a monk or nun hurrying to mass, my mind on spiritual matters. Beatrice must have had the leisure to consider if she wanted to simply sidestep this preoccupied person. But she stood her ground, right in my path.

I sensed someone blocking my way and vaguely swerved to the side. But Beatrice stepped sideways to stop me and as I looked up, perturbed, I was dumbfounded to find myself face to face with the very person who so preoccupied my thoughts. My first thought was to hide the paper bag, as if Beatrice could have known it was to her funeral I was rushing.

"Oh." Beatrice held my gaze with a steady, smiling expression. "I knew we'd run into each other sometime."

I was so shocked, so overwhelmed with the irony of our meeting, that I really could say nothing. Clutching my paper bag, I felt light-headed. My heart pounded, and I murmured something about my surprise. I couldn't get past the notion that I was caught up in some cosmic joke, that there was divine play here at work, perhaps at our expense.

"Are you in a hurry?" Beatrice inquired. "I have a class, but could we have tea for a few minutes together?"

"All right," I said dazedly.

I remember following my old friend to the table as if in a trance. I wanted to blurt out everything to her—that in my brown paper bag were *her* funeral objects. I wanted to open that little bag and show her each sad totem of our sisterhood. Then we'd throw our heads back and laugh, a little wildly, until we cried and embraced each other.

But I sat paralyzed, caught between a macabre guilt over burying her while she was still alive enough to physically stand in my way, and a growing realization that this was no real reunion. Beatrice, resurrected, so to speak, was still somehow lost to me.

I could see this in the calm, vaguely distant expression on her face. She was at her most maddeningly ethereal, her entire attention on pouring her tea as if she were some Zen master performing a tea ceremony. But what did I expect? That she would jump up and down and clasp me to her bosom? Certainly I showed little life, guiltily caught in my hubris of making funeral arrangements for the living.

It struck me as I studied Beatrice that she might have X-ray vision. Maybe she'd actually seen my paper bag with its symbolic ashes of her premature death. With my foot, I gingerly moved the bag under the next table.

Then this unlikely Lazarus at last finished with her tea ritual and faced me with a knowing smile. "I've really missed you." Beatrice smiled sadly.

At that I finally gathered myself. "Yes, it's been terrible . . . our silence." Suddenly I felt my daze change to resentment, as if we'd just picked up our phone conversation where we'd broken off a year earlier. "I don't understand why you didn't return my calls, Beatrice."

Beatrice's smile faded and her eyes filled with tears. "Well . . . I had some things I wanted to tell you and I didn't know how."

I tried not to let my exasperation show. I'm sure it did, though, as I asked, "Well, are you going to tell me now?"

Beatrice sighed. "No. I'd rather just chat. I'm on my way to a class and I can't get deeply into this, it'll be too much right now." She hesitated, her characteristic melancholy startling me with its familiarity. For the first time she looked like herself to me. "I've had a really terrible year," she said.

"What?" I couldn't help but press her. "What's happened?"

She held up her hands. "I can't talk about it. Another time, maybe in February after I've finished this new massage course."

Her despair and her old stubbornness deterred me from any more questions. I sat back and felt a strange sensation—one I'd never experienced before with Beatrice in person. I felt detached. The hidden observer in me was noting her face, her gestures, her clothes, all of which were familiar. But everything in me shrank back from her. It was as if there had been a window of opportunity when we'd first met for a true reunion, a deep clasping of one another. But the longer we hedged and avoided any true bonding, the more I felt myself stepping back and observing Beatrice with the dispassion of a stranger.

"What massage course?" I asked her, sitting back in my chair, folding my arms over my chest. I realized that as I did this, Beatrice moved forward, elbows on the table. For the first time since our meeting she seemed relaxed.

"You know, even as I signed up for the course I could hear you in the back of my mind telling me it wasn't a good idea, that I didn't need to go back to massage school since I already had my license, especially *this* school. I could just hear you warning me that it would be awful and I'd hate the techniques . . ."

I was surprised that Beatrice would imagine me as such a critic. Had I been that critical of her when we were friends? "What techniques?"

"Well," she said and paused, then smiled oddly, as if anticipating with pleasure my dismay. "Right now I'm off to work in the morgue and my cadaver class." She paused for maximum shock value, then announced, "We're dissecting dead bodies!"

I must have stared at her a long time. It took me that long to absorb all the levels, the sad and macabre ironies. Here I was on the way to bury her when I intersected her path on the way to a morgue.

Again, I wanted to blurt out everything to Beatrice, to show her the symbolic ashes in my paper bag, to let her regale me with morgue stories as my own nurse sisters were fond of doing at the dinner table. Beatrice, like my own sisters, would understand the black humor here.

But somehow I sensed that I dared not smile, that Beatrice would again interpret my laughter as belittling of her taking a stand. Still, it did strike me as grimly funny that Beatrice would take a stand over a dead body while I was sitting there over her symbolically dead body.

I kept my face very neutral, wanting neither to offend nor to show my true feelings. And it was at that moment I realized: Maybe our sisterhood really was dead. Because neither of us was resurrecting our true feelings for each other. We each kept our distance, disguising ourselves. Perhaps, I thought glumly, this rendezvous was the official postmortem of a friendship. Or was it a cosmic joke, a message that we mere humans can't assume symbolic death if that person is still alive?

Beatrice was very much alive. Her expression was mischievous as she awaited my disapproval over her morgue class—because I believed she was such a gifted massage therapist she had no need to work on dead bodies. But instead of delivering up the response she expected I just sat back and let that dizzying detachment take me.

I believe now in retrospect that I was in a mild state of shock that entire tea, that I had no time to really recover from my bewilderment over meeting the object of my funeral plans. What would have happened if I'd met Beatrice in the grocery store, the yoga class, during a theatre intermission? I'm sure I would have been able to connect with her more, or at least not step back so far from her.

But right then and there at the tea table over talk of dead bodies, my funeral bag underneath, I was overwhelmed. I actually pushed my chair back and shrugged my shoulders.

"Well?" she insisted. "Aren't you going to say I told you so? Because I do hate that massage school. But I want to finish it, now that I've invested so much money and work. Still, I'm miserable there."

From my remove I clearly saw this: that misery *was* Beatrice's constant companion—more constant, closer, and more familiar to her than any other friend. During our long friendship there had always been a crisis, a tragedy, a wrong or grief she was healing in herself. It was not that she was a professional victim or even melancholy; much of what I remember with Beatrice was physical play in our yoga part-nerships and gentle comfort in our ritual "at homes" together. Once I told her I believed she had a "genius for feeling." And I still believe that. But what I saw that day of her funeral was that her full range of feelings was limited. While she was truly gifted in compassion, empathy, grief, and an extraordinary healing mercy, she was not com-fortable with joy or expansive gladness. While she was generous and really kind in the face of suffering, she was not generous in giving of other parts of herself that drew her away from her role as healer. And what if I no longer needed a healer, but an adventurer or a playmate?

My own sister Paula may have summed it up when she said about Beatrice, "Your mistake, honey, was inviting her to an election-night prom. Some people are just more comfortable at a wake than a wild party. Now, the trick would have been to have convinced Beatrice that the party was really a funeral!"

So there we sat, Beatrice and I, at our own little funeral and I remembered the story my other nurse sister Marla once told me about two patients in her hospital who became fast friends and made their long hospital stay into a kind of perpetual party. But they didn't remain friends outside the hospital—they had healed together and that was enough.

Was it enough that Beatrice and I had come together for deep healing? As I gazed at her pale face and transparent eyes—often people remarked that we looked like twin sisters—I saw reflected much of my own sorrow. I also saw that there was a profound separation be-tween us that would not, perhaps should not, be healed. We were very different women: soul sisters, yes, who had shared and explored deep descents; but we had not climbed high together in the world, urging each other to take risks and perhaps fly.

Struggling to find something to say to Beatrice over our brief tea, I found myself instead thinking of my year-long stint in Girl Scouts down South when I was in grade school. We had bright badges across our proud, green sashes—symbols of rank and achievement. Wasn't there even a friendship badge? And wasn't it wonderful to be able to at last "fly up" and graduate into being a Big Girl? Those simple and clear distinctions were a comfort in the confusion of childhood cliques. We knew exactly where we stood and with whom.

But Big Girls grow up into mature women who know that badges and rank have little to do with lifelong friendships, that intimacy with a sister is so complex and ever-changing one is fortunate indeed to have any sense of exactly where we are in the long journey we take together.

I did not know then at our unexpected tea whether Beatrice and I were on a long detour away from our friendship or whether, in fact, that was our last meeting in this life. Perhaps we are resting from the lifelong dance; perhaps the dance is over.

"So you graduate from massage school in February," I finally said to Beatrice. "That's good."

"Yes." She smiled and stood up. "Listen, I'll be late for the morgue. How about I call you after February and we'll talk then."

"Sure," I said. "After that, then."

She stood up to embrace me and again I felt myself shrinking away from her. Maybe the funeral had already happened in my body, if not my mind. Maybe it was just too much to see her without any resolution or true reunion. I offered the briefest embrace and then smiled, perhaps one of my faintest smiles ever. "See you," I said.

And only at that moment did I realize I would not see her again. I knew it as I watched her grab her anatomy books and rush out the door. I realized it again when February came and went, and then another year passed by with no word.

If habit is half of love, then can the habit of silence also silence love? I still consider Beatrice a beloved, but lost sister. When I talk to my own sister Paula about Beatrice, she always asks meaningfully, "Is it finally the Iron Curtain, sis?"

She is referring to our childhood term for the many friends we'd had to leave behind in our transient years of crisscrossing the country following our father's career. At first when we were moved away from those elementary, junior high, or high school friends, we'd promise to write letters; but soon we were swept up in new worlds again. Without the habit of those friendships, we couldn't keep them up. Then there would come a day when we'd realize the Iron Curtain had come between us and our old friends; there was no going back to reclaim them.

In our adult lives, my sisters and I have referred to the Iron Curtain that rises when any relationship has become so unbearable or difficult, we don't know any longer how to make it work. "Yes," I at last told my sister this year. "I never would have believed it about Beatrice, but I think it is finally that . . . the Iron Curtain between us."

"Hopeless," my sister confirmed in her nurse's voice. But then she added, "Or maybe it's still just exile for that lost sister. After all, the real Berlin Wall *did* come down when we never dreamed it would."

I confess to still being very much mystified by my break with Beatrice. Often I have tried to guess what it was she felt she couldn't tell me and so lapsed into silence. When I really want to torture myself, I wonder if things I said before that last phone conversation directly led to our falling out. For example, when Beatrice asked me to give a workshop together with her called "Body Language" in which together we taught bodywork and writing, did my casual refusal to be a working partner with her feel to her like a deep desertion? Had I been overly critical or were my expectations overwhelming, much the way an older sister will demand too much of the younger ones? Or did our growing intimacy simply cross over into what I call "the demilitarized zone of modern love," so that we both got caught up in family and partnership issues, the likes of which destroy many intimacies?

I do not know whether the Iron Curtain between myself and my lost sister Beatrice will ever fall, if we'll take up our daily lives together, much the way a whole country on the other side of the world is now trying to find reunion after long political schism. I do believe that the personal is the political and that the barriers we erect between nations are simply larger versions of the walls we build between our more intimate friends and family. It wasn't national politics that separated Beatrice and myself that election night in 1992, it was personal politics.

But for many sisters around the world it is both personal and political walls that separate them.

8

Amor de Hermana:
Sisters in Exile

Perhaps one of the most devastating legacies of the past centuries of
patriarchy is the calculated exile of women from one another, as well
as from the lush territory of the feminine. For centuries, we've found
ourselves as women suspect whenever we have gathered together. This
demonizing and devaluing of female-female bonding at the same time
elevates male-male bonding to the status of religious sacrament (such
as in the Catholic Church) and political authority (such as our own
U.S. Congress). In other countries, violent male dominion has taken
the form of dictatorships which truly mirror the concept of God the
Father without a female partner.

This political-religious model of dominion rather than partnership,
as described in the book *The Chalice and the Blade: Our History, Our
Future,* by Riane Eisler, is "a social system in which male dominance,
male violence, and a generally hierarchic and authoritarian social structure [is] the norm." When dominance, not partnership, is the norm,
and violence overwhelms nurturing, then not only women, but both
sexes are in exile from the feminine. We hardly know how to heal the
excesses of the brotherhood by reuniting it with its true partner, the
sisterhood.

Recognizing that we are in exile from a larger sisterhood in our social systems is at least a starting point for change. In the writing of this book, one of the ways I've found hope for the sisterhood is in studying how women in extremes, such as political exile, have managed to bravely reconnect their sisterhoods, as if patiently reweaving a complex tapestry from tatters. Weaving is a particularly feminine art which requires deep attention to detail as well as to the whole tapestry. In these stories of sisters in political exile, one set of Cuban sisters endures physical separation by keeping alive their memories of each other; the other, the Chilean Isabel Allende, reconstructs the fabric of her own sisterhood by reaching out to a new world, a new sisterhood. Both these stories offer lessons to all women who have been in exile from the company of their own kind.

For the Cuban sisters Linda and Felicia Barrios, exile actually brought them fiercely closer to their tribe of seven Barrios sisters. When all the Barrios sisters were growing up together in Cuba, before Castro's revolution, Felicia (called affectionately Fela) was closest to the last daughter, Elda. They were like twins. Even after they married, Fela and Elda lived only two houses away from each other. Every evening when the husbands and children were settled, Elda would meet Fela on the front porch with specially brewed and scarce espresso coffee. They shared the ritual of porch-sitting on those warm, tropical island evenings.

"We would talk of all our problems and solve them right there together on the porch," Felicia said. "And we had so many problems. The revolution took all our property and much of our food. My sisters and I saved food for each other's families so that no one would starve. When my husband decided we must leave Cuba in 1970, Elda was the first to encourage me to go—although it was the most terrible idea for both of us. It was . . ." Felicia hesitated, then said softly, "my biggest wound to separate from this sister and to be away from her all those years." Felicia paused, her aristocratic, courtly manner barely concealing her sorrow. "My mother once told me, 'It's destiny, *mi niña*. If I were younger, I'd leave Cuba too. You have to believe in destiny, Fela.' " Felicia paused, her dark eyes brimming with tears. "Accepting my destiny has been the biggest challenge of my life. I don't regret coming to America because I see my sisters still suffering in Cuba. But I had to sacrifice my sisters to save my children and give them a better life."

Felicia was not the only Barrios sister forced to sacrifice her sister-hood; by coming to this country, Felicia was following in the footsteps of her younger sister Linda, who is now sixty-two and an American citizen. Where Felicia has her father's dark, Moorish looks, curly black hair, and black eyes, Linda is fair, with intensely jade-green eyes, a genetic inheritance from her Canary Island grandmother who, like many Spaniards, had light hair and eyes.

"My father was quite dark, a good, handsome man; we called him *uno negrito.*" Linda's fond laughter is light, as lilting as her quixotic Cuban-accented English. But there is about Linda, as about her oldest sister, Felicia, a melancholy that shows the stress of long exile. In Linda the sorrow over their lost sisterhood is more explosive than Felicia's, and Linda's longing sometimes takes the form of passionate idealism. Whereas Linda has learned English and taken a job in the community, Felicia has stayed close to her family and home. Felicia speaks no English, though everyone in her family suspects she understands it quite well. Where Linda has gone outward, Felicia has retreated in-ward. Interviewed with her daughter translating, Felicia said of her sister Linda, "When we were girls growing up in Cuba, I always ended up doing Linda's chores while she would be in her room reading. Now in this country, in exile, things are turned around. Linda did all those chores to help us come here—money, advice, jobs. She worked so hard to help us in this new country. And she still gives me so much hope." Felicia paused to consider a moment, then added thoughtfully, "Linda has what they call in Spanish *algo especial,* something special. She is more spiritual and emotional. And that helps me stay here."

Linda is the only Barrios sister to have learned English, having fled to America in 1960. For ten years, from 1960 to 1970, Linda was alone—a stranger in a strange land. And for nineteen years, she was forbidden to visit her sisters or her homeland.

When Linda Barrios first left her homeland on a student visa, she had no intention of becoming an exile. At the university in Cuba, where she majored in pedagolgy (education), she had gotten into some trouble for protesting the government-imposed revisions in the Cuban history books. She also disagreed with Castro's inclination toward Communism—a bent that the revolutionary leader would startle his country with by solidifying in 1961 with the Soviet regime, thus arousing widespread alarm.

"At first I had the idea of staying in this country for just a little while," said Linda, now a social worker who lives in New Jersey with her Italian husband, Franco. "When I first came to America I had to tell the U.S. Immigration authorities that Castro was turning Communist," Linda recalled. "At first they didn't believe me, then after five months they gave me political asylum."

Linda is perhaps the most charismatic of all the Barrios sisters, although she was born the next-to-the-youngest girl in a tribe that ranges from Anna, the eldest at eighty, to Elda, the baby sister who is in her fifties. "I have in me a part of each of my sisters, except the littlest one," Linda mused. "From Anna, who is so beautiful and peaceful, I learn to crochet—and this calms me. From Fela, I study how to dress so perfect always. Fela, she never goes out without looking just right. Then from Guana, I learn you can talk forever and also how to be a reading person. From Carida, I know how to be happy and find always the joke in things. Menza, the second to oldest, is like my second mother—and she teaches me much about love, *amor de hermana,* or what you will call here, sister love. When I was eight or nine years old, Menza marries, and I cry and cry like I lose my own mother. So what does Menza do? She comes back early from her honeymoon to be with me, and take me in her arms, and say 'I will never leave you.' "

Leaving her sisters, for Linda, was the most terrible ordeal of her long exile. "Sister love," she said softly, "is what you don't have with anybody else. It is a love that does not compare with love for a child, mother, even a friend. I share with my sisters a respect and such a strong feeling—if something happens to my sister, it happens to me."

What happened to her sisters in a Caribbean country whose revolution has failed, whose economy is in collapse after the Soviet-bloc disintegration, is a long and continuing story of daily survival directly dependent upon a vital, working sisterhood. It's one thing for a country to collapse, it's quite another for a sisterhood to be separated. Two of Linda and Felicia's sisters in Cuba have managed to save a small farm for themselves in a region where nowadays hunger is a nagging specter. In past years Cuba has been isolated from economic support, and has suffered severe food shortages. Linda and Felicia hear reports from their sisters of some families boiling shoe leather for soups, of women scavenging for rotted rice and overripe plantains. Gone are the days of rich *frijoles negros* and beef *barbacoa,* of caramel flan and giant wheels of *queso* made from one's own cow's milk. The only people in Cuba who are eating the traditional cornucopia of Cuban cuisine are the tourists, whose dollars Castro desperately needs to stay afloat. "But do you know this?" Linda commented angrily. "All those tourists, they are eating the food out of the Cuban people's mouths. In the country, all the food is going to the city resorts to feed tourists." Meanwhile, one of Linda's sisters reported last winter that her daughter was hospitalized for sudden blindness from a neurological disease that affected more than fifty thousand Cubans. The malady is linked to a vitamin B deficiency and lack of proper nutrition. Every month, both Linda and Felicia and many of the relatives here in the United States send care packages, small enough to pass through the corrupt postal system, full of vitamins, soap, aspirin, and chicken bouillon cubes. "If it is not for my two sisters and their little farm, my other sisters and all their families do not eat." Linda fell quiet, troubled.

When at last she continued, her characteristically lively voice was subdued. "I am not a strong person, but I can dream, and it is a dream that I have of sitting on my mother's porch that made me survive all those nineteen years when I cannot see my sisters in Cuba. Only by pictures did I watch them growing older, raise their children. In their letters they tell me now how bad it is, how they are hungry and how they fear for their children who are so skinny, like them. Each year in the photos my sisters grow too thin.

"And during the long years of my exile when I cannot go back to visit Cuba, I work my way through school in a sweater factory. And the other women at work, they always laughing of me and say, 'Oh, Linda, you were not here.' And I tell them, 'No, no, I am sitting on my mother's porch in Cuba.' They laughing of me and tease. 'You always dreaming. Do you think that you are going ever back to Cuba?' But I keep my dreaming, the same dream for nineteen years and when I finally return to Cuba in 1979, I arrive late at night. The first thing I do is go out and sit on the porch in my mother's old rocker. And

she comes out and says, 'Linda, what are you doing here in the night?'
And I tell her, 'I am breathing my grass and my flowers on my mother's porch.' And she laugh and say, 'You never change.' "

Though the dream did not change, everything else around her had.
"I recognize my sisters only by their pictures," Linda commented, a
certain tone of wonder in her voice. "I cannot ever explain that time
when I see them again after so many years. It is beyond my words.
. . . But I do tell you this, I come back to life again when I see my
sisters. I start again, like a resurrection. And I see how my life repeats
in them, even though I am far away. I see myself in their daughters
and sons." After pausing to ponder, Linda added, "You know, it is
right timing, sisters coming together again when we are old. I tell
my husband, Franco, before we even marry, that Cuba is my country,
and when it is free . . . I go back. He will come with me. As for now,
I can visit again and sometimes my sisters will come here."

Linda's husband is a jocular Italian who adores cooking and welcoming many friends and family into their home. Together the couple
speak a patois of Spanish and Italian, each having learned the other's
language. High-spirited and deeply involved in their extended families
and communities, the couple would easily fit into the large Cuban
tribe of Linda's sisters in her homeland. Linda has established herself
here as a natural leader and caretaker, the same role she played in her
large sisterhood. She works as an occupational counselor in New Jersey's Labor Department. Humor and a sense of play and caretaking
inspire her character. It was Linda who suggested that during a recent
enervating heat spell the workers in her office play Christmas carols;
it was Linda who made sure during their most recent painful pilgrimage to Cuba in 1991, that her older sister Felicia was protected from
some of the more tragic aspects of the struggle to survive in this island
left adrift in its shattered economy.

For example, Linda had not told Felicia of some relatives' deaths
before they visited Cuba. It was only right before they visited the
cemetery that Linda quietly explain to her sister how many more
had died. Felicia, who is quieter than Linda, more cautious and
inward-turning, was devastated by the discovery of so many more
family members who had died without her attendance, her help. To
be in exile from one's homeland and family is to endure many deaths
that happen seemingly offstage, far away. There are no funerals, no

deathbed embraces and farewells. There is just that phone call, often cut off by fickle Cuban phones which, like most of the island's infra-structure, are simply not working.

Felicia and Linda both heard news of their dear mother's death long-distance and were not allowed to return for her funeral. Felicia was particularly close to her mother, a Cuban matriarch who ran a successful plantation with her husband and who often depended upon Felicia for assistance with handling all the finances. Felicia was also her mother's confidante.

Both sisters have re-created strong sisterhoods in this country. In Felicia's Los Angeles home there is a continual stream of women through the house. Meals materialize as if by magic any time a chosen sister stops by for a chat. Together these women, from places as dis-parate as Ecuador and Mexico, talk of exile, of families left behind, of a new generation growing up without a homeland, between cultures. In lighter moods the women in Felicia's sisterhood argue over favorite characters in their *novelas* (soap operas), exchange tips from their fa-vorite *curanderas* (healers) or beauty shop. Theirs is a network that stretches from kitchen to homeland and every time a family member can escape for a brief visit there is a celebration, a long fiesta.

When another Barrios sister, Carida, visited several years ago she arrived very pale and frighteningly thin. The Barrios sisters met in Linda's New Jersey home. When Carida went to visit Felicia in her L.A. home, I talked with her briefly, because it was too painful for her to talk about those she had just left in Cuba and to whom she would soon return. She rarely spoke about politics; instead she talked of seeing her children starving, of foraging for wood to heat stoves because there was no fuel, of using bicycles because there was no gas, of doctors without medicine, of nights without electricity. Someone quoted a popular Cuban joke: "What are the triumphs of the revo-lution? Education, health care, and athletics. And what are the failures of the revolution? Breakfast, lunch, and dinner."

For the Barrios sisters in exile, it is not enough to be able to visit their homeland and receive sporadic, limited visits from their sisters. They see firsthand how the American embargo of Cuba has harmed the everyday lives of their families and has politically backfired. Carida showed her sisters snapshots of their nieces and nephews—all so ter-ribly thin, many like shrunken shadows of their American cousins.

"I just want my sisters and their families to be able to eat," said Felicia quietly as she glanced across at a frail Carida bent over wrinkled photos, some of children their aunts have seen only once or twice in the last decade of exile. "The exile goes both ways," Fela finished as she brought her sister another helping of food, encouraging her to have seconds, as if by feeding this thin, ailing sister she might nurture her whole, long-lost family. "In Cuba my sisters are exiled from us and we in this country have been so long separated from those we love most," Carida added, eating with gratitude and a soft, rueful smile. "Sisters should not be apart. We are each other's country."

Finding homeland in one's sisters, literally keeping each other alive with food and solace and the simple chores of everyday nurturing—whether it's coffee on a front porch or life-giving vitamins in a care package—is what many sisters in exile have discovered is a passionate raison d'être. The experience of exile often draws sisters closer together who might not otherwise have formed such an alliance. It also inspires women to find other sisters in their adopted country with whom they bond for life as if with family.

Though she is from Chile, where there is the opposite political situation from Cuba's, novelist Isabel Allende also found solace in chosen sisters during her long exile from the right-wing regime which overthrew her uncle, President Salvador Allende. I interviewed Isabel and her adopted American sister, the Berkeley jeweler Tabra Tunoa, in Isabel's Sausalito studio. We talked about Isabel's stepsister in Chile, with whom she had a pleasant but distant relationship, and about another adopted sister still in Chile who is decidedly right-wing, a supporter of General Augusto Pinochet who seized power in a 1973 junta, and ruled Chile with an authoritarian hand until 1990 when he yielded his presidency but not his military rule to general elections and the coalition government of Christian Democrats, Socialists, and Radicals.

"I haven't seen my Chilean 'sister' in twenty years, but we fax each other all the time and talk on the phone," Isabel said with a laugh as she served Tabra and me her special mango tea. "We are very close —though not in distance and not in politics!" She embraced me warmly and the movement sent Isabel's extraordinary earrings and bracelets jingling. "Tabra made all these for me. She's my real sister."

In Isabel's spacious studio situated just a block from San Francisco Bay, I was struck first by the wall of bookshelves adorned with photographs, a gallery of grandchildren grinning, portraits of Isabel's two children, Nicholas and Paula, and two striking photos of her beloved mother who is also her editor. In one picture, her mother is posed in an elegant evening gown beside Salvador Allende; in the other, she has donned boxing gloves and is preparing to throw a playful punch. Isabel's writer's studio could have been its own apartment it was so large, yet it was cozy—with beige couch and chairs, a desk so clean it seemed vacuumed, and huge windows that glowed softly with the liminal marine light off the nearby bay. Upstairs there were the rhythmic accents of Spanish as Isabel's assistant, her daughter-in-law Celia Graterol, graciously tended to Isabel's writing affairs. Several people streamed into the studio, including Isabel's husband of seven years, William Gordon. He is a tall, white-haired lawyer, fluent in Chicano Spanish from his years as a white boy raised in an L.A. barrio. Observing Willie, as Isabel called him, one understood why sometimes the most courtly of lawyers are also called solicitors: Surely he is solicitous of his wife, whose work he read and loved long before meeting her at a San José dinner party.

Isabel's studio is attached to her husband's law office in an elegant wood and brick building. When I first crossed the courtyard I'd noticed a striking dark-haired woman pulling up in an old Saab. It was Tabra Tunoa, whose gypsy clothes and jewelry, and exotic character, would make her comfortable in any Third World country. In fact, in Tabra's jewelry brochures, there is a photo of her walking among golden-veiled Indian women in a Pushkar marketplace—and Tabra blends in as naturally as if she has walked with these dark-skinned sisters all her life. In fact, she has spent most of her life in the Third World. Her childhood in Texas and teenage years in Nebraska felt like the real foreign countries for Tabra.

I expected Tabra, like Isabel, to have a lilting accent, but instead her soft voice had Southern tones; that slight Texas twang was the only thing shocking about this rare, fully cross-cultural woman. Isabel has joked that when her grandchildren watch *National Geographic*, with its images of primitive tribal woman, they excitedly point to the television and cry, "Tabra's family."

Isabel Allende's extended family is Tabra's chosen family. Here is perhaps an end to Isabel's exile—for she has married an American husband, brought her son's family here, and chosen her adopted sister in Tabra. And Isabel is now free to return to Chile where the political climate is safer; but she prefers to simply visit her homeland, where her mother still lives.

To meet Isabel Allende and Tabra Tunoa together, one might suspect they are biological sisters—they have the same deep auburn hair, with a rich coral cast to its sheen, like those semi-precious stones Tabra sets into her jewelry. Their dark brown eyes are also strikingly similar, both oval and wideset—a mark of generosity, say those who make a study of faces. Tabra wore characteristic black kohl, rimming her eyes as naturally as if she were one of those African beadmakers or Indian artisans with whom she spends so much of her time traveling and looking for inspiration and materials for her jewelry.

Isabel re-created Tabra in her novel *The Infinite Plan* as Carmen Morales. The real inspiration for this lively Allende character is delightfully close to the fictional creation. That day in Isabel's writing studio, Tabra wore an ankle-length skirt the color of bright rust; her graceful overblouse of orange and earthen browns was sewn around every long seam with small silver figures like fetishes. Her long cloth camisole was hand-embroidered with tiny bells at the neckline; they were an accompaniment to her glorious earrings of bronze, silver, and gemstones.

"Her jewelry always makes such beautiful sounds." Isabel laughed and shook her head, sending off a tiny tinkling from her own Tabra earrings—this pair was suns, moons, and assembled silver planets. "It's like my own private music I can hear all day long. Those earrings are the first thing I put on and the last I take off at night."

She wore a dark brown dress and woven shoulder shawl attached at the breast with a golden brooch. Her luminous black eyes settled on her friend's face as one gazes at a familiar landscape, perhaps a homeland. There was an ease and playfulness between them.

"We have several stories about how we met," Isabel began, teasing Tabra. "I have a much nicer one, but hers is the true one."

"I stretch it a little too," Tabra said, the bracelets that adorn her right arm from elbow to wrist shooting off light as she raised her hand. "I was getting my hair dyed purple in this place where I get my hair done all the time. I was complaining because they couldn't get it purple enough. They told me there was only one other woman who'd ever been in there who wanted her hair purple, too. They said she was from South America, Chile . . . Isabel Allende. And I said, 'No, that's the famous writer.' And they said, 'Yeah, she writes books.' I begged them to introduce me. Finally one day they called me and said she was there. And . . ." Tabra paused almost shyly, remembering that first meeting, "and she was wearing my earrings."

Isabel took up in her lyrical Chilean accent. "I like to tell the story with more elegance. I say that we just met in the hairdresser—she was reading my book and I was wearing her earrings."

Tabra had read Allende's books and loved them. With all her years of travels through South America in apprenticeship to her craft, Tabra's two political heroes were Salvador Allende and Che Guevera. In Isabel she found a sister traveler; both of them had spent many years away from their homelands. Tabra's exile was by choice and Isabel's was a political necessity. In the opening dance of their friendship, they did not rush upon each other like long-lost sisters; theirs was more a minuet of careful, delicate steps.

"We became friends slowly," Isabel explained. "I was new in this country. I didn't feel very comfortable at the time. I didn't have any friends. This was 1988 and I felt very alien. On the other hand, Tabra is a very cautious person, she doesn't open up very easily. So it took me two years to really have her trust me . . ." Isabel glanced across at Tabra. "That's pretty close to the truth, isn't it?"

"Yes." Tabra nodded. "But I kept wondering why she kept wanting me to come over for lunch." They both laughed like an old, sure couple remembering the first stumbles and falls of their shy courtship.

Listening to these two bejeweled, bracelet-jangling storytellers is like being privy to gypsies telling secrets of their worldly travels. There is much magic in the studio, and it is distinctly feminine, subtle, and mysterious. These two women could be any secret female society, exotic and ancient and knowing. They could also be descended from Isabel's Chilean grandmother's great friends, the Morales sisters, whose practice of spiritualism openly defied the Catholic patriarchal society. Isabel's grandmother, a clairvoyant, was a profound influence on Isabel's childhood and her sense of the feminine mysteries that abound, though they often are forbidden. Both Tabra and Isabel are rebels and visionaries. They are maturing into their own sense of spiritual authority as women. Both have passed through menopause and now in their early fifties they possess a self-assurance and depth beneath their nomadic, otherworldly personas. When each woman was interviewed for the book *On Women Turning Fifty*, Tabra clearly stated, "In your fifties, you can start concentrating on things that are really important and give up on those things that are unimportant, like trying to look very sexy and hoping to get a man by looking a certain way. You can start concentrating on things that have always interested you and that you've wanted to accomplish."

Both Isabel Allende and Tabra Tunoa have accomplished what their hearts desired as novelist and jeweler, and they come together as peers not only in worldly success, but as intimates. In Isabel's studio, they exchanged their syncopated stories about how they first navigated that seeming chasm between souls to find a cherished, everyday comfort. That comfort has seen them through the death of Isabel's daughter, the beginnings and endings of Tabra's love affairs, the tremendous stress of nurturing successful careers—what emerged was the deep surety of their bond, the daily craft and conscious care of their sisterhood. There is the sense that they each work on their intimacy, not because it is difficult, but because it is so fascinating.

What first drew Isabel to Tabra Tunoa was her work. "I was fascinated with Tabra's job," Isabel explained with a wide, wondering smile. "I saw her working." Isabel paused, giving her friend a direct look, as if to make Tabra visible to herself. "Tabra changed during the course of our friendship, but she used to be very closed and distant. For example, she doesn't like to be touched. And in Latin America we are always hugging and kissing. But I felt her become very stiff and cold if I tried to touch her—so I didn't do that. But I saw her working . . . and when she's working . . . she invited me once to her shop to put some beads in a necklace, and I felt so privileged."

"She is very privileged," Tabra said and nodded. "I don't let anybody else do that."

As Isabel worked alongside her friend, she observed Tabra as well as her craft. "I watched her and realized how she transformed her personality in the process of working. I realized that's the same thing that I do, in my case it's the other way around. She opens up when she's working and I close down, become totally mute, paralyzed. I'm in the story and can't do anything else. But Tabra opens up to everything, because it's all a story for Tabra. She knows where she bought each bead, who makes them, what country. Every time she put a bead in a necklace she'd tell me about them, the places she's been, her life. That was wonderful. We do that often now."

Tabra took up. "And Isabel told me about the time after Pinochet took over in Chile, which fascinated me. I've never been to Chile, but we're both going together this spring."

It will be the first time Tabra and Isabel have traveled abroad together on this trip that Isabel has made her yearly pilgrimage since General Pinochet loosened his stranglehold on the government.

It is a deep irony that Pinochet's coup (supported by the CIA) in September 1973, which ended the life of Isabel's uncle, President Salvador Allende, began Isabel Allende's life as a novelist. After the coup, when her diplomat parents fled to Buenos Aires under threat of assassination, Allende worked with the Chilean underground to give asylum to political refugees. At the time she was a successful journalist with her own television interview show in Santiago. A threat to her own life sent her in 1975 to Caracas, Venezuela, where her engineer husband and children, Nicholas and Paula, soon followed. What Isabel expected would be a short refuge became a thirteen-year exile. For a time, Allende, too, was silenced, mutely watching her country devolve into a territory of tyranny and terror. "I come from a land of crazy, illumined people," Allende has declared, "a Latin American continent where revolutions are made with machetes, bullets, poems, and kisses. . . . Hyperbole, extrasensory perception, the overwhelming presence of nature, legends, myths, traditions, forces of destiny, extreme passions and obsessions are some of the ingredients of Latin American literature."

Perhaps it was a natural next step for this journalist in mute exile who had lost everything—her country, her career, some of her family, many friends, her security—to take up storytelling. For by claiming her memories and so reclaiming herself, she could truly possess what no one could ever take away from her—her own story.

So Isabel Allende began to write a letter to her dying grandfather, from whom exile kept her; her letter grew into a stack of six hundred pages, which Isabel's mother read and pronounced a novel. After being rejected throughout Latin America, the novel was published in Europe under the title *The House of the Spirits*, to immediate recognition and acclaim. In the novel, two women adopt each other as sisters in a complex dance with a jealous, love-struck patriarch. Allende has remarked that she was fortunate to publish her work first outside Latin America, because many Latin American women have been ignored and silenced within the confines of their own patriarchal continent. It is interesting also to note that what began as a letter to a grandfather patriarch was edited by Isabel Allende's mother. It was also dedicated to "my mother, my grandmother, and all the other extraordinary women of this story."

The sense that her ancestors are spiritually embracing her is obvious everywhere in Isabel Allende's studio. Among the photographs that adorn her office like talismans is a beautiful portrait of her only daughter, Paula, a psychologist, who died at twenty-nine from a rare enzyme deficiency, after a year-long coma. In this picture Paula gazes out, her skin a darker shade than her mother's, her black eyes the same wide oval shape, with the same direct gaze as Isabel's.

Before Allende begins her writing day early in the morning, she lights some candles, gazes at these photos of her mother, her daughter, her friend Tabra, then sips her mango tea and takes up her storytelling. These women set the standard for her and it is to them that Isabel Allende turns for inspiration and nurturance. Sitting in her Sausalito studio now with her adopted sister, one feels there is no sense of exile here, only connection. "I have a little bottle that Tabra made for me to hold the ashes of my daughter," Isabel said with a lowered voice. "It's made of silver, very special, something she made only for me and no one else in the world will have it. So that's also an act of love."

"It has a little scarab on it." Tabra described the piece, tracing a delicate pattern in the air. "The Egyptian symbol for eternity."

The two fall silent, but in the air between them the conversation seems to continue as they both remember the year-long vigil Isabel held by her daughter's bedside. Isabel said that her daughter's death, the wasting away of a beloved child, was the worst thing that has ever happened to her. She wept when describing the process of letting her daughter go in a recent *New Dimensions* interview: "First you let go of the body . . . then the mind, because there was so much brain damage, and then the spirit." And when her daughter finally did die, in December 1992, surrounded by her tribe in a bedroom filled with flowers and family, Isabel said, it was a terrible surrender, yet "you don't love them any less for leaving."

It was Tabra Tunoa who sensed the exact days during Paula's coma when Isabel needed respite from her grieving vigil. "During the year when Paula was sick I was always at her bedside." Isabel leaned forward, clasping her arms as if chilled by the memory. Her voice was very soft, almost a whisper. Nearby Tabra leaned forward too as naturally as if they were not sitting, but moving together in synch, an inner dance choreographed by shared sorrow.

"I didn't do anything else, practically never worked." Isabel's eyes filled with unshed tears. "I was just with my daughter. Sometimes the sadness and stress was so unbearable I couldn't function. Then Tabra had this instinct; she knew exactly when I reached that point and I needed help desperately. She would never say, 'Talk to me.' She'd invite me over to make a necklace or play with the beads. So I could be with her and not talk, just play with the beads. Because I couldn't write at the time, it would take my mind away from the stress of Paula. And for a few hours I could be creating something— usually a piece of junk. But I was doing something with my hands that was a little bit like writing." Isabel paused, drawing her shawl closer around her shoulders. She managed a smile that was at once fragile and heartfelt. "It's strange how friendship develops and grows until it becomes a sort of sisterhood. There has never been any friend closer to me than Tabra . . ."

"Nor for me either," Tabra echoed with a grin and a strong nod of her head which sent all her earrings and embroidered bells singing.

"Tabra has the keys to my house," Isabel continued, "she comes and goes like my kids. It is her home. There are levels of friendship and there's a point . . . when you pass it, then it becomes like those old-fashioned blood promises among gangsters."

Tabra leaned forward and it was as if she'd touched Isabel's hand across the distance. "I think," she said tenderly, "what brought us closer was when I had to go to the hospital for surgery and she wanted me to stay at her house afterwards. She took care of me. I'm very independent and I'd rather take care of myself. And anyway, I wasn't sure she'd even show up on time to take me to the hospital . . ." Tabra hesitated, then said with some amazement, "And she showed

up! You know, the men in my life had never showed up. It really
made a difference. If it had been a man, the kind of man I've chosen,
they might not have gotten there at all. I stayed at her house, helpless
for a while, and let her take care of me. She absolutely spoiled me. So
much so that later when I had a new boyfriend I really liked—he had a
long black ponytail and an earring . . ." At this Isabel laughed uproari-
ously. "But I was sick one day and he wanted me to get up and make
him macaroni and cheese and he couldn't hear that I was sick. I
thought, Isabel wouldn't do this, she'd be over here with her little tray
and there'd be a flower on it and a bowl of soup she'd made . . ."
Tabra paused, then flashed a wry grin. "And so I left him! It took all
the courage I had to do that."

They talked about how calling upon a sister to set the standard by
which to judge all other intimacy is an idea whose time seems to have
at last come, as we move into a new century of equal partnerships and
place a higher value on the skills of relationship.

"There is a lot of sharing you do with another woman when you
have that level of intimacy," Isabel said. "Just buying clothes, talking
about clothes."

We talked about the feminine rituals of cooking, shopping, and
what my own sister calls "fashion therapy"—trying on each other's
clothes, styles, hair color (including purple). In this comfortable chat
with the sun and the mango tea pouring freely, the three of us settled
into playful banter that is the mark of many sisterhoods. Isabel teased
Tabra about her choice of men. Her manner was that of the protective
older sister, a role that Tabra grudgingly and perhaps gratefully acknowledged while insisting, for the record, that she is only a year and
a half younger.

"Tabra chooses these jerks; she has no taste for men!" Isabel declared. "Every time she appears with a new boyfriend we are all worried that he will be a serial killer!"

"No, no . . ." Tabra protested with a laugh. "I don't choose killers;
I just choose men who are jerks. But they're interesting and they're
cute . . . but immature."

Like the character of Carmen Morales whose luck with men is hap-
less at best, Tabra has spent much of her life with men—the more
exotic the better—who in her own words were "disasters." When she
was fourteen and living in Nebraska where her parents were both

literature professors, Tabra fell in love with a Samoan man with whom, four years later, she eloped to his native country. Her son, Tangi, was born in Samoa. When Tangi was five, Tabra divorced his father and began her world travels. Over the next fifteen years of travel apprenticing for her jewelry craft, Tabra would live with wildly different men, from Japanese, Trinidadian, to African and Chinese.

"My last lover was from Timbuktu," Tabra said with a straight face as Isabel laughed, bent double. "I had an affair with him because Isabel liked him, can you believe it?"

"It was a mistake," Isabel said and nodded, almost gleefully.

But where she has perhaps made some mistaken moves with men, Tabra has made herself and her business a deeply fulfilling success. From her street sales in Berkeley in the sixties to a multimillion-dollar international jewelry business in the nineties, Tabra embodies a self-made woman in more than her entrepreneurship. There is a strong sense about her that experiencing, understanding, and discovering herself has been her most important achievement. In a society that tends to judge women by their relationships and men by their accomplishments—it is refreshing to see a woman's success in standing alone, surrounded by friends.

"Tabra likes to be alone," Isabel commented. "She can walk for two hours on her own land just north of here and not see anyone . . ." With a meaningful nod, Isabel added, "We are going to spend lots of time this summer at Tabra's house, because she has a swimming pool!"

The image of Isabel's tribe descending upon Tabra's forested house north of San Francisco made Tabra smile; she herself spends two to three days a week after work with Isabel's family. Isabel's grandchildren think of Tabra as their aunt. And Isabel's husband, Willie, is as devoted to Tabra as is his wife.

"Willie is not at all jealous of Tabra," Isabel declared with a casual shrug. "He is very concerned about her; he teases her a lot and is very protective of her."

"Isabel's tribe and my son are my family," Tabra acknowledged. One senses, too, that Tabra Tunoa's jewelry business has a family feel to it. Her warehouse work space is draped with flags from every nation represented among the employees, 90 percent of whom are refugees from every country from Ethiopia to El Salvador. For two years running, Tabra Jewelry was named in *Inc. 500* as one of the five hundred fastest-growing small businesses in America. In 1993, Tabra's business joined Social Venture Network, a group of socially responsible entrepreneurs, including Ben and Jerry's Ice Cream and The Body Shop. In her interview for *On Women Turning Fifty*, Tabra explained, "I can't stop wars but I can make this company a better place for the people who work here. We must learn to not just tolerate other cultures but to appreciate and learn from them."

In 1991 Tabra's work won her the Women in Communications Award for the business that did most to promote women's concerns in the workplace. In her volunteer work with homeless groups and abused women, Tabra has said, "I try to show them how to get out of their situation, that they can find a way around male-dominated ideas and about how success happens. . . . The hardest thing I had to learn was that it is all right to have power."

There is also power in finding peers and equal partnerships, and that is what Isabel Allende and Tabra Tunoa have accomplished together. Recently Tabra published a small pamphlet entitled *In Celebration of Strong Women, Storytelling and Beautiful Jewelry*. On the cover is a photo of four women studying a silver belt; the women are Isabel Allende, Tabra Tunoa, and the novelists Terry McMillan and Amy Tan. All three writers have their say in the business brochure about Tabra's work, their own creative process, and their friendship. "Women understand that friendship between women is important," writes McMillan, author of the recent best-seller *Waiting to Exhale*.

In their novels, Terry McMillan, Isabel Allende, and Amy Tan have succeeded in portraying strong sisterhoods. Tan's two generations of Chinese-American mothers and daughters form a sister society in *The Joy Luck Club* that spans and connects two worlds as disparate as Asia and America; McMillan's wise and funny African-American sisters tell tales on their men that have struck a resounding chord among readers. Allende's magically real feminism illumines a Latin America too long dominated by machismo. It seems right that McMillan, Tan, and Allende should themselves share a sisterhood that supports them in their work. As friends and sister novelists, the three women often meet together (they all live in the Bay Area) and share everything from books to food. This alliance is central to their lives and work—and their many readers are by extension included in this spirit of celebrating cooperation and creativity.

Keeping the good counsel of one's sisters is exactly what Isabel Allende meant when she said, "It's not really about rivalry and competition." She glanced over at Tabra and for a moment they exchanged a smile. Then Isabel shook her head and her Tunoa earrings tinkled with their tiny music as she continued. "Real friendship or real love makes you aware of the other person's needs and the other person doesn't have to say anything. There is a way of knowing what is needed. Sometimes you are postponing your own needs. You never ask the question that is so typically American: 'What is there for me?' " Isabel shook her head firmly. "When people talk about relationships is this country—or at least in Marin County, in California—it's like an exchange, a deal: 'What am I going to get?' I think that's an obscene question. Because in human relationships, it's not what you're going to get . . . that may come eventually . . . it's what am I going to *give*. What can I add to this common meal that we are going to share?" Isabel mused quietly for a moment, then continued in a soft voice. "In Chile, there is the Indian potluck tradition of *malon*—that is what the Indians did. After the military coup there were many years of extreme poverty for half the population, especially in the urban slums. There people would get together twice a day and they'd bring whatever they had—a piece of bread, a bone, a potato—and put it all together so that everyone would have something to eat. You couldn't make a proper dinner with that, but it didn't matter, you could make a meal with it. Everybody had a little bit. You wouldn't worry how much you'd get that day; your worry was what am I going to add? So that is the first question: What do I bring into this relationship so that it will grow and make us better? I ask this question constantly with my husband and the intimate people I have around me."

Isabel Allende once said, "In order to survive in a patriarchal society, you have to be organized, you have to have good women friends. There is a network of female friends who survive in this patriarchal culture. . . . women do double the work and get half the recognition of any man in the job. They are usually much stronger and much more interesting human beings."

In her studio now, she laughed, and added, "Women also know more about intimacy. Remember the TV character the Lonely Ranger? Well, that's exactly what most men are about." Tabra laughingly corrected Isabel that it was "The Lone Ranger." But Isabel firmly nodded. "Same thing," she said. "Same loneliness and loss."

If we as women shape our ideas of power, intimacy, and relationship after the masculine models of dominance, hierachy, and survival of the fittest—the traditionally solitary, self-reliant male hero—we lose so many of our own natural skills. We adopt an alien and self-defeating role which separates us from our true allies, our sisterhood.

When we lose our sisterhood skills by trying to become more masculine, it is like losing our homeland, our native country and language. We are much the lonelier for it. To be in exile from ourselves and our gifts as women, as sisters, is to be banished from the very source that gives us strength and hope. Like the exiled Barrios sisters and Isabel Allende, women can learn to make their own country. We need not battle with the patriarchy we live within, but can exist quite independently and even flourish within it, if we claim our sisters. Inside this country of women that embraces the increasingly global sisterhood, there can be fewer lonely rangers and an end to the exile of sisters.

9

Sister as Shadow

Fifteen years ago, Jo, a dear friend of mine, who often referred to me as "her real sister," decided that her way out of depression after her divorce was to play racquetball. "I'll pretend that the ball is my ex-husband and my father."

Every time she slammed that fast blue ball against those four white walls, Jo imagined she was fighting back against the men in her life who had betrayed her love. There was much to revenge. Throughout her life, her father had warned her mother that she must never leave him. In the middle of her parents' divorce, when she was in her mid-twenties, Jo's father came over to the house where his wife was staying with a friend. He called her down for a talk. Suddenly there were two quick gunshots, one for his wife, the other for himself. And in an instant, both Jo's parents were dead.

There were times, those dawns in the Arizona desert, when I'd meet Jo on the outdoor racquetball court and it was so blazingly hot it might already have been high noon. The heat was like her anger, alive in that racquetball which darted out and richocheted off the graffiti-scrawled walls like bullets. We never kept score; our goal was to keep a volley going so long we'd often drop in exhaustion before the ball did. We'd collapse on the grass, gasping the hot, desert air, swilling water like drunkards. It was often during these racquetball games Jo would talk about her parents.

"This game reminds me of all those times my father took my sister and me to target practice," she'd say, trying to catch her breath. "We'd have to duck down while he fired round after round of ammo, then at his command like little soldiers we'd scamper out to change the targets. I remember how it felt tearing down those paper silhouette men punctured with hundreds of holes. My sister and I called it 'playing paper dolls.'"

While Jo would talk about her father's violence, how it hung like humidity over the rest of the family (all women), I would tell stories about my mother—her manic phases during which we sisters called her "a dangerous Lucille Ball," and her down cycles during which she rampaged after her children like our own domestic demon.

Jo and I would describe ourselves as survivors of childhood, of the war zone, the long march, the children's camps. We sometimes imagined that we were born prisoners of war, particularly the war raging inside one of our mentally unstable parents. There was one big difference between our violent parents: Jo's father never exploded to abuse his wife or daughters physically. Instead, they lived under the continual dread of triggering his rage as if he were a booby trap lying in wait. His explosion, when it came, came with the double murder, only confirming Jo's deepest fears.

"We could feel it, my father's rage," Jo would explain. "And because he never expressed his violence we knew it must be really big, limitless. We knew he was capable of anything, although we had no evidence. It's kind of like those women who go to the police and say they're afraid of their husband's threats but the police say until there is cause for arrest, they can do nothing. The cause for arrest is often death itself." It was for Jo's mother.

My own mother, like an intimate Kali, the Indian goddess of destruction, acted out her violence. It was daily, almost familiar—a resounding slap here, a kick or shove there. It always seemed like a short circuit in her brain; these episodes of physical abuse most always occurred when she had her migraines. She never seemed to remember her explosions; and we knew better than to tell our father, who would dismiss the wound with a warning that our mother was high-strung and we shouldn't "set her off."

The difference between my mother and Jo's father was that my mother was set off, and often. We witnessed and felt the parameters of her rage which, even to us children, seemed oddly impersonal, a misfiring of her inner mechanisms. And as soon as we grew tall and cunning enough, we could sometimes outwit or anticipate her ambushes. Often Jo and I would expand our childhoods as a metaphor for an entire generation of baby boomers who entered the world at the same time the atom bomb was exploded. I called us the "Baby Bombers."

Jo was obsessed with Vietnam, having spent much time around Vietnam vets. She had served a stint in the Peace Corps in Thailand and often dreamed about returning to Asia as a teacher. Jo and I were both teaching at Arizona State University and I was allergic to the desert. Those dry, arid sandy sea bottoms which nurtured some respiratory systems seemed only to suck all life from me; often I'd wake up feeling vacuumed from the inside out and rarely could I rest with the chilly whir of air-conditioning. Except for my beloved writer friends teaching alongside me and the nearby Hopi Indian reservation which mesmerized me, I knew I needed to leave Arizona and find a more watery world. For her part, Jo had a twelve-year-old son, a sister, and an ex-husband in Washington State; she'd decided it was time to go home again. So midwinter, we both made the sojourn through blizzards in Nevada and Idaho, to Seattle, Washington, where I would finish my second novel and she again take up the care of her son who'd been living with his stepfather while Jo earned her master's degree.

We found a house-sitting job on an island outside Seattle and settled in for the six-month stint. In our own minds, we were doing much more than surviving. I was writing full-time on a grant and enjoying a love affair with a film critic. Jo was finishing her first poetry collection and getting the house ready for the reunion with her teenage son. What I did not realize in those five months of sharing a home with this friend and sister was that Jo had no intention of surviving. Exactly when she had made the choice to follow her father's final solution, I will never know. All I know is that early one spring day I awoke to find that she had taken her own life—violently, horribly.

She had shot herself in the head. The target practice of her childhood was over—and she was both murderer and murdered.

Every moment of that May morning is etched into my mind as if with acid; I can still smell the burnt stench of gunfire, see that oddly sweet blackness that was blood congealing and closing her eyes as it swelled outward from her brain. Sometimes ten years later during the simplest of chores, I will suddenly remember that poignant arch of my friend's hand thrown back as if to wave, and the black stubby gun near her body like a small brutal bouquet—as if she were shot in the act of throwing a bridal nosegay, or a bomb.

Jo used to joke that we were terrorists because we were raised in terror. For me, Jo has been a terrorist whose suicide forced me face-to-face not only with my own despair, but also my capacity for violence. I consider Jo's death the end of my own childhood and the beginning of my maturing. That maturing has meant looking steadily at my own darkest and uncharted inner territories. It is sometimes quite frightening to face what is unknown about myself. But I have come to feel that if I sense where my own or another's shadow is lurking, then I am safer than when I am blissfully unaware of what darkness I am capable of doing.

If I had been more familiar with my own shadow, I might have recognized fifteen years ago some signs of Jo's despair. I will always be haunted by the memory of an Arizona morning racquetball game in 1980. After the game we returned to Jo's apartment for breakfast tea. Somehow we fell into a rare sisterly spat about an appointment with her I'd missed. Jo, who was estranged from her only sister, confessed she hadn't had a ripsnorting sibling argument in some years and she found herself enjoying it. I, who am accustomed to teasing, fiery, shouting matches with my siblings, suggested that we settle our disagreement with an old-fashioned pillow fight.

Pillow fights with my own siblings have continued throughout our lives—playful free-for-alls that almost always begin in yelling and end in laughing.

"I don't know," Jo said hesitantly. "Sounds dangerous."

I laughed. "It's not target practice; it's a game. Besides . . ." I teased her, "we're the same size, although I think I can beat you easy."

Jo was tall and dark-haired, with almond-shaped black eyes that at times seemed Asian. She was known among our university circle as a born dancer; in fact, she'd taught dancing to tide her over between teaching and the rigors of her life as a poet. She had a luminous red party dress left over from her ballroom dancing days and while the rest of us performed the rock-'n'-roll flailing and gyrating of our sixties generation, Jo would glide, sashay, dip her hips, and rhumba across the dance floor in a stunning display of steps——from cha-cha to tango. Often she was partnerless, no one able to follow her lead. More than one faculty party ended with Jo dancing in the middle of a tight, admiring circle who clapped in conga rhythms to her ecstatic, sensuous samba.

I, with my gymnast training on the uneven bars, was used to defying gravity and flying. Since my sisters were also gymnasts and dancers, we'd grown accustomed to almost choreographed pillow fights—certainly we expected grace and flexibility from our opponents. Any observer of our pillow fights would see that the *t'ai chi*-like feints and deft eluding of feathered weapons was as important as the landing of those light, laughing blows.

"All right," Jo agreed, even managed a grin. "Good thing starving artists have pillows instead of furniture!"

We divided her pillows in half until we each had a considerable pile —everything from fluffy down to short tie-dyed bolsters. I allowed her to keep her giant beanbag, knowing it would be hard to lift, much less aim. We put on the Beatles' *Sgt. Pepper's Lonely Hearts Club Band,* which, although it was more than two decades old, felt exactly right.

We bowed to each other in the middle of the room like martial artists, then Jo landed a surprise blow with a couch pillow on my shoulder. It delighted her so deeply she jumped up and down, clapping her hands. I took that opportunity to hit her with my famous one-two punch of pillows on either side of her head like great, downy cymbals. We both howled with laughter. Then Jo made a little battering ram with her bolster and dove for my belly. Like a bolero bullfighter, I stepped aside and let her fall into the big beanbag. Then I swacked her with a bright couch cushion that coughed out cotton batting as it caught her in the back. Though the blow wasn't painful, it suddenly enraged her.

She turned, furiously, "I had my back to you, that's not fair!"

"This is a pillow fight, not a duel," I yelled back gleefully, "there are no rules!" I socked her shoulder with another cushion and danced away like a lightweight boxer. As always in these mock battles with my sisters, there is what we call dancing in the lion's mouth—that delicious primitive power that can only be released in serious play. It felt wonderful to wallop her with all my might and know that it was only the weight of the pillow. I reveled in each feathered blow, whether giving or receiving. As always during these sister free-for-alls the destructive energy that is released is exhilarating. We feel very female and yet powerful in our own splendid fury and shadow play. In that pillow fight with Jo, I found myself growling, as I have done all my life—a low, guttural sound that is thrilling and, I've been told, menacing.

At that moment I was too caught up in the fight to note Jo's expression. Afterwards I would always remember it: She was utterly terrified. Her eyes were wide, dilated, and her face in one second went from a deep flush to pallor. Her lips and arms and whole body trembled as she turned her back on me again, consciously, and let me wallop her with the soft cushions. She seemed to bend, then collapse under the blows.

"Stop it!" she said with a deep voice I'd never heard in her before. "Don't push me around with your pain!"

Her loud voice startled me and I fell back, sensing for the first time that there was no element of play left here, that something else had been released and it was very big, very terrible—not something to taunt.

It was as if we had summoned up the violence of both our childhoods, as well as all our years of impotent rage. Between us, we had created a genie loosed by our play; we were, we realized at that moment, capable of anything. Anything could be lost, destroyed, and we would be responsible. We met each other's eyes and my vision blurred. The room went watery and I saw Jo bend to pick up that huge beanbag; I was not afraid of that silly bag of beans. I wasn't even afraid of Jo. But I remember that moment feeling deep fear as if I were finally safe enough to endure all those childhood terrors that I hadn't felt when I was little.

Jo must have sensed it, too, because suddenly she set down the bag and fell into it in a fetal position, sobbing inconsolably. "I'm so afraid."

I tried to comfort her and myself, stroking her back and cooing as if over another child, a sister. I have never heard anyone cry like she did that day—it was primal, the lung-bursting, heartbreaking cries of a newborn screaming out in the darkness. I told her and myself that she did not have to be afraid anymore, we did not have to be afraid. We were far away from our parents.

"It's terrible . . ." she finally managed to say after what seemed like an hour of weeping. "I'm so afraid."

When I tried to ask her who frightened her so, Jo just shook her head. If she had said then, *I'm afraid of myself,* if she had been able to claim the violence she'd been bred upon, that was within her, within all of us, and most particularly those of us who have been abused by violence—Jo might still be alive today. I might be calling her up for pizza or a pillow fight. Even after years of therapy following her parents' death after her own two suicide attempts, one before her parents' murder, the other after, Jo had not fathomed the depths of her own violence. Did she know that after years of living in terror with her father, the danger was now within her?

As if blindly anticipating the death that was only six months away, Jo wept brokenly. I held her and with a sixth sense asked her to promise me she would never kill herself, that she would not repeat her father's act of a decade ago.

"I would never do that," she assured me, tears streaming down her face. "I will never do to my son what was done to me. I swear it."

The pillow fight was over, the promise given. In the months after that Arizona morning, when we packed our separate belongings and moved to Seattle to share a house, when I watched Jo retreat into a private world of poetry and belligerent despair; when I saw her son's visit devolve into Jo's fears that she would not be able to be a good mother to him now—I always counted on her promise. It allayed my suspicions. Yet I knew something was terribly wrong with Jo and finally I demanded that she see a therapist or I would have to ask her to move out of our house-sitting arrangement. I didn't want to do that, because her son was due to come live the remainder of our house-sitting stint with us in two weeks.

The week after Mother's Day in May 1982, I gave Jo an ultimatum: I'd made an appointment for her with a therapist. If she didn't keep the appointment, she'd have to move out. Jo agreed and seemed relieved, even unusually upbeat. What I didn't know was that the next day, saying she had some chores in the city, Jo took a bus into Seattle and purchased a small revolver. There was a three-day waiting period, which meant she had a weekend to reconsider. Sometime in the night before the day of her mandatory therapist's appointment, Jo fired one shot in her bedroom down the hall. And it was there that I found her the next noon when I ventured into her territory of that big house.

For many years after Jo's death I could not think of her without witnessing again her dead body—that beautiful face filthy and bloodied by the bullet, her dancer's legs heavy with rigor mortis, those graceful hands grotesque and brittle as claws. We murder the whole world when we take our own lives—because everyone who survives us is harmed for the rest of their lives. Ask any sibling of a suicide, who knows that his or her chances of the same self-inflicted fate rise, and you'll hear the haunting sorrow, the fear, the rage. Self-inflicted violence is a realm of self-destruction that women know particularly well. Much of our feminine rage is turned inward, rather than outward on the world. The dearth of female serial murderers shows us that when women are enraged their options are different from men's. Few women go on shotgun sprees, gunning down innocent bystanders. The range of violence allowed women in our culture is usually infanticide, child abuse, and self-abuse. Female violence is usually more personal, private rather than organized around some group activity with a political goal. Even in the spate of abortion clinic killings, with one exception, all the killers have been male—and this over an issue which most concerns women and their own bodies.

Where the violence of the brotherhood is often impersonal, inflated, organized, such as military or political terrorism, the violence of sisterhood is personal, individual, and terribly intimate. It is also a subject that is under-explored in our storytelling. In fiction and film, female violence usually centers on the home and the family, portraying women whose Kali-nature overtakes the Angel in the house. *The Hand That Rocks the Cradle,* a film in which a baby-sitter turns violent, is a typical example of mother-violence, as is the real-life case of the South Carolina woman who drowned her two boys in a car, claiming at first it was a man who had kidnapped them.

Violence against one's sister is usually portrayed in our stories as sisters competing over a man and the sibling rivalry turns deadly. By depicting a sister battle over a man, the focus of the sister-sister bond, however dark, is diffused. Here again is an example of how our fictional and film stories trivialize the sister bond, as if between women there could be nothing important to kill for, except a man.

But there is a wide range of reasons why sisters often feel like destroying one another that strictly has to do with female-female relationships. A Jungian analyst, Louise Bode, once commented that the deepest destructive relationships in her professional experience have been between siblings, not parent-child; and that sister-hate has been the most damaging of all. "Sometimes it's a lifetime of struggle," she said. "And there seems no end to the dark levels of despair and violence."

Sister-hate and sister violence are much more common than our mainstream stories let on. In the same way that we sisters often die in each other's arms more than romantic movies let on, we also die, whether literally or figuratively, at each other's hands. When I saw the movie version of *Little Women*, I had two responses: One part of me wanted simply to live in that movie, to celebrate and luxuriate in the deep bond of sisterhood. The other part of me rebelled, saying, "Yes, but we're not just Little Women!" We are so much more! The sister relationship can be blissful, but also hateful; it can be divine and dangerous, supportive and destructive. In fact, the sister bond is capable of all the wide range of emotions that are usually reserved in our culture for the romantic or the parent-child bond. The sister bond is, in its own way, a lifelong marriage, for better or for worse.

And until we explore and plumb the depths of our violence, as well as our love, we will continue to trivialize and underestimate this enduring and essential intimacy. To simplify our female relationship to violence as one only of victimhood means that we remain unconscious of our own power, both to create and destroy. There are signs that this exploration of female violence is deepening. In another movie, *Heavenly Creatures*, the story of two girls who conspire to murder the mother of one is based on the real-life history of the mystery writer Anne Perry; its tagline reads, "Not All Angels Are Innocent." And in another film, *Death and the Maiden*, the advertisement shows the strong-jawed Sigourney Weaver strong-arming a man, obviously her prisoner, with a gun raised over his face. She has recognized him as the South American soldier who tortured her during the years of her country's dictatorship; Weaver's character now has the power to use the same violence against him that he supposedly wielded against her.

The power to decide life and death is a power long denied women, as the abortion struggle still shows us. Women have not exercised this power for so long that we are often appalled, afraid, and disclaiming of that power to deny or choose violence. Trapped in the role of mother nurturer or femme fatale, we are again limited to roles that show us only in relationship to the masculine, not the feminine—not each other. The fact is that emotionally and sometimes for life, we women hold guns to our own and our sisters' heads.

As record numbers of women arm themselves with guns, claiming self-defense, it is absolutely crucial that women stop to consider our own capacity for violence, especially given the statistics that guns in the home greatly increase the chances of suicide and homicide. As the violence of our culture increases, as women themselves are victims of increasing violence, our chances of becoming victimizers also increase, if we do not integrate our own feminine shadows. If we do not do this shadow work, acknowledging and exploring our own female violence, we may well turn this unexplored shadow against our sisters or ourselves.

My friend Jo could not participate long in a pillow fight because she had not explored her own violent limits, because she could not face her inner demons and survive. Women most often act out the violence against themselves. Flor Fernandez, a psychotherapist, commented recently that after giving a workshop in "Healing the Sacred Womb" for women who had experienced sexual abuse, as well as mastectomies, hysterectomies, and all manner of scarring (from the Dalkon shield to silicone implant injuries), she was alarmed at the disfigurement of the female body.

"Women are allowed only to turn upon themselves, their own bodies. Because they've been assigned roles to create and caretake, the darker elements in their human nature have been denied, driven inward. The only way women have been allowed to destroy under patriarchy is by going crazy, out of control, or getting sick and suicidal."

It occurred to me, listening to my friend, that if one were to take photographs of generations of nude women, our recent generations would indeed look battle-scarred: lost breasts, multitudinous C-sections, bald chemotherapy-ravaged skulls. An alien suddenly dropped here might wonder what war women had survived.

Is there a physical price we pay for our culture's denial of the Kali aspect in women? What happens to women if they are not allowed to integrate their dark Kali energy, if they are instead limited to roles of benevolence and creation? What will we destroy in ourselves if we are not aware of and open to claiming our shadow, our violence? If the work of the twentieth century, as C. J. Jung maintained, is to become conscious, both of our inner and our outer worlds, then meeting our shadows is as heroic a work as any conquest of new worlds. Jung also wrote that "one does not become enlightened by imagining figures of light, but by making the darkness conscious."

We are all individually responsible for our small part of knowing the shadow as well as the light. There is much life force in the shadow we've so long denied in our religions and social roles. Jung calls it "pure gold," which can only be discovered through an inner alchemy of descending into the realm of one's personal shadow, reckoning with one's disowned demons, and integrating these elements into the whole, conscious Self. In the recent anthology *Meeting the Shadow*, the philosopher Sam Keen notes that making enemies of those we refuse to recognize as much like ourselves is perhaps why our scientists named us *homo hostilis,* the hostile species. He argues that "the wars we engage in are compulsive rituals, shadow dramas in which we continually try to kill those parts of ourselves we deny and despise."

I wonder sometimes what part of Jo she was destroying when she took a gun to her own head. Was there another part of her that simply wanted to live, but lost out in the inner war? Was target practice so familiar to her since childhood that she could not live without finding a target, even if it was herself?

Another dark memory of Jo haunts me still. At a dinner party with other writing teachers in Arizona, after dancing and drinking, we all engaged in a philosophical debate on the subject of evil. It was all very abstract and political, until someone said, "Do you, any of you, believe you are capable of doing evil? I don't mean petty evil like the little, everyday murders of manners and words and mild hostilities . . . I mean, do you believe you could do great evil, like a Hitler or Stalin, if you had the chance?"

There was a deep silence. We were in Jo's apartment sitting around on her pillows. Slowly, haltingly, every one of us confessed that given a terrible upbringing, a betrayal, a war, a deep loss, that yes, we might be capable of becoming Hitlers or Stalins, although we hoped we each might not succumb to that evil within.

"But it's there, all right," a poet said. "We all know about it. We all try to find ways to balance ourselves."

"Sometimes I can feel a real tyrant inside me," I found myself confessing and shifted uneasily with the dark, toxic feelings that rose up that moment. "After all, I was raised by fundamentalists and I always have to keep watch on the part of me that is a crusader, the part that might destroy for my beliefs." Then I found myself telling a story I'd never told anyone, much less a group of people. But it spilled out, and as I told it, I could feel a deep shame burning in my belly and face.

"I was living in New York City," I began, my voice shaking. "Everybody told me to walk down the middle of the street if I was coming home late at night, but I didn't listen." I had been mugged twice, but was not physically hurt so I still walked with that confident city girl's stride, my Frye boots making a satisfying noise on the sidewalk. It was after midnight and I was walking to my brownstone apartment after a play. Suddenly, midstep, I found myself bodily lifted up and dropped to the ground on my tailbone. A hot bolt of pain went up my spine and I turned to find myself lying next to a drunk in the alley. He'd reached out and caught my left leg midstride and pulled me down, groping for my purse that was slung across my shoulder. He smelled horrible, like vomit and piss, and I jerked away from him and managed to jump up; but he grabbed again for my legs, pulling me down again. I felt something warm and wet against my jaw and believed that it was my own blood. Terror and rage and adrenaline shot through me and I kicked out at him savagely. My boots had that steel shank in the soles and I couldn't even feel my foot hitting him but I heard it: *thunk, thunk, thunk!* I don't remember how many times I kicked him, my foot just kept striking his body. There was only the muffled sounds, the disgusting smell, my terror and fury. I was screaming with each kick like some martial artist—guttural nonsense sounds, so loud it hurt my own ears.

"I barely heard the man shouting, 'Lady! Stop! You're gonna kill me!' And he was right. I could have killed him, stomped him to death. He was drunk, puking, trembling; he had never once stood up to fight me and how many times had I kicked him as he lay there in the alleyway? My fear and rage had been so overwhelming I had lost any perspective as to his power versus my own. I had lashed out, assuming I was the weaker, fated to lose this battle as I had lost every physical fight with a larger-than-life parent.

"But this man was not my abusive parent: he was pathetic," I confessed to my friends that night. "As I ran away from him, he screamed out, 'Jesus Christ, you kicked the shit out of me, lady!' " I told myself that at least he was still alive, as I ran the several blocks and climbed those many flights of stairs as if I were an Olympic high-jumper. But how badly had I hurt him? I felt my own face for the blood which had stained my gloves a dark brown. Heart throbbing, I bent double, trying to catch my breath. At last I walked into the bathroom, my knees buckling as I looked into the mirror to assess the damage. There were dark, wet smears all over my face and a funny smell that at first I couldn't place. "It was chocolate streaked all over my skin," I explained, " . . . melted chocolate. Not blood."

"Mugged by a Milky Way," one of my friends said, not unkindly, and reached for my hand. He was a writer who'd often written about hunting with his father. He was a man familiar with the intimacy of predator-prey relationships. "Poor baby," he soothed. "Poor old bum."

Several others joined in with stories, some savageries and shames from childhood fights, some domestic squabbles that degenerated into black eyes and punches. One man wept while telling how he'd turned on his brother in high school and they'd never really made up. Another man was an ex-con who'd been busted for cocaine and who broke another inmate's arm in a prison scuffle. All of us had our shadow stories. Far into the night we shared them, often with tears.

Jo was very silent, listening as she often did in groups with a certain characteristic aloofness. Her face was candlelit and quite cold and there was contempt in her voice when she spoke. "I do not think of myself as capable of great evil," she said firmly. Then she let it be known that it was time for everyone to leave her apartment. "Party's over," she pronounced.

For a moment nobody moved. I was somewhat surprised, even though all of Jo's friends were accustomed to her odd mood shifts and abrupt dismissals. On good days, Jo would confess that it was very difficult to take her leave of those she loved so she simply cut things off. Another form of distancing was her trademark black humor and contempt. Oftentimes she had taken my breath away with her dead-on descriptions of people that, while they made me laugh, also secretly shocked me. And yet, I enjoyed this part of Jo, this dark view of life that I lacked.

Jo had a self-acknowledged cruel streak, while I was comfortable and had long practice playing the caretaker. It would take me years of therapy and searching my own shadow to claim what I call "the dark side of the nurturer," which at that time in my life I let others around me act out. It would take me years of descent into my own inner darkness before I would come to accept that the shadow side of compassion can be contempt; and unless I claimed my own contempt I would always find myself playing the compassionate roles while letting others do the dirty work of my shadow.

Fifteen years after Jo's own shadow swallowed her whole, I look at her squarely and feel both compassion and contempt for her. I have a deep understanding of her despair, I even honor it; I also hold her accountable for the lives she has harmed, including her own.

Every year on the anniversary of Jo's death I write her a letter; some of my own epistles make her terse, generic suicide notes to me and her best friend and her son seem placid. I have raged and howled and screamed at her beyond the pale. And it is through the dark lens of this one event in my adult life that I have been able to look at my own darkness. It is considerable. One of the last things Jo said to me before she climbed the stairs for the final night of her life was, "You have more life force than anyone I have ever met."

I sat sprawled out on the couch watching an episode of "Brideshead Revisited," slightly surprised that my friend was turning in so early. "Brideshead" was one of her favorites, identifying as she did with Sebastian, the brilliant, doomed, decadent choirboy. I was struck by Jo's expression, desultory in her silk kimono, smoking a cigarette as she leaned against the doorjamb. But there was also about her an alert air, emphasized by her intent gaze and comment.

I laughed, trying to tease her out of her mood. "I guess I'll take that as a compliment," I said.

Jo shrugged, but there was nothing casual about her expression. "Sweet dreams," she said and slowly climbed the stairs.

For many years I tried to remember the exact slant of her smile, for she was smiling, as she took her leave of me and of her life. I do remember noticing her smile and thinking that there was little warmth to it. Jo, who could be very warm and attentive, also seemed perfectly detached, the way she often watched others eat with that odd, critical half-smile. Friends had often commented on Jo's habit of not eating with others. I rarely saw her eat, and I lived with her. But we never made fun of her self-denial and asceticism because we could sense her hunger, even as she appeared indifferent. And always, at the end of every meal, she would ask if she could help herself to the small leftovers on our plates. This was such a characteristic Jo ritual that I'd once placed a sign over our kitchen toaster that read, "Up From Crumbs," in the hope that she'd simply allow herself the whole food, the deep nourishment, not the dregs.

That night I remember my exact thought when she wished me sweet dreams. She's not hungry, I thought, and this was so unusual that I registered it deeply, even found comfort in it, because sometimes Jo's hunger dragged on me. What did not comfort me was that contempt in her smile. It froze her face and it froze something in me that wanted to hug her good night as I might my own sister. Instead, I sat on the couch and frowned. "Good night," I said. "Sleep tight." As she climbed the stairs I sighed, grateful that she had agreed to start therapy the next day. It would be a relief for me.

When I'd made the therapist date for Jo several weeks earlier, I'd wept as I told Jo about it and gave her my ultimatum. We were walking together on an island path overlooking a calm Lake Washington. "I just can't do it, Jo," I'd told her. "I can't carry you. I won't."

She'd turned to me with an expression I'd always loved in her— fond, concerned, frank. "I know," she whispered and companionably took my arm as we walked. "I know. Don't worry . . . Big Nurse is on duty."

Big Nurse was the imaginary character she'd created in herself who was the ultimate caretaker and comforter. As writers we often played character games, summoning up within our imaginations all manner of characters. I still play this game with my siblings, my friends, even my students. Sometimes we're the critics, sometimes the imaginary secretaries, sometimes the alter egos we've never in real life claimed. I trusted Jo's Big Nurse and believed her equal to any Executioner.

I was wrong—so terribly wrong that for years Jo's death left me confused and distrustful of my own intuitions. How could I not have known that night when I felt her lack of appetite that it was life she no longer hungered after, that it was not detachment but death that shadowed her face as she wished me into dreams, into a nightmare?

For several years after Jo's suicide, I did have a recurring nightmare: Jo stands at my bedroom door in shadows, much the way she looked the last time I saw her silhouetted against the stairwell. In her hand is a loaded gun as she contemplates entering my room. Will she take my life or her own, the way her father took his wife with him? In my nightmare I am hovering somewhere above—watching, waiting, witnessing. Suddenly I see Jo's cold, dark-of-the-moon face change from contempt to grief. She is bending double, holding herself. There is no gun now, simply a woman in the shadows embracing her own belly, weeping. Her hair is matted and there is even a smell in the dream, a vegetable rot like rich compost. I realize that this suffering, shadowy Jo has decided to let me live.

I do not know whether this nightmare that stalked me for several years after Jo's death is a half-memory of an event that night or my own coming face-to-face with my self-destructive shadow. The literal truth doesn't matter, because this nightmare of the deathly shadow outside my door is an inner reality—the dynamic tension between life and death. This struggle is my own, just as it was Jo's, just as it is anyone's who is conscious of the human struggle to reconcile our life wish with our death wish, and so find wholeness.

After Jo's death—and in equal parts to my mourning—I felt an unexpected energy. At first I felt terribly guilty about having even more of what Jo had termed my great "life force." But then I realized that Jo was also saying that she believed my light was great enough to equal the darkness about to descend upon me. I do not think this was simply an excuse she gave herself for leaving me to face her death. One thing I've learned about suicides is that their last days and hours are often choreographed with exactitude and care. Many times the suicide wants to make an impact on family or lover or friends, much the way a resentful, vengeful Huck Finn imagined attending his own funeral, as if to insist, *Now, aren't you sorry for what you did to me?* In these cases, the suicide is not thinking about the pain or evil he or she is commiting—the outrage is too all-consuming. Suicides are victims making victims of others; and so the cycle repeats itself. Jo had become her father, leaving a legacy and life script to her son and sister and me that we will have to face for the rest of our lives.

Because Jo is not my family, because I endured her act as an adult, having known her only a year and a half, perhaps she assumed that I could bear her death in a way others dear to her could not. It is obvious from the poetry, letters, and requests she left me that she needed to know that someone would receive her death, that she would make a deep mark on someone, without perhaps consigning that person to her fate. I suspect that in Jo's mind, I was a stand-in for her sister, the only survivor now of her original family. This sister was much in Jo's thoughts during the time I knew her; she believed her older sister was the "perfect one," the sister who took everything in her stride, never acted out the shadow, but was in Jo's word, "good and true and false." The sister, Rosamund, had chosen a career in psychotherapy and had a thriving practice, "caretaking the multitudes," as Jo dismissed her sister's work.

I never met this Rosamund who was good sister to Jo's bad sister. I'd only seen pictures; she was fair where Jo was dark: almost typecasting. The stories Jo told about Rosamund were so full of fury and despair that I kept a certain distance. What I did see clearly was the two had early on been polarized, both by their parents' roles for them and by their own acting out of only one side of the light/shadow dynamic. Jo told story after story of Rosamund's fabled kindness—that is, to everyone but Jo. In each story Jo was left with only one part to play—the screwup, the despairing girl, the shadow. Instead of bringing the sisters closer together, their parents' suicide-murder further separated them.

"Rosamund rises above everything so often that she only makes rare appearances on this planet," Jo would complain. "I'm the one left down here in hell, feeling everything . . . everything she doesn't!"

"Maybe it's the way she survives," I suggested. "Maybe anything else is just too painful for your sister."

"She doesn't feel anything," Jo would protest. "Certainly not pain." The implication was that feeling pain was Jo's job.

I do not know whether this sister portrait was true; I do know that Jo saw all her actions in the mirror of the perfect/imperfect sister— Saint Rosamund, she grimly called her older sister. I'm sure in Jo's mind, her own suicide was directed at this surviving sibling and in that there was murderous intent. There was also a cry for balance and reunion, as there always is when the denied shadow calls out for its luminous twin soul.

Recently on an international scale, we witnessed this good sister/ bad sister shadow play in the previously pristine world of Olympic figure skating. For weeks during and before the winter Olympic games in Lillehammer, Norway, the world watched, mesmerized, as the American skaters Tonya Harding and Nancy Kerrigan exemplified this split. Why was it so fascinating to follow the daily unraveling of the Tonya-Nancy skating sisters? Not only was it crackerjack soap opera, there was something deeper at work, just as there was during the judicial hearings of Clarence Thomas and Anita Hill, the William Kennedy rape trial, and the violent John Wayne Bobbitt and Lorraine Bobbitt episode.

What began as the standard sibling rivalry of sports—Tonya in her bad-girl, white-trash toughness threatening Kerrigan and promising to "whip her butt"—trespassed into real violence when Kerrigan was attacked and Tonya Harding and her ex-husband were implicated.

Before the attack, Kerrigan's persona was that of the fragile, sweet-tempered ice princess who some portrayed as Snow White to Tonya's truck-driving, hunting, tacky, tell-it-like-it-is Wicked Witch. The Kerrigan-Harding sister mirror was the subtle shadow play beneath all the much-emphasized duality. Again, these images of women doing violence to each other is such a long-hidden area of our society's feminine portrait that it was as if Pandora had once more opened her infamous box as the world watched, transfixed. The fairy-tale world of figure skating turned the myth inside out. We saw not only a female victim of abuse but a female victimizer. Even if Tonya hired her hit men, she was doing violence against her sister, as violence had been done to Tonya by her mother, her stepbrother, her husband. The cycle was spiraling down right before our entranced eyes—and we reveled in its dark, dervish energy.

The shadow is a mess, that's her very essence. Her shoelaces break, her cheap costumes come apart, her leaps land her on her buttocks; and most of all, she is mean-spirited and just low-down nasty. This shadow was onstage, stealing the show from the women who dance on thin blades of steel but never stab each other in the backs, who twirl and defy gravity but don't ever break the law, who smile as good sportswomen should, even standing second-down on the podium.

But what happened to Nancy Kerrigan, who was supposed to embody the good sister against Evil Tonya's tricks? After losing the gold medal by one judge to the lovely Oksana Baiul, there stood a suddenly sarcastic Kerrigan. She thought she was waiting in the wings, before the medal ceremony, for Baiul to redo her makeup; Baiul had been weeping in physical pain and joy over her victory. Kerrigan and bronze medalist Chen Lu (along with the rest of the world) were actually waiting for someone to find a copy of the Ukraine national anthem to accompany the medal ceremony. In the wings, in true shadow form, Kerrigan groused, her expression contemptuous. "Oh, come on," she said. "So she's going to get out here and cry again. What's the difference?"

Kerrigan's soured Snow White continued to startle the public as she skipped the Olympics closing ceremony to travel to Disney World; she had just made a ten-million-dollar deal with Disney, including a movie, commercials, and Magic Kingdom parades. What's wrong with this picture? There was Nancy Kerrigan participating in a Disney World parade grumbling aloud that she hated it and thought the whole Magic Kingdom act was "corny." She didn't want any part of this fairy tale—as a bummed-out princess, she didn't want to kiss the prince, no matter how much they paid her. She wanted to go home, more like Grumpy the Dwarf than Snow White.

The Olympics' main act was over, but the shadow play between these skating sisters showed no sign of subsiding. And Americans particularly could not get enough of the Tonya-Nancy drama. The first round of the women's figure skating competition at the Olympics was rated the number-four television show of all time, and the highest-rated sports event ever. Women were reading the sports pages of daily newspapers as well as men. Many of the male sportswriters were bewildered. George Vecsey of *The New York Times* mused, "I never used words like 'chiffon' and 'frilly' when describing great athletes." William Grimes, also in the *Times*, grimly marveled, "Say this for hockey fans. They may throw hot pennies onto the ice, but no one ever talked about whacking Wayne Gretzky before the Stanley Cup playoffs. And the players punch each other out during the game. Usually they do not waylay each other in the parking lot. Figure skating, it seems, is a much tougher arena."

Nancy Kerrigan is only twenty-four years old; Tonya Harding is twenty-three—of course, neither of them has the life experience to understand that the shadow side of being elevated is being devalued. It's the "feet of clay" dilemma and the fairy-tale simplicity of dividing darkness and light between the Witch and the Princess. Figure skating, like fairy tales, suffers the same dangerous duality; its heroines are rewarded for youth, not maturity.

Anyone watching Germany's Katarina Witt skating her final tribute to the people of Sarajevo accompanied by the haunting antiwar classic "Where Have All the Flowers Gone?" recognized the powerful depth of the mature feminine vision. For me, watching Witt's tribute, there was only one woman on the ice. She was the only one who made me weep. I certainly didn't have to weep over Tonya and Nancy— they were too busy crying for themselves.

If the bombed-out 1984 Olympic stadium in Sarajevo was not shadow enough for the glistening white Lillehammer games, if the distinctly feminine violence stalking Olympic figure skaters was not enough to open our eyes to the denied darkness that we as women can no longer keep hidden—what is to be learned from this drama which transfixed us? More than unconscious fascination, we need to understand that women are not only victims, they are also abusers; they are not only luminous and lovely, they are also dangerous and ugly; they are not only ice maidens, they are also Kali-like hags. The mature feminine can embrace all of these seeming polarities; we can reckon with the shadow by acknowledging it and bringing it into the light. That is balance. When Katarina Witt brought the shadow of Sarajevo onto the blazing white mirror of ice, her beauty was a balancing act for the horror of that war-ravaged country. It is the admission of the shadow that heals, contains, and finally transforms it.

The Tonya Harding–Nancy Kerrigan story was a great lesson in integrating the shadow. In a way, Kerrigan's character was stretched and deepened. The attack which struck her with all the painful force of any shadow forced her out of her fragile, fairy-tale sweetness into finding her own inner toughness. She did not crumple and despair; she healed her body and offered up the performance of her life. It may not have gained her the gold medal, but it showed the whole world her grace and stamina and genuine spirit. Her shadowy sulking and mean-spiritedness after the Olympics was a good sign: Even the simpleminded, mythologically corrupt Disney machine couldn't parade her around as Snow White. The Magic Kingdom is neither magical nor spacious enough to embody any maturing feminine vision— a vision in which the Sleeping Princess is kissed by the terrible witch within and so wakes up to her own wholeness.

As for Tonya Harding who out-victimed everyone, both on ice and in the courts—she, too, gained much from this Pandora's shadow loosed among fairy-tale women. Tonya's encounter with her own dark side continued in the courts. She was finally convicted as a felon, having pled guilty only to hindering the police investigation. Will she ever claim the violence within her own psyche that she has projected onto everyone else in her life—from mother to boyfriends to husband? Stay tuned. The shadow knows.

On the day after the women's figure-skating finals, the front page of *The New York Times* had a photograph of Oksana Baiul's gold medal performance right next to the headline AT LEAST 40 SLAIN IN WEST BANK MASSACRE AS ISRAELI FIRES INTO MOSQUE. In that same issue of *The New York Times* ran a full-page political ad of civil rights umbrella groups sponsored by the American Jewish Committee. It pleaded for tolerance and quoted Martin Luther King's visionary words, "We must all learn to live together as brothers or we will all perish together as fools."

And what about sisters recognizing their part in all this escalating violence? What might happen if women claimed their Kali impulses and stopped projecting it completely onto men? This is not a popular proposition in the face of all the statistics of violence against women by men. How, for example, to ask a battered wife with a broken jaw to claim her own violence?

And yet this is exactly what women must do if we are going to begin the work of balancing ourselves and our brothers. Louise Bode, a Jungian analyst, once remarked to me, "Almost every time I counsel a battered wife I find violence in that women's past—childhood violence or sexual abuse between siblings. That woman may not beat her kids, but she will allow herself to be beaten. One has to consider the fact that perhaps that woman is allowing her man to act out her own violent shadow."

If we allow men to act out our own violence we will have no control over balancing it. If my friend Jo had been able to claim in that close circle of friends that indeed she was capable of evil, that in several months she would in fact commit great harm against herself, her sister, her son, her friends—would she have begun to balance and so survive the target practice of her childhood?

In their introduction to their anthology *Meeting the Shadow*, as Connie Zweig and Jeremiah Abrams wrote, "Perhaps . . . [we can] refrain from adding our personal darkness to the density of the collective shadow." There cannot be birth without death, just as there will not be any balancing of violence in our world without women taking their part in that struggle. We are now debating the role of women in the military, and new Pentagon rulings permit women in limited battle roles. But the real battlefield is the psyche, where all the dreams and demons and projects begin long before the arms are taken up against our own kind. It is in this netherworld that women have long had much power and say—the dark-side-of-the-moon world where intuition and Kali can be guides away from the descent.

If one believes that the integration of the shadow into our daily consciousness is an evolutionary step in human emotional development, then the next step is to claim on a personal level that same shadow. Instead of watching the Bobbitts, we must look at our own marriages; instead of watching *Oprah* like a daily freak show, we must identify and embrace the freaks within each of us. As we follow the rape trials, and sexual harassment statistics, and the skaters' world of violent retribution, we can also remind ourselves that these modern fairy tales are the grim grist of our own everyday dilemmas. We are the Witch and the Princess, the Heroine and the Villain. As women and as a sisterhood, we embody all extremes and we inhabit a profoundly moral universe—a passion play with the full range of human emotions and actions.

There are some sure signs that our culture is beginning to recognize this feminine fullness and the wide spectrum of good and evil in our sisterhoods. More than a year after the Kerrigan-Harding Olympian ice drama, a *New York Times* sports-page article reported that these women's rival sibling roles "once in stark contrast have become more complicated. What was once Nancy in white and Tonya in black—good girl vs. bad girl—has bled into gray." This is progress, albeit painful progress for both skating "sisters." As the article concludes, "The banned skater gets a public redemption. The hero shows flaws." This more complicated vision of the women's roles is what the ancients understood long ago when they imagined their Olympian gods and goddesses as siblings engaged in divine rivalry and shadow play, as well as in heroic acts of grace. When the Olympian siblings were replaced in our religions by a parent-god, and only a father at that, both the divine and human range of roles or relationships were lost. We were left with polarities and a separation of shadow from light. We were either saved or damned; we were certainly not gray, not somewhere in between struggling to reconcile our souls to a bewildering range of spiritual and moral dilemmas. But in these times, when coming into consciousness of both our potential for evil and good is a heroic responsibility, gray is an exemplary color; as we mature, gray seems most to sum up the human condition with its paradoxes and difficult reconciliation of opposites.

Our sisterhoods are now on this threshold, as our old notions of limits and roles are giving way to the light of a new self-consciousness, one which embraces our dark and our luminous natures. Snow White sleeps no more, she is wide awake and remembering that she has us as modern sisters. We are not all evil, just as Snow White is not an innocent ice queen. Ours is a sisterhood of brave gray and mature women—sisters of the shadow.

10

Sister Acts

I first met the DiGrassi sisters a decade ago at a wedding of mutual friends. Suzanne and Gracie DiGrassi struck me immediately as I glanced around the festive wedding reception tables. Amidst the swirl of celebrants, these two dark-haired women leaned close, listening to each other with cupped ears. At first I thought they were riveted in some deep family or wedding gossip, but coming closer, I realized they were singing, practicing their harmony for the entertainment they would later offer us all.

What intrigued me the most about these two sisters was their absolute attention toward each other, like two tuning forks vibrating at the exact same frequency. Their intense concentration reminded me of how fierce and strong was the collaborative bond; also how exclusive. Several times when someone tried to engage the sisters, each waved them away with a dismissive hand.

"Let us just figure this out!" one of the sisters said, stalling a fan or family friend.

I was impressed by the sisters' passion and self-possession. Unlike many women when interrupted during a deep discussion with their sisters or friends, the DiGrassis made no sheepish apologies for being otherwise deeply preoccupied. I thought of all the times my own sisters and I have been rudely intruded upon by a solitary man who, upon spying three sisters talking together, will think nothing of walking over and demanding, "You girls alone?" This happens particularly in the South and my Southern-belle sisters have a well-prepared comeback to any would-be interloper. "We're not alone," Paula or Marla will remark in their best Southern-lady accents. "You are."

It was obvious as the DiGrassi sisters swung into their reception performance that they had practiced their singing act since childhood, because their timing was synchronized and smooth, their jazz riffs respectfully interwoven, their blues numbers gutsy and self-assured. They each took turns singing lead so that they didn't fall into the rut of one taking alto, the other soprano, and staying with their own predictable, linear parts ad infinitum—the danger of any duet. Since Suzanne played a mean electric fiddle and Gracie the piano, they often backed each other up on a solo—everything from the Irish folk classic "Danny Boy" to a sultry Etta James number, "At Last."

Suzanne DiGrassi had a fragile face with a lush mane of dark brown curls, which she wore delicately cinched back by tortoise-shell combs in pre-Raphaelite splendor. Her low, alto voice was as ravishing as her looks; but her wit betrayed some shyness. On the other hand, her Sicilian black-haired sister, Gracie, was high-spirited, with the mischievous charm of the younger sibling-trickster. The sisters kept up a fond banter between numbers, and I envied them what seemed like lifelong play together. I wondered, what would it be like to carry one's childhood games, songs, and theatricals into adulthood? What happens when the imagination of siblings grows side by side into a full career act together? Such popular sister acts as the Roches, the McGarrigles, Heart, Wilson Phillips, the Pointer Sisters, and Sisters With Voices prove that the "family sound," as they call it in the music industry, is enduring. I remember reading an interview with Nancy and Ann Wilson, whose band, Heart, wrote and recorded the classic songs "Dreamboat Annie" and "Dog and Butterfly." When a reporter asked the younger sister, Nancy, if she ever took an important talisman for luck on her performance tours, Nancy nodded to Ann and said simply, "I only have to take *her*."

I wondered as I listened to Suzanne and Gracie DiGrassi swing into a sassy, original song, Was their easy intimacy onstage true to their real-life sisterhood? Had they as artists always been so serenely matched?

Now after ten years of friendship with both the DiGrassi sisters, I've learned that their sister act, like any bond between passionate, creative women, has as many complexities and layers as any marriage of true minds and voices—perhaps more, because they have been harmonizing and struggling with each other since they were children. And their serenity seems directly linked to resolving their struggles.

Suzanne DiGrassi, the eldest sister, was in her early thirties when she and Gracie finally got their big break and were offered a record contract with a major label; Gracie was three years younger. After decades of hard work and sacrifice, the DiGrassis seemed about to gather the professional garlands of a sister act begun in girlhood choirs.

As teenagers in Philadelphia, the DiGrassi sisters first began singing duets in their Catholic Church pageants. In the sixties, they each took up the acoustic guitar and formed a folk-singing group with their two brothers, calling themselves the Family Four. At first the DiGrassis' singing roles mirrored the sibling roles: Suzanne as the eldest was a second mother, Donnie, Gracie, and Alfonso. Separated from her brother by only eighteen months, Suzanne still felt much older because her assigned duty was to take care of her siblings—so much so that she often wondered if her fate as a nurturer was a sign from God that she was called to the vocation of the nuns. Certainly her mother expected Suzanne to follow a female tradition in their family and take her convent vows. Maria DiGrassi, their mother, had wanted to be a nun until she got pregnant by Tony DiGrassi, a trombonist in a Big Band orchestra.

Maria gave up her convent aspirations and instead became a fervent secretary in the local diocese; for his part, Tony sacrificed a life on the road with fellow band members and instead opened his own restaurant, giving music lessons on the side. Both Maria and Tony were devout Catholics who taught their children that family and God came first, but each in their own way nurtured their children's musical and artistic talents. By the time the four DiGrassi children were in their teens, each one of them played several instruments and when they were not singing in church, they were performing in Tony's restaurant.

All the young DiGrassis took to music with their father's passion; but the boys drew the line at learning opera, something their mother kept blasting every waking hour in her huge kitchen.

The day Suzanne DiGrassi announced to her mother that she had decided not to be a bride of Christ, she asked her sister to stand with her for moral support. Everyone in the family knew without saying that Gracie was Maria's favorite child. It was not only that Gracie was a mirror image of her mother; it was also that Gracie's temperament, flirtatious and flamboyant, was more her mother's style than Suzanne's pensive, shy nature.

That day when Maria DiGrassi glanced up from the calamari she was marinating for her husband's restaurant, she was startled to see both sisters standing stolidly, as if about to perform one of her tragic operas. Maria was taken aback by Gracie's uncharacteristic somber manner and Suzanne's surprising lightheartedness. It was as if her daughters had suddenly switched roles. She was further confused when Suzanne confessed without a shadow of guilt, "Mama, I'm not going to the sisters. So you can stop waiting for me to become the nun you never were because you got pregnant with me."

It all came out in a rush, just the way Suzanne and Gracie had practiced it, as if this were an intricate harmony that must be performed just right. Suzanne felt an intoxicating rush of freedom. After all, she was seventeen, old enough to tell right from wrong. She had already confided her choice against convent life to Sister Antoine, her favorite teacher, and Sister Antoine had assured her there were many ways to serve God outside the convent walls. With Sister Antoine's blessing and her younger sister Gracie's staunch support, Suzanne felt immune from her mother's disappointment. She waited for Maria to come back at her with judgments, pious hysterics; she was shocked when her mother considered Suzanne very deeply, then unexpectedly turned to Gracie with a demand.

"Is this what you want, Gracie? Does this mean you'll both be devoting yourselves to your singing?"

"Yes, Mama," Gracie said firmly.

Suzanne was too startled to say anything. She had expected anything but her mother's focus on their singing.

"Good." Maria nodded as if that was all there was to it. "Suzanne, you and your sister will be stars, I just know it. And that is serving

God, too." She wiped her hands on a kitchen towel and came over to embrace Suzanne and Gracie. "Besides, if you were a nun, Suzanne, what would Gracie do without you?"

Suzanne would never forget that moment—her mother's scent of garlic and sweet-sour capers, her unexpected blessing. But there was also an undercurrent that Suzanne would not understand until many years later when she and Gracie were on the verge of breaking up their act. It was an uneasiness at having agreed to some role that in its way was more servitude than any convent. For at that moment, Suzanne accepted without knowing that she would continue to be her sister Gracie's caretaker long after childhood and into a roller-coaster career.

That momentous day in their mama's kitchen, neither Suzanne nor Gracie foresaw the tumultuous and troubled singing career that awaited them; they only knew they had scored a major triumph by gaining not only their mother's permission to focus on their music, but also her strong support. At times Maria DiGrassi's encouragement of her teenage daughters took the form of overbearing stage mother. When Donnie and Alfonso started chasing girls instead of singing gigs for their Family Four performances, their mother dismissed them from the group. Since the Family Four had recently shocked the chaperones at the Catholic Youth dances by playing a steamy rendition of "Lay, Lady, Lay" and a mocking, rebellious version of "Eve of Destruction," their mother packed the boys off to military school in upstate New York and focused all her attention and hopes on her daughters.

The DiGrassi sisters sang at weddings, convent school graduations, and continued their weekend performances in their father's restaurant. "Just you wait," their mother would predict with such force Gracie and Suzanne half-believed she was foretelling their future. "One night a music rep or producer will come in to eat and instead he'll gobble up your act. He'll sign you on the spot, right before our eyes. Maybe, if you're still young, I'll come along on tours and cook for you."

"Mama," Gracie would protest, "if you tour with us, we'll get fat."

Unlike her tall, slender sister Suzanne, Gracie had found to her horror that she'd inherited her mother's curves—"Sicilian hips," her mother called them proudly. "Good for carrying weights, like children."

"Mama," Suzanne would say and laugh, "you should have been an opera star; you'd never make a roadie or a rock groupie."

No music rep or producer ever discovered the DiGrassi sisters in their father's restaurant. Instead, Gracie was sought out by a young man who announced to her the first night they met that he had only two ambitions in life: to be musical director of a large Catholic church, and to marry Gracie DiGrassi. Gracie was still in her Catholic girls' high school and Suzanne was attending a Catholic college near home; they sang together on weekends and practiced three times a week. Gracie's admirer, Ray Salvatori, was a skinny, bespectacled boy, who listened to Gregorian chants while others his age tuned in to the Grateful Dead. For all his eccentric choirboy ways, he was oddly hip and considered by his Catholic crowd a shoo-in for any priestly position. His passion for Gracie deflected him from the monastery where he might have been happiest, but he courted her with a determination akin to religious zeal.

"That boy should be with the saints," Maria DiGrassi said fondly. She knew his mother from her diocese work and strongly approved of Ray's courting her daughter, as long as he took an oath also to support her singing career. Ray, who had been a church organist sought after in all the Philadelphia churches since he was barely older than an altar boy, swore to Maria DiGrassi that he would make Gracie's career as much a priority as his own.

Maria was satisfied. She had positioned her favorite daughter between a doting choirboy and a devoted older sister—Gracie would be the singing sensation that Maria knew she might have been had she not taken the path of "mortal flesh" and gotten pregnant with her firstborn daughter. "I don't regret you," she'd solemnly tell Suzanne. "I gave up my life for you and your sister. . . . The boys, well, they can take care of themselves. But my girls are going to sing like angels and the whole world will hear them."

The DiGrassi girls did sing like angels during their Catholic school days, but as soon as Suzanne was only blocks away at college, she discovered the delicious sensuality of blues and jazz. Her dorm room was adorned with Billie Holiday posters and on weekends she'd persuade Ray and Gracie to abandon their Catholic dances to crash nightclubs in South Philly, where all the best blues and jazz singers passed through on their way to the Big Apple.

While Gracie had been going steady with Ray Salvatori since they were both sixteen, Suzanne was often a third wheel to these weekend dates. It's not that Suzanne didn't have suitors, but Suzanne had blossomed into a dark-haired beauty who was so quietly charismatic that shyness was her only defense against the sudden onslaught of freshmen men. "Most guys think you're stuck-up," Ray would advise Suzanne in a brotherly way. "You're so drop-dead gorgeous that a guy thinks he's automatically out of the competition. The way I see it is, you've got two choices: Either you stay shy and end up some corporate lawyer's trophy wife or you let guys see you're not so superior and serious and then you can call your own shots."

Suzanne did call her own shots. Between her studies, her singing, and her family's demands, she kept herself in the center of a tight, possessive circle, none of whom complained that she didn't have many dates. "Outsiders," their mother called anyone who was not family or an accepted friend. "Keep 'em in your audience, not your home."

When Gracie joined Suzanne at college, the sisters returned to their duo status, with Ray off at seminary where he was studying music. It was during this time that Suzanne took on the major burden of Gracie's high-strung and demanding moods. Whenever Gracie was not with Suzanne she experienced terrible panic attacks, calmed only by Suzanne's presence and soothing voice. Often Suzanne sang her sister out of her hysterics and they'd fall into laughter. At the same time Suzanne noticed how different Gracie was from the other girls in school; somehow it had not been as pronounced when they both lived at home with their mother as ever-present ballast. But alone together as sisters on campus, Suzanne began to see a disturbing pattern with Gracie around other women: Gracie seemed incapable of making real friends. She'd go through intense, all-consuming bonds with other students, then suddenly drop them at the hint of any slight or suggestion that she was not the center of their universe.

"You can't be someone's friend by bullying them, Gracie," Suzanne would attempt to explain to her little sister. "You've got to give and take. This is not family, where we have to love you and put up with your demands and moods. . . . You are not Mama's magic child out here." Then Suzanne would add darkly when she saw Gracie ignoring her advice, "And I'm not your guardian angel!"

Gracie would always burst into inconsolable sobs at the hint that

Suzanne might desert her. At every turn, Gracie challenged her sister's closeness to other friends, insisting that they practice their singing instead of hanging out. "If we're going to be artists," Gracie would remind her older sister, "we've got to be the best. What would Mama say if she saw you going to all those stupid antiwar rallies? They're not asking you to sing, they're wasting your time with petitions and politics. In a few years, no one will have ever heard of Vietnam and we'll be washed up as singers because you chose your hippie pals over our act. Mama would never forgive you and neither will I, if we miss our chance because of your protest rallies. And another thing, no more antiwar songs on stage. I don't care how much the audience wants us to sing 'Blowin' in the Wind' . . . it's a boring song, not upbeat, and if you try to sing it one more time, I'll walk offstage and leave you alone up there."

"I wouldn't mind," Suzanne retorted. "I can be up there all alone. You can't."

That threat always silenced Gracie, but it also reduced Suzanne to penitence and deep guilt. She'd always say her rosary many times and ask Gracie's forgiveness after such an outburst. And then she discovered something about her sister which made her hold her tongue even more, for she truly began to worry about Gracie's stability.

One midnight when the sisters were home for a weekend visit, Suzanne was awakened by sounds downstairs in her mother's huge kitchen. Bleary-eyed, she descended the staircase and stopped cold. In the kitchen sat Gracie, hunched over one of their mama's banana cream pies. With a serving spoon Gracie was scooping big pieces of pie into her mouth, eating like a starving criminal who'd broken into Maria DiGrassi's kitchen and was eating as if this were his last supper. For years after that night Suzanne would remember that pie, how the meringue was whipped up into tiny mountains like a topographic map of the Swiss Alps and in each valley were small pools from her sister's tears.

Suzanne had always thought of her sister as a snacker. This was a decade before the particularly female obsessions with food, anorexia or bulimia, would become a common theme in our culture. In the early seventies, women who binged were most often seen as obeying some drug-inspired mood of the moment; very few people were aware that increasingly large populations of girls and women were bingeing or starving themselves. When Suzanne saw her sister eating with such desperate hunger, even she recognized that this was not one of Gracie's moods or a high-school eating binge—this was like being sick, only no one noticed it. In fact, everyone from their mother to Ray to all their chums praised Gracie's hard-won hourglass figure and fad diets.

That midnight in their mama's kitchen Suzanne felt at once guilty and horrified—guilt over her own effortlessly slender body and horror that Gracie was so secretive and sick. Without a word Suzanne glided into the kitchen and sat down next to her sister, helping her eat the pie. Suzanne didn't even like banana cream pie; it was too sweet. But the moment she began eating it, Gracie caught her breath and sat back gratefully as if awoken from a nightmare. Chin propped on her hands, Gracie smiled and watched her older sister eat the pie.

"You feel it, too, don't you, Suzanne?" Gracie demanded, with deep relief, falling into their old camaraderie as if they were children again, defying their mother, stealing goodies from her kitchen.

"What?" Suzanne managed between mouthfuls of the stiff, sticky meringue.

"The hunger . . ." Gracie said in a whisper. "Almost like you could eat yourself to death and still be hungry. You know, right?"

"Yes, Gracie," Suzanne lied, "I know."

Then Gracie showed her sister how to throw up without making noise; it was as if she were sharing a secret, holy ritual, much like those arcane and unfathomable rites that martyred saints enjoyed. Suzanne was never able to make herself vomit as Gracie did, effortlessly, as if from long habit.

"How long have you been . . . doing this?" Suzanne asked tentatively, not wanting to criticize her sister.

Gracie laughed. "Never knew, did you? You always had it easy, no hips! But I had Mama's body and would be as wide as she is if it weren't for learning to ride the bus."

"Ride the bus?"

"You really are a nerd, Suze . . ." Gracie laughed and delicately wiped her lips on one of their mother's guest towels. "Riding the bus, you know . . . puking. The toilet bowl is like your steering wheel." Gracie smiled when she saw the effect this had on Suzanne. Her sister shied away from vulgarities. Even though Suzanne prided herself on being bohemian, she had no stomach for truly low-life details.

After that guilty night together in their mother's kitchen, Suzanne took it upon herself to oversee Gracie's eating habits. Since they shared a room at the dorm, it was easy to coordinate her classes to meet Gracie at the cafeteria for lunch and dinner. Gracie seemed to relax more, knowing she'd share mealtimes with her sister. She even found herself getting along with Suzanne's girlfriends and feeling for the first time since she'd left home that she had a circle of friends. That they were Suzanne's friends mattered only if the sisters had a fight and the friends were forced to take sides; few ever defended Gracie. Most of Suzanne's friends tolerated her out of loyalty to Suzanne. If pushed, the friends would confess that while Gracie had a beautiful singing voice, she was "a spoiled brat." But no one dared venture this opinion to Suzanne, knowing that she'd cut them off if she had to choose between her sister and her friends.

When Suzanne was a senior and Gracie a sophomore they had an offer from a record company to cut a demo tape. They were experimenting with the folk music sound and had attracted a large local audience. The demo tape went nowhere, but it was enough to assure their mother that they were on their way to stardom—a conviction Maria DiGrassi took to her deathbed soon after the sisters graduated from college in 1974.

It was Suzanne who had the idea of recording a series of songs— from Italian peasant folk songs to an aria arranged in a jazz version —to honor their mother's memory. It was this combination of deeply felt and intricate duets that first attracted real interest from a recording label who signed them to do an album after hearing them perform at a New York club known for launching new talent. Those years of early performances and writing their first album are remembered by the sisters as some of their best times together.

They lived in the same apartment house in Philadelphia near their father's restaurant, which was now being run with the help of their brothers. Ray returned from seminary and with his music degree was even more popular in the diocese than when he was an organist. He was not so much devout as devoted to the resonant, trancelike moods of religious music. Gracie and Ray married in 1979, the year the sisters' first album was released to critical success, but except for their local following, it was widely ignored. Suzanne and Gracie began the difficult work of a second album.

It was then that Suzanne fell in love with a Jewish civil rights lawyer, Alex Fine. Alex had gone south for the integration struggle in the sixties, and returned to Philadelphia determined to make a difference. His idealism captured Suzanne's latent liberal yearnings and further separated her from her sister's more conservative politics. "I don't get it," Alex had laughed after watching their sister act on-stage. "At the microphone, Gracie's a total temptress and yet offstage she's a neurotic choirgirl." Alex respected Suzanne's tight bond with her sister and family, having very little family of his own who had survived the Polish concentration camps. At times he even idealized the large Italian brood that belonged to his wife body and soul. But he was also the first to see that Gracie's demands on Suzanne were endangering her own health if not her career.

"It's always *Gracie's* throat and *Gracie's* stomach—everyone in your family monitors her like they've got invisible IVs plugged into her body," Alex told Suzanne in 1982 when the sisters were about to wrap up their second album. "But what about you, Suzanne? You're work-ing too hard; you're falling apart and no one takes care of you, ex-cept me."

One afternoon Gracie showed up in the recording studio, her face pale with dark circles beneath her eyes. Her singing was erratic, not at all in synch with her sister's soprano flights. Suzanne suspected it was a drug hangover. Angrily she dismissed the band for the day and took her sister into the bathroom. The two sat on the edge of the long porcelain countertop, glaring at each other.

"I might as well have been a nun." Suzanne threw up her hands. "Look at you . . . what is it this time, cocaine, downers, or uppers? I thought this was just a stage, an experiment, but maybe it's more . . . maybe it's a habit."

Grace frowned and turned away from her disheveled reflection in the mirror. "Mama's already got a sharp eye on me in heaven, and Ray's no slouch. He keeps me in choir practice so much I don't have time to be a drug addict!" Gracie laughed harshly. "Then there's my dear big sister, Suzanne . . . always spying on me. . ."

"I'm not spying, Gracie," Suzanne protested. "I'm taking care of you . . . since you can't seem to do it for yourself."

"Give it up, Suze," Grace said wearily. "Give up your nun-big-sis habit . . . and . . ." Here Gracie paused and spun around to stare at herself in the bathroom mirror. Gingerly she touched her face, the hollows in her cheeks. "And . . . I'll give up my habit."

"Listen, Gracie," Suzanne fumed. "I don't believe you anymore. It's just another promise to me that you'll break . . . to Mama . . . to everybody who loves you . . ."

"Love me less," Gracie murmured, "let me *be* a little more."

"Oh," Suzanne asked, "so you can get your act together? Without me, there'd be no act. I'm holding it all together now, no thanks to you!" Suzanne stood up and headed for the door. "All our lives I've had to take care of you, Gracie. I'm sick of it! When a man wants to save the world, he joins the priesthood or the Foreign Legion or something. But when a woman wants to save the world, she takes on an impossible relationship and tries to save that person instead. You're impossible for me now, Gracie. . . . you've made me never want to sing again . . . just give up the music business . . ." Suzanne stopped, frozen at the open door. She was shocked at her own threat.

Gracie was quiet, eyeing her older sister with an expression at once thoughtful and daring. "Just give me up," she said evenly.

Suzanne shut the door and leaned against it, bursting into tears. "I . . . I can't."

"Am I *your* drug?" Gracie asked, amazed and knowing.

Several months later, after Gracie had voluntarily undergone a month-long drug rehabilitation program, the DiGrassi sisters were in the final throes of finishing their second album. Suddenly Suzanne collapsed in the recording studio. She was hemorrhaging badly and the doctors finally diagnosed her wasting illness as Crohn's disease; Suzanne was advised to cancel all performances and learn to rest and control her sickness, a lifelong ailment. In the hospital recuperating from her collapse, Suzanne had an encounter that changed her career —and her sister act.

She was drinking camomile tea in the hospital cafeteria with one of the orderlies who told her a story worthy of the tabloids. It seems one of the patients on another floor, a man in his mid-fifties, had been brought in with what seemed a routine heart attack. When the doctor studied the emergency X rays he saw an unexpected shadow in the man's chest cavity and decided to operate immediately. As the surgeon opened the man's rib cage he found to his astonishment a tiny fetus curled around the man's heart, constricting its function so terribly that the prognosis was life-threatening if the undeveloped fetus were not removed. The surgical team removed the tiny fetus as if it were a tumor or destructive growth. A "deadly symbiosis," the doctor called it.

"It was a parasite, pure and simple," the orderly told Suzanne, who was so struck by the story she asked for every detail. She didn't know at the time why the story both appalled and comforted her. "Had to be taken out," the orderly continued. "But that man, when the doctor told him about the undeveloped fetus, just took to hollering and sobbing like there was no tomorrow. He had always wanted a sibling, the man screamed, and now we'd taken away his brother or sister from him and left him alone again. He'd rather be dead." The orderly paused, not noticing Suzanne's pale face. "So next thing we know the guy is piling up his pain pills and he overdoses the minute he gets back home on his own. In his suicide note he said we'd, the doctors, I mean, stolen his life-support system!" The orderly shook his head and stood to go, leaving Suzanne sitting dazed and silent at the table. "Some thanks we get for saving a guy's life." The orderly shrugged and was gone.

As she stared out the hospital window to a courtyard below, Suzanne felt that dizzying physical sensation that often accompanies any shock of recognition. *Epiphany,* that's what the nuns had taught them about that moment when the doors between divine wisdom and the mundane mortal world open wide to reveal some personal truth. She identified with this man's story of discovering a parasite within that at once endangered his own health and at the same time was somehow his life-support system. Her relationship with her sister was like that: Gracie depended upon Suzanne for her well-being to the point of demanding from Suzanne what Suzanne needed for herself. But Gracie also supported Suzanne in a profound way that the elder sister had never quite understood. Symbiosis, but was it deadly?

Suzanne knew she couldn't blame her incurable ailment on Gracie alone—part of it was simple: Her body had broken down. She couldn't change that fact, but she could change the future. As soon as she was out of the hospital, Suzanne quit her part-time job as a music librarian and also put Gracie on notice that their second album would have to be on hold until she gathered her strength again. Gracie was surprisingly acquiescent; she even seemed relieved. She threw herself with her usual abandon into helping Ray arrange and produce a record album of citywide Catholic choirs.

For six months, Suzanne navigated the new, narrow confines of her illness, understanding for the first time at the age of thirty-five that she had mortal limits and that what she had always reached for— both in dealing with Gracie and in their singing act—required resources that she no longer physically possessed. Finally, as Suzanne emerged from the cocoon of her chronic ailment and her energy increased, she found herself looking at the world with new, shrewd eyes. Everything had an energy price tag—from singing to cooking to listening to giving advice. Suzanne woke up in the morning and planned activities according to each day's allotted quota of energy. It was her body that had put her on an energy diet and Suzanne found herself carefully observing her daily physical exertions. For the first time ever she understood something about her sister—Gracie's teenage binge-and-purge eating habits had been rooted in this terrible private knowledge that she was starving emotionally and needed to be filled. Suzanne now understood what it was to feel starved—starved for life force, for abundant physical energy and drive. Suzanne knew in her body now what it was to feel old. Her job was to find a way to feel thirty-five again and to find that full sense of well-being that comes from good health.

Suzanne turned for help to the last person she thought would ever take care of her—her sister. Since they lived nearby, it was Gracie who often drove Suzanne to doctors' appointments, Gracie who helped her clean and shop and perform the multitudinous details of daily life. Without the pressure of their singing act, they were free just to be together without a focus, without their mother's driving ambition and plans.

"I had to get sick for us to have a real life together," Suzanne told Gracie one day when they were running around—"trooping," they called their daily chores, which no longer included endless recording sessions, performance gigs, and travel. "Sometimes I think we've had to choose being sisters over being singers."

Now when they sang there was not as much pressure, they could enjoy themselves. One day, while riding together to do their shopping, Gracie suddenly burst out with, "I'm glad Mama's dead! Oh, I know the nuns would never forgive me and I'll have to say a bezillion Hail

Marys, but you never knew what it was really like, Suze. I loved
Mama, but she just used me up. You never felt it like I did . . . how
her eyes followed me with all those big expectations and . . . well, it
was weird, like desire. I didn't recognize it until boys started noticing
me when I got this woman's body at twelve . . . but it was like that,
desire from Mama!" Seeing Suzanne's shocked face, Gracie rushed on:
"It's not sexual, Mama didn't want incest, for God's sake . . . she
wanted . . . my life. The day I finally got it big-time was when I was
in college and a friend told me about her father's incest stuff with
her. The worst, she said, was not the sex, the worst was walking about
her own house feeling her father's eyes always on her, his *awareness* of
her every move. She could never escape. It was like living with a
voyeur.

"It was the same with Mama, like she tapped into me somewhere
so deep I didn't know how to fight her off. I had her face, her figure,
her voice—and she was always pulling on me . . . like the way someone steals gas by siphoning off your tank with a hose. That's why I
ate so crazy those last years at home. . . . I was eating for two, I just
didn't know it!" Gracie paused, breathless, then added in a quiet voice,
"You always say I was Mama's favorite, Suze, but that's like saying a
vampire loves me best. One of my professors told me when I tried to
explain about Mama once . . . she said, 'Don't you know that the dark
side of the nurturer *is* the vampire?' " Gracie stopped, taking a deep
breath. "And . . . and I'm so glad you got sick . . . don't hate me,
Suze . . . but it stopped you cold . . . stopped you from taking over
where Mama left off . . ."

Horrified, Suzanne would have walked out on her sister had they
not been traveling together in a car to the grocery store. Instead, she
unbuckled her seat belt and demanded, "Let me off at the next stop
sign. I don't have to listen to any more of this, not about Mama, and
not about me."

It was Gracie's turn to be horrified. She was about to fight, to yell
and pitch a tantrum as she had much of her childhood, but instead
she simply pulled the car to the side of the road and turned off the
engine. Steadily, she turned to her sister. "Did you hear what I said,
Suze? I said that we can't do to each other what Mama did to me or
wants you to do to your own life. You can't take care of me first,

instead of yourself . . . and I can't fall into the old role of the bad baby sister who uses everybody up!"

Suzanne was very still, eyeing her sister as if for the first time recognizing an equal, and not only that, a threat. When Gracie was the spoiled brat, the dependent younger sister, Suzanne held the power for the two of them. Now that Gracie was the independent, perceptive peer, she was a person to be reckoned with, even sometimes surrendered to—and the idea of yielding to Gracie's wisdom, her strength, sometimes even if it was just physically more sure than Suzanne's own, made the older sister begin to weep. She wept with gratitude, from fear, and out of a sense that their future singing act might be wildly different from what their mama or they themselves had ever planned.

One thing stayed the same: their intense collaborative bond. After a stint doing a nonprofessional solo act in Europe, Suzanne returned to the States and finished that difficult second album with Gracie. It is strikingly different from the first—more balanced and darkly nuanced; there is only one mention of their mother or their Italian roots in a song the sisters wrote together. The rest of the songs are eclectic and heartfelt, as if something in the DiGrassi sisters has been set free from their Catholic girlhood mythology and has moved into mature, feminine territory—that intersection between loss and surrender. Though their harmonies are still astonishingly tight, each sister's voice is now distinct.

"We've lost some of the 'family sound,'" Suzanne explained recently. "And we're not there yet musically, but both Gracie and I are searching for our own styles. That's why sometimes I sing lead and she backs me up, and then we reverse roles . . . kind of like what's happened in our lives."

Gracie agrees. "When Suzanne and I really get in a groove, it's like knowing someone's soul . . . Ray says it's a religious experience, but then *he* would read something spiritual into it." Gracie paused and sipped a diet Coke. She is still more voluptuous than her older sister, but Suzanne has filled out with the beginnings of her first pregnancy and because of that, the family resemblance between the sisters is more pronounced.

"For me," Suzanne took up, "singing with my sister, when we're really cooking, is thrilling."

Gracie smiled, with a contemplative nod. "That's the best of us," she said. "That's the very best of us."

Without another word they shook their heads and smiled at some secret they shared and were not about to tell. Instead they sang a song they hope to record on their first CD. It was a rousing rendition of a 1950s hit, but the DiGrassi sisters sang it with a distinctly hip and ironic playfulness. In complete dissonant harmony, they sang the classic Mills Brothers song "You Always Hurt the One You Love."

Then they collapsed in a heap on the couch, laughing.

Part Four

Loving Ourselves
as Women

11

Slumber Party

When Lynettie, Alix, and I first moved in together as housemates, we were all recovering from broken hearts and failed relationships. We'd dubbed our big bungalow "Heartbreak Hotel." And that summer we decided to throw a slumber party. Our first plan was a small party, just my housemates Lynettie and Alix, then a few of our best girl-friends. But as word of our gathering got out, we were swamped with women inviting themselves along.

"Heard you're having a party . . . well, count me in!" was the typical call. We did call a halt at fifteen women, simply because of sleeping arrangements and the fact that we wanted some intimacy, especially as we envisioned there might be all-night "girl talk."

Our rented two-story beach house on Washington's spacious Puget Sound was perfect shelter for our slumber party. With its expanse of beach for a backyard, its spacious and ramshackle rooms someone had adorned with fishnets, giant starfish, and driftwood, its cozy, reclusive location on a dead-end street—our house was the perfect place for healing our wounds. And our neighbors, both amiable retired couples who spent most of their time traveling around in their Winnebagos, were sweetly tolerant of our summer dance-and-volleyball parties.

One of our elderly neighbors, Dorothea, found it charming that we three "girls" were living together, "just like sisters," she said, and she often brought us brownies or homemade cream puffs as if we were a band of Girl Scouts or ladies-in-waiting. We did not feel demeaned by her old-fashioned treatment or the fact that we were always "the girls" rather than women. The simple fact was that nothing seemed so much a balm to our womanly thirty-something broken hearts as to be seen as young and spirited, with the whole world of romance still ahead of us. And we were grateful to our elderly neighbors for their many kindnesses; they were like the best of parents, all tender concern without any judgment and expectation.

Certainly we sometimes gave our neighbors cause for bewilderment. There were the barbecues in which we symbolically burned our ex-partners in effigy; there were the holidays when we had our wild "orphans' orgies" in rebellion against what Alix called "the Noah's Ark of couples, two-by-two, trooping up the gangplank into Christmas" or what I bleakly thought of as the "perfect family" holidays that were more like Hitchcock than Hallmark.

"Oh, you girls . . ." Dorothea shook her gray head with fond bemusement when we announced our plans for a slumber party. "You keep this beach from becoming a retirement community." She smiled. "It's so good to have young people around." Then she told us that we reminded her of her four sisters, all of whom had died. "That's what happens when you get to be my age," she breathed. "Every time a sister died, I lost a part of my childhood. Now, there's not one soul alive who knows me, how I was when I was growing up. It's like a kind of weird senility when I lost my sisters—at the same time you have complete recall of your childhood, you lost the very sisters who shared it with you."

Like a much older, wiser sister, Dorothea never disowned us, no matter how weird we might have seemed to her at times. One night, just before our slumber party, we particularly startled her with our famous Egg Incident. Lynettie had just broken up with yet another boyfriend and was downstairs in her room, with its inherited nautical decor; she was weeping inconsolably and half-expecting that Alix and I would notice and come down to comfort her. But Alix and I were upstairs on a completely different track. Alix had also ended an affair, but it was she who had done the dumping so her mood was celebratory, slightly wild as one often feels when, as she said, "the dead weight of another body is lifted off you." She was referring to her hefty partner, whom we'd always thought a dullard anyway. I was having the time of my life, dating and playing and unpartnered for the first time since I was a teenager and still living with my sisters.

Where Alix and I were feeling subversive, untamed, and mischievous, Lynettie was miserable. She did not recognize the bumps and thumps from upstairs as anything but another night of Motown on the stereo as we perhaps cleaned the house or just danced because it was summer, because we lived on a glorious beach, and we were free women.

When Lynettie finally realized that neither of her house-sisters was coming down to comfort her, she dragged her sad self, still snuffling, up the basement stairs. As she opened the kitchen door she heard a *splat* and then felt something whizz past her face and splat again on the wall. It's important to note here that Lynettie is a clean freak and her favorite form of therapy is scouring, sweeping, or vacuuming. We might have been renegade women living there on the beach, but our run-down house was immaculate, thanks to Lynettie. Imagine her dismay when she peered into the kitchen to find Alix and me hurling eggs at the walls and windows. Stalactites of gooey egg yolks hung from the ceiling in eerie yellow globs. Lynettie gazed at us in shock as we hurled eggs overhand, pitching them at a blown-up photo of some hunk movie star a former occupant had left behind on the door. The kitchen was a disaster area. I will always remember Lynettie's tear-streaked, startled face as she eased into the kitchen, darting and dancing around our barrage of eggs. She made a feeble attempt to reason with us, pointing in horror to the egg glop above our heads.

"Don't you want to throw an egg, too, girl?" Alix cajoled her. "Just imagine you're exploding or deep-sixing everything about your life that holds you down, keeps you back, does you no damn good!"

"Yeah!" I chimed in. I tossed her a perfect white-shelled missile and yelled, "Women to the beach!"

And that's what kindly Dorothea saw when she looked out her window to find out what all the fuss was about—three women on the beach, screaming and hurling what she thought were Ping-Pong balls into the waves. "Surely they wouldn't be *polluting* Puget Sound," she told herself as she wiped her sudsy hands on her apron and came out on her deck to observe us on that starry, summer night. Her husband, Ralph, stayed inside, observing us with his portable telescope. Later Dorothea would whisper to us conspiratorially that he'd thought about dialing 911 but he decided he "didn't want those gals locked up with common prisoners and drunks. They just need some other kind of help. They're . . . they're women out of control."

Dorothea said she'd laughed at her husband and told him there was Animal Control for dogs at large, but no controlling women, that certainly he'd learned that from her and her own sisters. "Ralph is an only child," Dorothea explained to us. "He doesn't really know how to play . . . and he doesn't know women at all."

It was the first time she'd called us that, women. Perhaps that night we graduated in her mind; it was our wildness and abandon that matured us from girls to women. For even Dorothea recognized that we were not rebelling against our parents, we were breaking the same tether that she and her own sisters had struggled against. "Remember," Dorothea was fond of reminding us, "when I was born, women couldn't yet even vote. We hardly knew what to do with ourselves, we'd been kept quiet and down for so long. Like those slaves when they were first emancipated; I'll bet they wandered around for years, trying to figure out how to be free."

Figuring out how to be free is what those house-sisters taught me in our years of living together on the beach. And that's why we put so much stock on our slumber-party plans—we were celebrating a teenage ritual that reminded us of a girlhood when we were not yet mated, not yet married, and we were reenacting this as adult women having chosen again not to be mated or married.

Our slumber-party guests were about evenly divided among single women, married women, and mothers. One was even a new mother who was so stressed and sleep-deprived she saw our slumber party as a chance for a good night's rest. There were artists and writers, corporate execs and lawyers, journalists and computer whizzes at our slumber party—but that night we made some impromptu first rules: No shoptalk! And No Going Home! Everyone agreed, we were in it for the night. About half of us began the slumber party in our pajamas, as if to remind those still in street clothes that we were gathered for a party that was more intimate, more feminine, more open.

"Anything goes!" Lynettie announced as we sat around the huge living room, sleeping bags splayed out across the floor. "And just think, we don't have to have any designated drivers, so drink up!"

There was sangria punch and beer, elegant dry sherry, and fine wine. Even though I rarely drink, I was busy in the kitchen with homemade margaritas. I will never forget the extremes of nightwear, from red silk negligées to flannel pj's with feet, which made one of my friends look like a female Harvey. Most of the women wore nightgowns, long and cozy, floor-length cotton. Every time I'd walk through the living room to distribute my margaritas in the elegant glasses Lynettie had bought especially for this occasion, I'd start grinning to see so many women in nighties making toasts, draped over pillows or couches as if we were all in some ancient temple or sister society. Certainly it was no harem, for there was an attitude about all these women friends that suggested our birthright was freedom, an emancipation earned for us by generations of women struggling before us. We stood on the shoulders of suffragettes and birth-control crusaders, the stories of which we'd heard from Dorothea, who had herself declined to come to the party. She was extremely pleased we invited her to the "gala affair," as she imagined it, but she thought she might be too old for us.

Like the pizza delivery, however, Dorothea did pop in with her famous brownies and had a quick cup of rich mocha coffee. As she stood in the kitchen gazing into the rooms full of languid, laughing, and relaxed women, her eyes blurred. "Oh, my sisters would have *loved* this," she murmured. "I'm just next door if you need anything." She finished her coffee and stood at the doorway, hesitating.

"Oh, come on and stay for a while," Lynettie said. "There's a mean Scrabble game out on the deck."

Dorothea declined regretfully. She glanced back to her house where we wondered if Ralph were tracking her progress with his small telescope. "You know, my sisters and I always thought we'd live together in old age. I always counted on that . . . and now they're gone." Then she brightened. "But I do have you girls. And that's a blessing."

We felt very blessed to be in one another's company that night. Though many of us met weekly for coffee or walks or yoga or classes and some of us were in a book club together, we'd never had the luxury of not going home to our separate houses and partners, instead of lingering long together.

"It's just like summer camp," said one of my friends, stretching out full on the sofa and downing another brownie. "But the food is so much better."

There was angel food cake drizzled with peach brandy, dark wheels of chocolate decadence, pecan tarts, and warm pretzels; there were mountains of tortilla chips and hot, homemade salsa, as well as pizza made from scratch and Domino's at our door. Some of the women had decided to have a sub-theme for the slumber party and that was Tacky Foods We Love but Never Allow Ourselves to Eat Anymore. So here were all these health-conscious women reveling in Cheez Whiz–drenched Doritos, red licorice ropes, and Halloween-sized packages of M&Ms and Snickers. On the table was one glass punch bowl full of sinful cashews, Hershey's Kisses, and Good 'n' Plenty pellets. This was dubbed the "trail mix" of our slumber party.

"After all," Lynettie reasoned, "we need fuel for the long night ahead of us."

Some of us indeed needed fuel for the passionate conversations all around. As I cruised through the beach house in my flowered night-gown and flip-flops, playing hostess, I observed dramatic dialogues that fondly reminded me of my own sisters'. There was the deep abortion debate between two women giving each other a manicure; there was a group of rule-breaking women strategizing local environ-mental politics while making Toll House chocolate chip cookies to-gether; there were several women organizing an ad hoc artists' project to support the homeless while mixing more margaritas; and on the deck two women had spread a deck of tarot cards, questioning the fate of their law firm. Along with the more worldly, weighty matters being solved at that slumber party, there were those of us who were determinedly superficial, luxuriating in girl talk. I'd provided free copies of the *National Enquirer* and *World Weekly Star*. My friend Re-becca Claire and I were giving dramatic readings from these blissfully sordid pages while we debated which nail polish to adorn our toes. I was partial to "Passion Peach," and Rebecca Claire was debating be-tween a hot red called simply "Longings" and an equally flamboyant "Frosty Apricot." Our favorite tabloid story was about a woman who had traded away her twin boys for one package of Oreo cookies.

With all the sugar, sensation, and tequila, our happy, pampered feet were soon doing the talking as we rolled back the rug for a ripsnorting sock hop. I'd made a special dance tape dubbed "Sisters" as a sound track for our party. Aretha Franklin began the dance set with "Pink Cadillac," followed by the Supremes suggesting that "You Can't Hurry Love."

There was absolutely no hurry for anyone that night. Time folded in on itself, just as above our rocking house, the sky seemed to set out new constellations we might study as we rested between dances, lying on the deck, some of us drunk, all of us delighted.

"Don't you think there are some different stars out tonight?" Alix asked with a contented sigh. Her face was still flushed from drink and a mean version of "Twist and Shout." She laughed, that familiar wild edge to her. "Hey, why don't we steal old Ralph's telescope?"

"No." I smiled, watching Orion's belt twirl around the sky. I'd only had one margarita, but that was enough to send me reeling—a "cheap date," as my sisters always teased me. "We've already scared Ralph too often. He'll think we really are banshees and this time call the cops."

"Yeah," Lynettie chimed in as she jumped up for yet another dance. "I want to attend one slumber party in my life that's not crashed."

"Why do you think the boys always crashed our slumber parties?" I asked.

"It scares them, of course," Alix answered. "Women having fun without men is the most subversive thing we can do. They can't imagine we might have something to do together besides talk about *them*."

"Boys get together all the time," Muriel, another friend horizontal on the deck, joined in. "And we don't assume they're talking about us. In fact, they usually aren't!"

"Oh," Alix laughed, "my ex-boyfriend—may he rest in peace—always said that men had more important things on their minds than women. The subject of women rarely came up with his guy buddies. I suppose they were too busy talking about really big issues, like sports."

"Well, if women are so meaningless," I asked again, "why would they always crash our slumber parties?"

"Because," Lynettie said, "men know that women can get along without them just fine and that terrifies them."

"Right," Alix said, "and men always imply that women who like the company of other women are lesbians. Whereas a *man's man* is considered a real hero."

"Well, I'm a woman's woman," I announced.

"Oh . . ." The others playfully made as if to swoon. "Our heroine."

"Let's dance!" Lynettie said.

"And let's have a slow dance," someone called.

One of my book-pal friends presented herself before me and made a slightly tipsy bow. "May I?" she invited.

I was somewhat amused by her request, for this was Eleanor, one of my most repressed friends. Shy and bookish, she was married to a stockbroker who was as fastidious as Eleanor was distracted. She often blushed during our book club confabs when the subject turned to sex or eroticism and Eleanor had never once joined us in the hot tub. "I'm about as sensual as Saran Wrap," she was fond of saying.

I thought of her comment that night as Eleanor draped herself around me, admitting, "I only know how to lead. I haven't danced since I was a teenager with my sisters. They gave up on me because I don't know how to follow."

"Fine," I laughed. "I'll follow you."

She was a surprisingly graceful dancer, gliding and swooping in and out of other couples who stayed within the box steps of a waltz. "Can you tango?" Eleanor astonished me by asking. "I taught myself by videotape, but never found a partner."

"Lead on, Ellie," I barely had time to say before she practically carried me across the floor in a gliding tango that was so sensual and knowing that all the other dancers stepped back in wonder. They began clapping slowly in time as Lynettie hurried to put a sultry flamenco on the stereo.

Eleanor is a tall, slender woman who looks so much like a librarian that she walked into a Seattle library without any credentials except being an avid bibliophile and she was hired as a library assistant on the spot. But this woman could dance! I have never before or since been so literally swept off my feet as Eleanor eased us across the pinewood floor, our wool socks almost hissing, nightgowns flared at our feet, our hot cheeks together, eyes straight ahead in that passionate trance of tango.

To hear Lynettie tell it, that tango was better than the ballroom dancing she watches religiously. "That tango was so terrific, it set the tone for the rest of the night."

When Eleanor and I finished our long, slow, and sultry dance, we found other slow dancers around us, but most of the women were collapsed on sleeping bags or couches, leaning against one another easily. Two women braided another's luxurious black hair; on the deck were languid sighs over head and foot massages; the kitchen sink was transformed into a beauty salon with women rubbing Lady Clairol ash-blond color into their dark roots. Several women were perched on the edge of the bathtub drying their multicolored toenails, eight bright bottles of polish between them. In the bedroom four women with faces green from cucumber-clay facials were playing drums and looking downright aboriginal.

The easy sensuality, the familiar, female touching, the tender massages we so rarely allow ourselves these days—all those tribal gifts of the sisterhood, just like the sinful foods we declare off-limits, no matter how they delight us. Looking around at my slumber party mates, I felt so comfortable and cherished, so connected and restored—we joked that our slumber party was an emotional makeover.

Sensuality belongs most to the world of women. And to lose the skills of touching other women's bodies is to lose mastery of our own feminine bodies. The same shame we accept when we abide by the patriarchal fear of women's rituals together is shame we turn upon ourselves and our female bodies. Ironically enough, female sensuality is allowed to flourish within societies determinedly male-dominated, such as in Middle Eastern countries only decades removed from enslaving their women in harems.

In her gorgeous book *Harem: The World Behind the Veil*, the Turkish author Alev Lytle Croutier, whose grandmother was brought up in a harem, writes, "Eroticism in the baths was not reserved for the master alone. For women who were bred in the ways of pleasure and who rarely attained the sultan's bed, it was a chance to feast their eyes on beautiful bodies and satisfy each other. While washing and massaging one another . . . the women often became lovers as well as friends."

Friends *and* lovers, that's a part of the sisterhood spectrum that often keeps us apart, keeps us participating in the male fear of female-female bonding. Of the many women I have asked about whether they've ever made love with another woman, a majority of them report that they have, though that may not necessarily be a life choice or preference for them. Of those who have not, many of them have had erotic fantasies about other women.

Before I moved into the beach house with Lynettie and Alex I had told them, along with many other things about myself, that I was bisexual. Alix laughed and said, "Aren't we all?" Lynettie, a true Midwestern gal, looked at me in bewilderment. "But . . . but . . . ," she, who is never at a loss for words, actually stammered. "But what do women *do* together, I wonder?"

This wonderment was not meant as judgment or fear; Lynettie simply couldn't imagine women making love without men. "Is it like masturbation?" she asked with all the innocence of a child trying to understand her first description of sex.

I told her it certainly wasn't like being alone; but it was like being with oneself.

"But, well, you don't look like a truck driver." She laughed. "Most women who make love with other women look just like men to me."

"Some of them do," I countered, "but I'm not attracted to them. If I wanted to sleep with someone who looked like a man, I'd make love with a man. What I find beautiful in women is the sensuality, the curve and grace and fluidity. We don't really know yet what feminine beauty is as defined by women for women. I'd like to find out."

The night of the slumber party as I watched my dear friend Lynettie do a slow dance with another woman, with no fear, no hesitation, no bewilderment, I felt she had become a true sister. I knew that Lynettie would never actually make love with a woman; but making love with another woman is not a prerequisite for loving women. It is not so much about sexual preference as it is about self-acceptance and praise of one another. This means also celebrating all forms of love between women, whatever the bond. That is what fully embracing the wide spectrum of sisterhood gives us—the dignity and permission to love one another as we love ourselves.

It was almost midnight when the music stopped and we all lay around in that pleasurable fatigue of any successful slumber party. Someone was in the kitchen making a pot of SleepyTime tea when the phone rang. There was a brief, hushed conversation and then Linda guiltily crept in to announce that she suddenly had to go home. Her child had a cough, "or so my husband says." She shook her head. "I knew he wouldn't really let me stay the night."

We all argued with her as she climbed out of her nightgown with a sigh. There was a strange murmuring among us all and then another woman leapt up. The mood was broken as surely as if one of our husbands or mates or children had come crashing in through the window. There was a rustling, a restlessness, and some of the women disappeared into the bathroom and reemerged in their street clothes.

"This is a *slumber* party!" Lynettie protested.

"We're just . . . well, not used to it," one of the women said as she hurriedly pulled her blue jeans up under her red negligée. "It's . . . it's maybe too much."

"Too much what?" I asked softly, abandoning any effort to convince the women to stay.

No one answered as there were brief embraces and thank-yous all around. "If we were going off to war, you'd see women with more courage," Alix muttered under her breath.

What were we afraid of that night of our slumber party? At the end of the midnight stampede only three brave souls opted to slumber at our slumber party.

My theory about that party is that we got scared of ourselves. In the same way that we are afraid of intimacy with men, we are also afraid of intimacy with women.

As adult sisters and friends, we have been behind closed doors with one another so seldom that perhaps in this century it is "natural" to actually fear the company of other women. This is not so in tribal, indigenous cultures such as the Native Americans or the Australian aborigines. In Hispanic cultures there is also acceptance of strong female allegiances to balance the *machismo* of male bonding.

My Native American sister-writers Linda Hogan and Joy Harjo both tell me that in their tribal culture, Chickasaw and Creek, the women's societies are still strong and resonant. Sometimes they have carried on the traditions while the tribe was in decline and helped restore the tribe to its true vision. "We don't grow up and away from our tribal sisters," Linda says. "We take them with us wherever we go. And we always come back to these women's societies for wisdom." Joy has written in her poem "The Blanket Around Her":

> Oh women
> remember who you are
> it is the whole earth.

Remembering who we are means reclaiming our biological and natural birthrights—and that is the lifelong company, the sensual and spiritual companionship, of our sisters.

Slumber parties celebrate all forms of love between women, whatever the bond. They cherish confidences and play; they nurture freedom and also companionship. Spending a long night in each other's company, we reveal secrets and share our silly or sacred rituals. This deepening intimacy also means that we risk rejection, affection, pleasure, and pain—as in any reconciliation of long-lost love.

In my own search to restore the tradition of slumber parties, I've been delighted to discover several sisterhoods whose motto is: "When the going gets tough, real women go to slumber parties." These girls' nights out include the biyearly weekend of my Bad Girls' Book Club, which meets every month to celebrate books, food, sex—sometimes in a hot tub. Bad Girls' overnights are even more irreverent, kind of like a Wyf of Bath weekend. Another gathering is my women writers' group; every nine months we journey from all corners of the country to meet in some beautiful natural setting for several days of what we call "conversation and reclamation"—the natural resource being ourselves. We take time off from demanding careers and partnerships and children to nurture one another, and most of all, to play together with our true peers.

Last time we met on a high country ranch—a dude ranch with no dudes—and, except for one hike, we never exercised once. Instead we swapped stories, sang, and baked. Over elk chili and apple crumb pie, we stayed up half the night predicting one another's futures. When it came time to say good-bye, we formed a fond circle and, arms encircling one other, we sang "Happy Trails."

Even now my writers' group is planning its next weekend away. It will be a deep forest cabin on the water and midwinter we'll sit cross-legged around the warm-bellied stove, taking up a tradition as old as storytelling or sleep—women dreaming together. Until we meet again.

12

Excavating Esther:
When First Love Is Female

We were on a road trip, my friend Libby and I, when she surprised me with a story. It was the summer of 1992 and we were roaring along the Northwest back roads en route to a long-awaited island retreat at a Puget Sound cabin. This would be Libby's last vacation before her marriage to a man with whom she'd lived happily for the past five years.

"Kind of a Thelma-and-Louise trip without the desertions, the murder, the robbery, or the double suicide," Libby explained it to her fiancé, Francisco, from a pay phone where we stopped at a burger stand.

"Why don't you just come out and admit you're on a vacation, Libby?" Francisco had shot back good-humoredly. "You're allowed."

When Libby climbed back in the car, arms piled with greasy fries, shakes made from locally grown raspberries, and home-cooked double cheeseburgers, she was grinning—a smile that was so relaxed and open, it showed she had finally made the three-day transition from anxious New Yorker to country girl. "You know," she said, "Francisco reminds me more and more every day of my first love. It's taken me over twenty years to find another love who is as playful and passionate, as fascinating to me as . . ." Here Libby suddenly caught herself, glanced over at me, mid-milkshake, then laughed. "Maybe this is a story I meant to tell you . . . but never had time in New York with all the rush and business. But I want you to hear it because . . . because I'm at a time in my life when I need to fully understand and embrace it myself." Libby gave me a fond pat on the shoulder. "Consider it your wedding present to me . . . hearing me out and helping me excavate a long-buried first love."

I was so curious. "This first love . . . ?" I prompted.

"A girl," Libby said, and laughed. "We were very much girls. Esther, that's her name—you know, after the good queen Esther in the Bible." Libby laughed dramatically. "We first met at camp when we were both fourteen. She was only four months older than I was, but Esther came from divorced parents; she had an older brother and lived on the Lower East Side in the city, while I lived with both parents and had a younger brother and lived in the Westchester suburbs. So she was more sophisticated, outgoing; I was painfully shy, even more self-conscious than most adolescents. I was also incredibly naive, though I had a poetry-inspired passion in me which could pass for intellectual worldliness."

"Still do," I teased her.

"Right, well . . . I didn't fool Esther, either. She was very bookish, too, but extroverted. Where I wrote poetry, she wrote novels and acted them out. Soon I was starring alongside her in all the roles. We met at a geeky Zionist hippie camp in the Catskills; it called to me like an adventure novel."

"What did Esther look like?" I asked. "When you were ninth graders?"

Libby smiled and suddenly she looked very young herself—her kinky black hair pulled back in a ponytail, her vacation face without makeup, her green eyes wide. "Well, Esther was tall and what they call willowy, though she hated that word. She was very fair with straight blond hair like California girls we always heard about. But nothing beach bunny about Esther. She had a pair of reading glasses she wore around summer camp, even though they hurt her eyes, because she thought it was horrible the way boys equate blond with stupid. Once or twice I even permed and dyed her hair different colors, not like the punk rainbow hair you see on kids today, but our own version of beauty. Esther wanted to look like Audrey Hepburn, but she really looked just like Meryl Streep. And I deluded myself into thinking I could be a stand-in for Grace Slick, who even then was fading along with the Jefferson Airplane; but I really looked like a bookish Debra Winger—an actress who hadn't even come along yet. This was 1972—Watergate—and the country was upside down in its loss of innocence. We prided ourselves on our disaffected youth, rebellious teen stuff, but we were really just kids, virgins at that, who got stoned." Libby stopped, frowning. She was quiet awhile, then continued. "At camp they took their Zionism seriously, though it wasn't conservative at all. Esther, another girlfriend, Heidi, and I called ourselves the 'Bad Girls,' and we holed up in our segregated bunkhouse, smoking and talking about boys in the other bunkhouses. I had an obligatory boyfriend, Eric, who worked as a dishwasher in the cafeteria where Esther and I were also on work-study. Eric was completely uninteresting to me except that he was also friends with Esther, who liked him okay. So most of my time with Esther during the days was often spent with Eric. Esther had a series of boyfriends. Anyway, I lost my virginity with Esther . . ." Libby stopped and howled with laughter. "Oops, I mean with Eric. Talk about your Freudian slips! I wanted to lose it with Esther, I lost it instead with Eric."

"Were you conscious of this at the time . . . that you wanted to make love with Esther instead of Eric?" I asked.

"Oh, no," Libby said and sighed. "I had hardly even kissed a boy and along with being painfully shy, I was also woefully inexperienced. Just as I never would have initiated sex unless Eric insisted, I would never have imagined that it was Esther I wanted to be with. I was fifteen, not unaware of homosexuality—sometimes 'The Bad Girls' joked that we were bad-girl lesbians—but we never for a second believed that. I mean, we had a deeply physical relationship, we teenage girls—we'd roll around in the same bed, tickling each other, borrowing each other's clothes, kissing on the lips when we parted company, holding hands like we'd seen European fashion models do. I can even remember purposefully asking Esther for her favorite blouse not only because it made me feel Number One to wear it, like going steady or something, but because it smelled so good . . . like Esther. She wore

White Shoulders, which her mother always gave her for birthdays
. . . and to this day whenever I smell White Shoulders, I feel happy,
loved, the way I felt wearing my best girlfriend's blouse."

"Did Esther lose her virginity at camp, too?" I asked

"No and I hardly even noticed I lost mine. Eric was inept, but
sweet, and we never got a chance to do it again after that one night.
You see at camp we had this universal garden on the front lawn and
all the boys and girls made out there at nights; then we separated and
returned to our bunkhouses to gossip and brag about what we did."

"Was there a lot of eroticism in the bunkhouse?" I laughed.

"I didn't think so at the time. You know, it seemed so natural.
Esther was a person who, if she talked to you and liked you, she'd
touch you whenever she told you a story. I loved that, because it was
her touch, playful and familiar and never pushy like the boys. She'd
tap or touch or teasingly push or even roll over you on the bunk, all
the while telling some hilarious story or imitating someone. She was
a born performer and so graceful with those long limbs. Remember I
was both shy psychologically and physically; I remember thinking
once that if it were anybody else but Esther touching me all the time,
I'd be turned off. It would feel invasive. But Esther's touch was so
light. Knowing what I do now about trained massage therapists, I'd
say that she actually had a conscious touch—very knowing, but not
invasive. All I knew then was that it made me happy and open when
Esther held my hand or walked arm in arm with me at camp. I felt
chosen, very grown up, cosmopolitan, and . . . and adored."

"Did she adore you?"

Libby laughed and I saw a remnant of that old shyness from her
teenager days. "Yes, I believe she did . . . back then."

"What happened to Esther?" I asked. "Is she still in your life . . .
did you become lovers? Where is she now?"

"Whoa!" Libby threw up her hands. "Not so fast. Everything goes
so fast. But remember how slow some years are, some special years?
My whole Esther story really takes place in one year, but it feels like
it was a very long time. That's because so much happened that was
new and so painful. Suffering slows everything down, ever noticed?"

"Yes, I've noticed," I said. "Want to stop for dessert?"

"Right . . . pain and sugar, perfect together."

We pulled into an A&W Root Beer, the kind of place neither of us had been since teenage days. There was even curbside service, though no waitresses on roller skates as I remember from my Southern teenage days. As we sipped our root-beer floats, Libby sighed. "The story gets pretty sad and weird from here on out, sure you want to hear it?"

"I'd kill to hear the rest of it," I laughed.

"Okay, but I have a request. I want to hear a story from you before I go on, to make me feel less . . . well, exposed." Libby said very seriously, "I want to hear the story of your first love because I'll bet it's complicated, like mine."

"All right, I'll tell you my first-love story if you promise after that to finish yours . . . with all the details."

"I promise." Libby slurped her iced float glass for emphasis. "Now, do tell!"

I told her she was very precocious compared to me—and I was coming of age in the wilds of sixties' Berkeley, between People's Park and the Vietnam War, at the University of California, Davis, which was experimenting with its first coed dorm. "I lost my virginity almost simultaneously with a girl and a boy," I told her.

"Same bed?" Libby demanded.

"No, not even the same month, but the same year."

"Who came first, boy or girl?"

"Girl. My first love, like yours, was female."

It was 1968, I told Libby, and I was a freshman in a dorm turned upside down by coed living, drugs, and raging hormones. Because we were taking part in a live-in sociology experiment that included mandatory encounter-group sessions and weekly dorm-wide seminars called "Self and Society," any romance between dormmates quickly faded. "At eighteen, most girls don't want to see their boyfriends in their morning-after glory, unshaven and bleary-eyed at the same long dormitory mirror," I explained to Libby.

She agreed. "It's a real downer. At eighteen a girl wants dashing and mysterious and fantasy. Save the shared bathroom mirror for marriage."

There were very few romantic couples in my dorm, myself and my boyfriend, Daniel, being the exceptions. He was Polynesian and very sensual—his mother had been a trained island dancer and he inherited her grace, her almost feline strength. But what was most exotic about

him was not his looks—it was his erotic curiosity. Unlike any other
boys I'd been with who were awkward and like physical pinball ma-
chines when it came to sexual exploration, Daniel had an exquisitely
slow and luxurious sense of wonder about our bodies. It was his idea
to find an old Chinese erotic arts book, so we could make our way
chapter by chapter through the exercises, most of which we didn't
understand at all. We only knew it had something to do with
breathing and arousing each other, right up to the moment of orgasm
when we'd hold ourselves as if on the very edge of a waterfall—then
stop, suspended in an ecstatic, tingling trance. I can remember my
entire body thrumming with electricity and desire, my belly hot and
pulsing in waves as up and down my legs ran a warm rivulet of
pleasure.

"Teenage tantra!" Libby said. "Did you know back then that's what
you were doing?"

"No," I answered. "We thought everybody was playing with their
bodies like us. It wasn't until I started telling my best girlfriend
Natalie about what Daniel and I spent our supposed study nights
doing that I realized we were unusual." I stopped, then continued.
"Natalie was also unusual. Unbeknownst to me she had enjoyed a
high-school love affair with her closest girlfriend, as well as her boyfriend . . ."

"So everybody in your teenage world was bisexual," Libby laughed.
"No wonder we preppy, bad-girl East Coasters gazed west to California
like it was an adolescent mecca!"

"But we didn't know we were bisexual," I insisted. "We didn't
think in terms of those labels or definitions. You have to understand
first of all that it was the late sixties, California, and that we were
participating in a college freshman program which encouraged experiments, sexually, psychologically, in daily living structures. It was
weird, a window of opportunity really, because there was no judgment
outside of us, so we didn't judge ourselves."

"And why should you?" Libby interrupted, then caught herself. "I
mean, why did we? Why did Esther and I judge ourselves and . . .
and do so much damage?"

"All right," I said, relieved to switch the focus back to Libby.
"What happened with you and Esther?"

"Not so fast!" Libby punched me playfully on the arm. "You said your first love was female and all I've heard about is Daniel. You said you lost your virginity first with a woman. 'Fess up!"

"With both Daniel and Natalie I lost my physical loneliness for a peer. We were each the same size. It used to almost make me cry with happiness when I could fit into Daniel's old jeans or wear Natalie's silk caftan."

"So what about Natalie?" Libby demanded. "Are we ever going to get to her?"

"She got to me," I said softly. I was shy about telling this story to Libby even though I knew she would understand. I have always been shy about revealing this first love, not because of shame or fear, but because it was so unexpected, yet natural; and because it remains one of my happiest memories. "Natalie was my singing partner before she was my lover," I began slowly.

I knew her voice as surely as if it were another body—I knew how her voice trembled on the high notes and fell into full, almost visible curves of sound, on the low, vibrato notes. Following her movement was like synchronized swimming with someone—you're in a kind of musical trance as if underwater and there's this voice alongside yours that you have to follow and fit with so exactly. It always required my complete attention—like meditation. I'd close my eyes, open my ears, and imagine my skull was an empty cave, acoustically open and echoing.

On the eve of Easter that freshman year, after eight months of singing, studying, sleeping, traveling, and enduring our experimental dorm, Natalie and I were practicing a duet for an Easter sunrise service, not a religious ceremony, but a spiritual celebration some dorm-mates planned on our rooftop. As often happened, Natalie and I fell asleep in my bunk after practicing for hours; usually we slept like sisters, arms wrapped around each other in spoon poses. But this night I woke up very early in the morning to find Natalie moving against me as if we were in a horizontal slow dance to some song that was in her head or dream. As if in a trance, eyes still closed, she swayed her hips against my buttocks and she pulled me close, her hands tenderly stroking my breasts.

Was she lovemaking in her sleep the way some people walked when dreaming? I wondered. Did she think I was her boyfriend, Stuart? Did she know it was me, her best friend and singing partner? Because I was so familiar with her body—hadn't I danced with her, followed her lead voice so long it seemed a part of my own—I easily moved with her in a kind of lying down, feminine samba. We were all hips and breasts, and soft bellies and thighs, so unlike Daniel's braided muscles and jutting pelvic bones. I liked the difference, the dreamy luxury of another body so like mine, except Natalie had broad sloped shoulders from years of swimming. When I turned to face her, to find her blue-green eyes wide open seeking mine, I laughed because, like our voices, our bodies fit so well together.

"I want you," Natalie said softly and her breath was so familiar. Hadn't I followed this mouth, inhaled this exact breath myself when we sang close together? "It's you I want now." And I smiled, taking her weight upon mine easily. We had the same faintly sweet scent. I loved her sexual smell as much as I'd always liked her gardenia perfume.

"White Shoulders," Libby said softly.

"I had never felt anything like it," I said, "even with Daniel. The arousal was the same and the delicious, slow exploration of each other's bodies. But the difference was that her body and smell and even the way she came was so familiar—it was so moving, it made me cry. And I'd never cried before with pleasure."

"When you're young, everything makes such a deep impression," Libby mused. "I can remember Esther's exact way of flipping her hair over her shoulder—that blond hair that was supposed to belong to a *shiksa,* but was her Russian-Jewish heritage. She had this mannerism with her mouth, an expression of barely suppressed laughter, especially when she was noting some teenage stupidity. We hated being teenagers, but everybody who wasn't our age was also considered a real loser!"

"And what else did you memorize about her, your first love?" I asked in a low voice, sensing some pain in Libby.

"I regret to this day that Esther and I were not really lovers, not in the way you were with Natalie and the way teenagers today are so much more open to sexual play and gender roles. What I know about Esther is much more than a girlfriend, but less than a lover. What I wish I'd known about her was the way she looked after lovemaking or the smell of her body, that scent unique to everyone which is so haunting ever afterward." Libby fell silent. "But I don't know those things, except through some chaotic, half-glimpsed fog."

"Tell me about the fog," I said. We drove now through deep, ancient forests on the Olympic Peninsula. Some had been clear-cut into jagged crazy quilts of stumps and bramble.

"The fog is both from drugs and from unconsciousness," Libby began. "Everything overtly sexual really began and ended so quickly." Libby shook her head as if it ached. "But that was just the obvious sexual groping. Inwardly and unconsciously, Esther and I were always reaching out to each other on so many levels. It was like an under-current of electricity."

Libby sighed. "First love should come when you're forty and have the maturity to recognize it." Libby stopped herself. "But that's wrong. I *knew* who Esther was to me even at fourteen. I just didn't know what that meant, or how it would work out in the world. So I fit her into the role of my best, best girlfriend and we were inseparable. At camp, if it hadn't been for Esther I would have dumped Eric as I did most other boys. But because of the emotional high pitch of our girlfriend relationship, my thing with Eric functioned as a way of diffusing sexual energy."

"How exactly?"

"Well, I had everything I needed emotionally from Esther and it was to Esther every night I returned in the bunkhouse. So my lawn time making out with Eric was just because that's what a girl did at the camp's universal garden. But I remember having nothing to say to Eric, except for physically. He did teach me more sexual confidence, but remember, I never made love again with him after the first time. I didn't need to. I was in love with Esther and I knew it, but I had split off my emotions so completely from my body that it never oc-curred to me that what I did with Eric sexually I could also do with Esther back in the bunkhouse."

"And what about Esther? Was she split off, as well?"

"Hey," Libby said suddenly, "you're really sneaky! How did we get back to my story? What about your story?"

"It's the same story," I said quietly. "Different endings, different choices, same first love story."

The drive was darker now, as the dusky light in the old woods filtered down from a sunset obscured by towering pine and fir forests. There was a sense of enchantment about these woods, as if we were returning to something we only dimly recognized as our roots. As if feeling the protection of these ancient trees, and breathing easier because of them, Libby leaned back in her seat and rested her feet on the dashboard.

"I was utterly grief-stricken after summer camp," Libby began again, "when I left Esther after a Central Park concert. She took the D train back to Brooklyn and I got on the wrong train to take the Long Island Rail Road home. My parents had to pick me up at a strange stop and I was weeping inconsolably." Libby paused and sighed. "That was the beginning of a deep mourning for Esther. Even though we talked every day after school and I saw her every weekend, I knew I was beginning to lose her, or else I was anticipating that loss."

"How?" I asked softly. "How did it happen?"

"We had this crazy teenage party when my parents left for a Thanksgiving trip to Europe. We invited all our camp friends and even some strangers. Esther announced that she had met a guy whom she'd known before and was bringing him to the party with the explicit intention of losing her virginity. She said it wasn't fair for me to have made love before her, even though I told her it meant nothing. She arrived with this guy, Tino, in tow. He was really tall and good-looking, but right away I could see he couldn't keep up with Esther; he wasn't as bright or articulate. He was, however, very savvy sexually, the kind who would boast about it in a locker room. I'll always remember Tino as a sleazy guy, the kind who dropped out to work in casinos in Atlantic City. Even Esther seemed a little bored by him, that is, until he played with her hair or kissed her neck as they sat on the couch. That stopped her cold, almost put her in a trance like she was listening intently to something—not him, but her own reactions to him.

"I don't remember what I did except dance while Tino and Esther disappeared into my parents' bedroom. I couldn't believe they'd do it in my parents' bed—it was disgusting to me. But I was also insanely jealous and kept drinking myself silly. When suddenly Tino appears and grabs me from behind. 'It's done,' he said, as if Esther's virginity were some sort of business deal they'd finished. Then Tino whispered,

'Now we *both* want you . . .' " Libby made a face and fell silent for a long time.

Trees whizzed by in a dark green blur as the sun faded from this vast forest. I drove quietly, not wanting to disturb her. At last she shook herself and said, "I had no interest in a three-way thing. But I was so jealous I would have done anything to get Esther back in some way. So I followed Tino like some sort of sleepwalker. In my parents' bedroom I saw Esther naked in their big bed; she looked tousled and tired and some part of me wanted to comfort her. But it seemed not cool, especially with Tino there looking so triumphant. Slowly I took my party clothes off and slipped into bed. I don't remember the first time I kissed her, it's all very blurry. What I remember is feeling sort of a combination of panic, fear, anxiety, and wishing that *he* wasn't there, because it was clear to me even then that this was all about her and me, it had nothing to do with him. Yet he intruded . . ."

"You invited him in," I said quietly.

"Esther invited him!" Libby shot back. Then she caught herself and shook her head. "All right, all right, he was a catalyst. We both needed him, I suppose, to face this thing between us that we weren't facing. But I'm sure this threesome thing was his idea. Remember this was the first time Esther had ever made love and only my second time. It was old hat to Tino. But Esther and I were in way over our heads. I was petrified. Esther did initiate some kissing and stroking my breasts, but every time she reached out to me, Tino would immediately intervene. He wanted both of us—he was not at all interested in seeing the two of us together. Once he saw it happening, he stopped it. His plan was to be in the middle and have us both—never for us to be together with him watching. Esther must have seen this clearly long before I did, because about five minutes into all this mess, she jumped up and left us." Libby turned away.

I couldn't read her expression, but the feeling in the car was one of deep regret and even after all these years, bewilderment.

"I don't know why I stayed in that bed with Tino. Maybe I was too drunk or stoned or too weirded out to move. I just lay there and let him screw me. I didn't even see the door open and Esther walk in again. Next thing I knew, sex was over, he got up and dressed. In a trance I put my party dress back on and went to find Esther who was absolutely hysterical. She couldn't believe I had done this, gone through with it—with *her* first lover. She had thought when she left the bedroom that I would've followed her out. Esther just cried and cried and there was nothing I could do, except feel horrible."

"Do you know why you felt so badly?" I asked. "Did you understand it then?"

"Oh, no," Libby said. "You see, Esther was depending upon our bond, our sisterhood. We were so close sometimes people had joked we were the same person. One of her earlier boyfriends had teased us that he would take my top half, my breasts, and Esther's bottom, her lovely curves, and then he'd have the perfect woman. With all this identification going on, Esther assumed I would know exactly what she was feeling and follow her. But I didn't know that night. A third party, a boy, had come between us and separated us so profoundly we no longer knew *what* the other was feeling! And this recognition horrified me most—that I suddenly couldn't fathom her. For the first time, I couldn't get a pulse on Esther. And I couldn't get a pulse on myself either! I wondered if I was gay, knew that I had erotic feelings for women, especially Esther. So I overcompensated by really giving power to men over me. I was terrified that I was weird and no one would want me. Especially not Esther."

"But hadn't she wanted you?" I said. "She lost her virginity with Tino and you all at once, in the same bed . . . your parents' bed. You were with her in that. Didn't she also invite you to be with her?"

"I don't know," Libby said, deeply disturbed. "All I knew then was that once Tino got into our picture, Esther's and my groove started to come undone. She felt so betrayed by me for sleeping with Tino . . ."

"Without her."

"All right, without her. And I was so full of longing and regrets. This was not the way to introduce eroticism between Esther and myself. If it was going to happen, it should have happened with just the two of us, not through the catalyst of a man. Because with that third party, especially Tino, it was just voyeurism and betrayal. That night was a deep disservice to what our true feelings were for each other, which were more sensual and tender than sexual. What it was about for me and Esther was love, and we hardly even knew this guy, Tino." Libby hesitated, then said bitterly, "But after that night, Esther and I hardly even knew each other. We were unsure and really freaked out when we were together, which was hardly ever because now Tino was the third wheel. I always saw her in the context of him."

"You mean, you never talked about it, about what happened between just you two, the passion?"

"No," Libby said briefly. "We talked about Tino! Esther worried about him—bad crowd, flunking out, all that. Remember, we were only fifteen."

I thought about how little help Libby had had in recognizing and claiming who she and Esther were to each other, how few mirrors among their peers or grown-ups or teachers that might celebrate that great experiment our young hearts open to in first love, male or female.

How many adolescent girls, I wondered, like Esther and Libby lost their first love simply because it was female? In her groundbreaking work *In a Different Voice*, Carol Gilligan focuses on what gets lost for girls in adolescence: "Girls' initiation or passage into adulthood in a world psychologically rooted and historically anchored in the experiences of powerful men marks the beginning of self-doubt." This hesitation on the threshold of puberty, a passage that really should give her her feminine power, causes the adolescent girl to lose her voice, to mistrust her instincts, and to forget what she knows. Gilligan argues that because men's experience has long been equated with all of human experience, without integrating or recognizing the female story, a young girl's sense of self at adolescence is fractured, split off, and disassociated from the very connections she needs with herself and her female peers to flourish. "I saw," writes Gilligan in a new preface to the 1993 edition of this work, "that by maintaining these ways of seeing and speaking about human lives, men were leaving out women, but women were leaving out themselves." In order for girls and women to listen and tell their own stories, they must allow themselves a different voice—"a voice that insists on staying in connection and most centrally staying in connection with women . . ."

But how can an adolescent girl stay in connection with other girls her age if at the moment she becomes sexually mature, she is also taught that her sisters must take second place to boys, that girlfriends are just a developmental stage on the Pilgrim's Progress toward Romance and Marriage, the "real" bonds of love and devotion? Perhaps the terrible loss of self-esteem among adolescent girls is directly related to the denial of sisterhood as being unworthy or even illicit, compared to the boy-girl bond of romantic attachment. It is not only that teenage girls begin to believe they are unworthy compared to boys their age, it is also that they lose their main emotional connection to other girls.

So many confluences like treacherous river rapids converge on teenagers at a time when they are often the most vulnerable. What if our psychologists and social workers and parents began to focus consciously on ways to reassure and celebrate this adolescent rite of passage, which is very different for boys and girls? A new bimonthly, international magazine out of Duluth, Minnesota, called *New Moon*, with an editorial board of adolescent girls (ages eight to fourteen), addresses itself directly to this audience of girls on the threshold of maturity. With an eclectic and cross-cultural offering, the girls' magazine is dynamic and has been widely welcomed. It also offers an adult guide called *New Moon Parenting: For Adults Who Care About Girls*. In a recent issue of this parenting guide, Harvard psychologist Annie Rogers spoke about the difficulties facing adolescent girls: "Starting around ages twelve and thirteen," she noted, "it is common for girls to begin to stop speaking about what they really know and what they feel—and to really doubt themselves." Even when these girls can find their voices, they often go unheard by parents who find their daughters' stories discomfiting. When a woman listens to these adolescent girls' voices, Rogers warns, "she's likely to come up against . . . the compromises she's made herself as an adult woman in this culture— in terms of her own honesty with herself, her relationships with men in power, and what she lets herself know and voice." But if we can continue to listen to adolescent girls talk about their fears, their self-doubts, their losses of self and sisterhood, their romantic experiments and confusions, their terrors over AIDS and violence in the schools— then we will begin to change ourselves as adults, as well. Rogers concludes, "I just think that to really attend to girls means to upset the fabric of society."

What if our society began to value sisterhood and the passionate devotion between females from childhood all the way to death? What if we celebrated the intimacy and alliance of adolescent females by way of helping them to carry their sisters through the puberty rite and into mature adulthood? It is in adolescence that the official second-class citizen status takes its terrible effect. But what if a teenage girl equates her girlfriends and boyfriends, and so keeps her own and her sisterhood's identity intact, even as she loses her virginity? Adolescence is difficult enough without a girl's loss of self-esteem; it is a tragedy to lose her entire sisterhood, especially if those were the girlfriends who once mirrored, defined, and adored.

It was dark now and the narrow, curved country roads were empty except for an occasional startled deer or oncoming car's headlights. "You know," Libby continued her story musingly, "Esther was the first person I believed when she told me I was pretty, funny, and smart. I knew she was telling the truth; why should she lie to me? I felt so special and valuable. But when Tino came into the picture, I was trashed. I couldn't believe it. One minute I was the best; the next, I was just there to listen to her real-life romance with Tino. *But what about us?* I wanted to scream out at her."

"Did you?" I asked.

Libby's expression was lost in the darkness. "No," she said after some silence. "I never asked her what happened to her and me, our friendship, because I knew the answer already. We were kaput, kids' stuff. We were, after all, just girls together."

"Just girls," I echoed. "Together."

I well knew that feeling, but I also knew I had been so much luckier than Libby. She had no sister to stand with her in a subversive, feminine solidarity through adolescence, whereas I had been blessed with two staunch sisters, neither of whom ever dreamed of trashing one another for a simple date. Then again in college when Natalie and I became lovers, we welcomed unusual encouragement and acceptance from our sociology-experiment dormmates. What was distinctive and different about my first love affair with Natalie was that it was not seen as some lifelong choice or preference or same-sex love label; it was seen by ourselves and those around us as a playful, passionate experiment. We were not forming ironclad gender identities; we were expanding our experience. We were also not exclusive, because both Natalie and I had boyfriends. I kept my tantric evenings with Daniel and she her romantic camping trips with Stuart. We all four even socialized together. But there was one big nod both Natalie and I made to social norms—neither of us told our boyfriends about our concurrent female first love. Natalie would tell Stuart only after her and my dramatic breakup; and I told Daniel after he had left me for

a stint in Scientology. This information would, in fact, seal my freshman fate with both Natalie and Daniel.

"Okay." Libby scrounged around the backseat of the car for her
sweater. "Let me get settled. Then I'll finish my little tragedy and
you can finish yours."

"It's not a tragedy," I insisted. "Not now."

"But it was then!"

"Yes, first love always is, has to be, don't you think?"

"No," she said fiercely. "I believe that if I met Esther now, she
would be as magnificent a person to me as she was at fourteen. I still
love her now as I did then. That never changes. My love for her exists
in a kind of parallel universe now right alongside my love for Francisco. In fact, I tell him all the time he comes the closest to Esther
of any lover and that's why I'm walking down that aisle with him."

"So Esther is not in your life at all anymore?"

"No," Libby said in a flat voice. "I haven't seen or heard from Esther
in twelve years."

"I'm sorry," I said softly.

"Last time I saw Esther I was with a man I liked, but who was too
old for me. We went up to see Esther and her husband, Theodore, for
a long-overdue New Year's reunion. When we left, my boyfriend told
me, 'You care for Esther much more than she cares for you.' It was
my worst nightmare. It was the story upon which I had built every
other love since Esther—that I'd lost her because I cared too much
and she too little. That I had also somehow betrayed her love and
been punished by losing her. That I would lose the people I loved the
most. These are all the assumptions I've built my relationships on
since losing Esther. Until Francisco, they were proving eerily true."

"And what if it's not a true story?" I suggested. "What if your
relationship was truly equal, and you were also Esther's first love?"

Libby turned to me and even in the dark I could see her astonishment. "Then my whole life would be upside down!" she said. "I
would've told myself a false story all these years—that my first love
for Esther was not reciprocated."

"Seems to me it certainly was returned and then some," I offered.
"It feels too intense between you both to be an unrequited love. Esther
adored you at fourteen, at fifteen she asked you to be there the night
she lost her virginity; even if she repented it, she invited you in. And

I'll bet the sexual stuff didn't end there." I stopped, then added ruefully, "It never does."

"No, never does," Libby agreed. She settled down in her seat, heavy-knit sweater wrapped around her like a camp blanket. "There was this one night I always keep forgetting, but it's so important. It was right before Esther met her husband, when Esther was still with Tino. We were on one of those awful double dates Esther and Tino were always cooking up for me with one of Tino's dud friends. We were at Tino's house and his parents were there, so at bedtime we had to segregate like the teenagers we were. Esther and I ended up in the same bed. Now, remember, we'd slept together zillions of times, but that was always before Tino and her sexual coming of age. Now she was lovers with Tino. In bed, Esther turned to me and said, 'I'm really horny, let's make love.' It was so shocking to me. With all my veneer of precocity and experience, I was really very young sexually and emotionally, always still painfully shy with my body. I also had my period, which I couldn't even tell Esther!

"Esther initiated, put her arms around me, ran her fingers through my hair, kissed me and caressed my belly. She asked me, 'What do you like, Libby?' And I was absolutely dumbfounded, couldn't say a word. I went rigid and finally mumbled, 'I don't know.' This made Esther laugh and she said, 'Libby, that's like saying which do you like better—peanut butter or tuna fish? How can you *not* know? Of course you know!' I was so uncomfortable, still had a problem saying no to her like I had with Tino. I put the onus on her to end it. Finally, Esther sighed and shrugged. 'I guess we can't do this, huh?' she said, and turned away, went right to sleep.

"I lay there, traumatized. It wasn't that Esther had reached out to me sexually that wounded me the most. It was that she was saying, 'If I can't make love with Tino, I'll take you. You're second best.' Also, I was shocked that she came on to me just like a man—that's never the way I'd envisioned it. So I suppose, telling this to you right now, twenty years later, I really had envisioned making love with Esther as a teenager. But the fact is that more took place between us in not being explicitly sexual than when we tried lovemaking. When she tried to be sexual with me it was all wrong. Besides, here it was all over again—us reaching out to each other only in the context of a third party, a boy."

"Did you ever show your passion for each other when just the two of you were alone together?" I asked.

"No," Libby said with so much sorrow I turned to see if she were weeping. But in the dark, I couldn't see her face. "What's going to happen between fifteen-year-old girls in the early seventies, both male-identified women? It wasn't going to happen, unless we'd given it special status and let it develop outside of male influences." Libby stopped and was quiet awhile, then turned to me and demanded, "Did it happen with you? Did you and Natalie find time and a place for yourselves? Did she leave you for a boy too?"

The question took me by surprise and I surrendered to a sharp pain in my chest that was so acute I marveled at how little protection I had from it, no matter how far the memory was in the past. I sighed, and settled into my driver's seat, feeling anything but in control. "No," I said finally. "Natalie left me for another girl." Libby exploded with laughter, then apologized, but her black humor helped me breathe better. "Natalie and I were lovers from Easter to almost the very end of that freshman year. It was wonderful. I felt wealthy inside because like you say about Esther, I knew I was adored. I can still conjure up the exact look in Natalie's eyes when she gazed at me over her guitar and we were in perfect harmony. It was like being the chosen one, known and cherished. I felt like I had everything—Natalie's love and our music, Daniel's sweet, erotic arts, and my studies."

"Did you also lose your virginity with Daniel?" Libby asked.

"No, we had a waiting period to get on the birth control pill, so we just played sexually, without intercourse. It was fabulous, foreplay heaven. I didn't lose my virginity with a man until six months later when I was a sophomore. He was sweet, but not gifted as a lover like Natalie and Daniel."

"So . . . Natalie left you," Libby prompted.

"Yes, she began disappearing into another dorm across campus. I didn't think much of it because I was writing this huge history term paper and disappearing myself into the library. I didn't realize that both Natalie and Daniel felt abandoned by my long hours at the typewriter. Well, it turns out that Natalie's old high school girlfriend-lover was living across campus and they'd gotten caught up with each other again. I had no idea until I got locked in the library one night with Natalie's old girlfriend, quite by accident, and I discovered Natalie's betrayal. It shocked me to the core. I immediately drank a fifth of gin—and I can't hold my liquor at all. I banged on Natalie's door. It opened. I held up my finger, pointing it at her in a rage—then I fainted dead away, fell onto my face. Broke my nose!"

"And your heart," Libby said softly.

"Yes, that hurt much more. I turned to Daniel, but he had taken his revenge upon me for deserting him for my books by getting caught up in this weird cult. So I was suddenly an outsider to him."

"You lost both your girlfriend and boyfriend at the same time," Libby commented.

"It was good preparation for being bisexual," I said, with no mirth. "Knowing that I could be hurt by both sexes."

"So you broke up with them simultaneously, then what happened?"

"It wasn't clean. It was very messy. Somehow or other, during my missing-in-action study time, both Natalie and Daniel had gotten together to commiserate over losing me to the library. One of those nights, they actually made love."

"So Natalie had intercourse with Daniel before you actually did!"

"Right," I felt a hot bolt of anger running up my spine. "I'm still furious about it. And when I found out back then I raised holy hell. They both felt so badly, said that I was really there with them, that they were thinking of me the whole time. Then Daniel actually suggested that we try being a threesome. He thought it was great Natalie and I were lovers. Unlike your Tino, who wanted to be the center between you and Esther, Daniel was excited about Natalie and me together with him. He was always a very open guy, very feminine in his own way, tender. Actually, he fit right in . . ." I stopped, then found myself laughing. "It's something people dream about, to be the center of attention between two lovers—because I was the center and they both were very generous with me. But it was, it was just exhausting. That's all I remember about that long night, how weary I was from all their lovemaking with me. The next morning I felt like I'd been moving heavy furniture!"

"I don't feel sorry for you," Libby said dryly.

"No, it was lovely. But I knew that I couldn't go through it again—that I had lost something special, which I had with each of them alone. This one-on-one intimacy couldn't be replaced by a threesome with all its gymnastic pyrotechnics. Besides, I think we all knew deep down that it was over between us. That this lovemaking night was also a way of saying good-bye—it had the kindness and deep courtesy of leave-taking."

"Lovemaking as leave-taking," Libby whispered. "Yes, I know that. So, did you ever see Natalie again after that freshman year?"

"See her?" I practically shouted. "I had to be her roommate my sophomore year. Turns out it was too late to cancel our roommate selection for the new dorm and we ended up together *again*. We'd each separately canceled our choice of each other for sophomore room-mates, but I'll never forget that first day back to college when I walked in and saw Natalie's emerald green comforter on her bed and her guitar! I was appalled. We tried to have our room assignment changed, but couldn't. So we were stuck with each other. Couldn't even break up living together, even after we'd broken up as lovers."

"Kind of like marriage," Libby remarked.

"Well, we struggled all year fiercely. She had another boyfriend by that time, Jacob, a brilliant, charismatic, hippie dope dealer; I had lost my virginity, such as it was, to Ivan, a poet and psychology major. Natalie and I lived in the same dorm room, but avoided each other."

"Sometimes . . ." Libby began ruminatively, "sometimes I think it's as simple as emotional readiness."

"Will you ever reconcile with Esther?" I asked.

"You're saying I should invite her to my wedding!" Libby asked incredulously, then fell into deep thought. "Well, I do have to ask myself what if this story I've told myself all these years is false—what if she did love me as much as I did her? What then?"

"What then?" I echoed.

"Have you kept in touch with Natalie?"

"End of our sophomore year we finally had it out and decided simply not to see each other. By that time we hadn't been lovers in half a year. She was off into travel and geology, I was deep into the arts. We parted ways, but always kept loose contact over the years. She dropped out and disappeared, like Daniel had, into some intense religious group for a while. When she emerged years later in 1974, she was in graduate school, had gone through two abortions, traveled the world, and was one of the sanest people I'd ever met. I was de-lighted to hear from her when she tracked me down in New York City. Then we wrote letters. Since that reunion by mail I've seen her about once every two years, especially now that we're both on the West Coast. About ten years ago, she decided she wanted to commit to being only with women and to have a family; now they have two children. Natalie's singing again and sends me cassette tapes of her new group. Someday maybe she'll do a record and I'll sing backup harmony. You want to hear her voice?" I reached into my dashboard for one of Natalie's latest song tapes.

"Whoa!" Libby held up her hands in the dark. "I need to keep at this excavation. How 'bout I hear Natalie's singing on the trip back. Right now, I've got to figure something out."

"What?"

"The letter I'm composing in my head to Esther."

"Wedding invitation?"

"No," Libby said slowly, "but an invitation nevertheless. After I'm married and back from the honeymoon I want to test your theory. I'll write her and invite her to meet me in New York . . . then we'll see if my first love was also hers!"

Libby did send that invitation to her old schoolgirl love. She wrote Esther her warm greetings and request for a reunion; she told Esther that though she was happily married, with a close circle of female friends, she'd come to realize that Esther was a very important, irreplaceable person in her life. She missed her terribly. Would Esther meet her again?

Within a week, Libby received her answer—a fond phone call from Esther, agreeing to meet with Libby after these twelve years of silence, midway between her home in Abington and Libby's in New York City. They chose a teahouse in Philadelphia.

"Like those tearooms during World War I." Libby called me cross-country to report on her meeting with Esther. "You know, where all those war widows went to gossip and dress up for one another and have tea together, tête-à-tête, while the men were off with their male-bonding war-buddy stuff." Libby laughed, clearly delighted by her recent reunion with Esther. "When you stop and think about it, those women in their ladies' tearooms really understood something about sisterhood. Those women didn't just do lunch, they did lifetimes!"

Intimate lifetimes together is the focus of recent research by Carroll

Smith-Rosenberg on nineteenth-century women and their "female world of love and ritual." In rediscovering the Victorian bonds of female devotion to each other, Smith-Rosenberg cites the long residencies women shared with each other before, after, and during marriage. Many times "sisters, cousins, and friends frequently accompanied newlyweds on their wedding night and wedding trip," comments Smith-Rosenberg in her book *Disorderly Conduct: Visions of Gender in Victorian America*. She goes on to remark that the bonds between Victorian women were "often physical as well as emotional. An undeniably romantic and even sensual note frequently marked female friendships." Women were constant and close to each other through marriage, birth, and in death. Sometimes women even "slept with the dying woman, nursed her, and prepared her body for burial." Such lifelong intimacy would of course have a deep sensual and passionate nature that was not a taboo at a time when Victorians were supposedly repressed. While male-female sexuality may have been repressed, female-female bonds were in fact socially recognized and encouraged.

It is ironic that during our so-called sexual revolution, which began in the 1960s, the taboos against female sensuality were more rigid than for Victorian women. This may be beginning to turn around for adolescent girls today. In a 1993 *Village Voice* article called "Queer in the Streets, Straight in the Sheets," author Ann Powers chronicles the emergence of the "queer straight" among her young friends. Reveling in the deliberate sexual ambiguity of such role models as Madonna, the late Kurt Cobain, and U2, Powers cites the playful "rise of mass drag," which defies labels and gender definitions. Many of her peers, while choosing straight sex, play at passing for gay in public display. In analyzing this post-adolescent trend, Powers comments, "Just as whites in the African-American civil rights movement needed to recognize the racism that ran through them as an inheritance, so must straights accept that the modes of sex and romance in which they still participate carry the seed of homophobia. . . . A full embrace of queer culture wouldn't expand the boundaries of straightness, it would dissolve them." Powers concludes that her scrutiny of her own pleasure in passing for gay while practicing straight sex has "helped me understand ways in which my star-struck, sensual friendships with women during my teens and early twenties counted as love, even though we'd never made it into the sack. Passing, I realized that sex didn't have to mean going all the way; that, in fact, sex was being redefined all around me as the expansive and ever-present field of physical and spiritual growth it has always been."

Perhaps a new generation of adolescents will not have their puberty marred by shame and denial of their sisterhood; perhaps they will feel the openness and expansiveness that rightfully belong to adolescence if a society is not bent on labels and taboos. The average teenager now starts having sex at the age of sixteen and the threat of AIDS is on the rise among women and teenagers. I fervently hope that as our society's youth come into sexual maturity they will have every option and opportunity, every compassionate continuum of gender relations open to them—for their choice of lovers may literally save or destroy their young lives.

Libby exulted as she continued her reunion story. "Esther's just ahead of me as usual. She already has these two beautiful girls, one who looks just like her. If I have a daughter, I hope she'll get to know Esther's and maybe they'll like each other as they grow up, too."

"Full circle," I said.

"Yes," her voice softened. "You know, I told Esther that I'd always loved her and that every relationship after her was all about her. That my choice of her as my first love was the very first story I ever told my analyst. I told Esther she was the paradigm, the precedent, and that it was terrible to have lost her." Libby paused, then continued gladly, "She looked at me and smiled—you know, that crooked kind of trickster smile I'd always admired—and she just said, 'Coming here to meet you made me so nervous, like seeing an old boyfriend after twenty years.'

"I said, 'We had a romantic relationship, Esther, we weren't just best girlfriends.' And she nodded her head, with the same smile. 'Yes, we did.' I asked her, 'Was it ever like that with any other woman, the way you felt with me?' Then she laughed. 'No, it wasn't, only with you.'" Libby was quiet on the phone, but even cross-country, I could hear her triumph.

"So it *was* reciprocal," I said softly.

"Oh, yes," Libby said. "And it still is. Esther is still beautiful to me, I'm still very attracted to her. This has nothing to do with categories or gender—it's beyond labels. That's how the erotic is, I'm finding out—beyond gender and narrow confines. You know those great T-shirts the kids are wearing these days? On one side the T-shirt says DON'T THINK I'M STRAIGHT and on the other side, DON'T THINK I'M GAY. I just love that playfulness and wide-openness. I envy it. Now, maybe I can enjoy it in my own life."

"And what about Francisco?" I asked. "Does he welcome Esther back into your life?"

"Francisco is wild about her—they're kindred spirits," Libby said with a laugh. "Though Esther's husband isn't too blissed out about me. But he has no choice. Esther has let him know I'm very important in her life and that we're both monogamous in our marriages. This doesn't soothe Theodore; he's too possessive. So it just means we probably all four won't socialize much. But Esther and I intend to go on and on together."

"Well," I commented, "we have long lives . . . and men usually die before women."

Libby howled with laughter. "How subversive, but of course I've thought of that. You see, when I met Esther at fourteen, I would have been just as afraid if she were a man—it's that emotional readiness thing again. Ours is not a story about gay identity, it's a story about human love. And sisterhood has this same sensual love in it—sisters fall in love, just like parents fall in love with their children. Love is not a developmental stage—it simply exists and doesn't go away. I know now that if my life had worked out differently I could have ended up with Esther. And Francisco would be the relationship I now have with Esther." Libby paused, then concluded, "I don't think anybody gets through adolescence without going through this deep same-sex love; and why should we have to abandon or deny it? Real love is all about differences and knowing who we are separately, as complements—that's also why love between adult women can be so satisfying—like what you have now with Camille."

"I know," I told her, "that partnership is certainly all about differences—and it may take us another six years to figure out how to keep balancing each other. But I've learned so much from her—perhaps more than any other lover, male or female."

"And what I've learned from Esther is that it never stops, this loving. And for me, first love is female—it never went away. Love is about a person, not a sex."

"Maybe that's the future," I mused. "Maybe the kids have it right . . ." Then both Libby and I laughed as we said it together.

"Don't think I'm straight . . . don't think I'm gay!"

"So what are we?" Libby asked. "Where are we?"

"I don't know," I answered. "But I like it. It's a mystery. It's like adolescents say today, *awesome.*"

13

Backstage Girls: Opening Nights

This is the story of a lifelong love between women whose power struggles are matched only by their erotic fascination and abiding friendship for each other. When I first met Helene and Misha we were all in our twenties living in New York City in the seventies. I was working at *The New Yorker*, Misha, a French actress, was staging her first one-woman off-off Broadway show, and Helene had published her first novel to critical acclaim.

Even after I left New York more than two decades ago, I kept in touch with Misha and Helene's turbulent coming together and falling apart. Their story has intrigued me because not only are they both like chosen sisters to me, but also their romance seems a lifelong puzzle. They have met in each other a mirror and a match. Now they are in a phase of finding some kind of sisterhood that is at once passionate, nonsexual, and a lifelong commitment. It is rare to find ex-lovers who remain devoted even when that bond is the most bewildering and complicated relationship in their lives.

Right before Halloween of 1990, I spent several weeks in New York City listening and interviewing each of them as they nervously prepared to meet each other again face-to-face for the first time since their dramatic breakup in 1987. Though Misha and Helene had lived in the same city, shared the same artistic careers and several friends, neither woman had ever once seen or spoken to the other since that opening night four years ago when everything between them was broken, lost. "Miscarriage," Misha had sadly named it in one of the many letters they each shared with me. "We have miscarried our love."

This Halloween evening, Helene walked nervously through Manhattan's theater district toward the reunion that she and Misha had carefully choreographed through several postcards and one call.

"Now that the Berlin Wall has fallen," Helene had written Misha, in 1989, "can we end our own little Cold War and at least lay eyes on each other?"

" 'Yes, she said, yes, she said, yes . . .' " Misha wrote back. "The Great Divorce is over. Shall we send the governesses to tea since Misha and Helene are such spitfires and would just walk out on each other all over again?"

The governesses were two characters Misha and Helene had created among a large cast of personas that had first made their love affair so protean and playful. The governesses were characters from what the women called "our cool, blue period." They wore pale blue Victorian vintage dresses and high-collared nightgowns. Helene played a virginal but sensual British governess; Misha was a French mademoiselle well-schooled in genteel seduction. Privately playing at governesses, they decided, was like *Les Liaisons Dangereuses* meets *A Thousand and One Nights,* for each woman had to tell a love story before she could tenderly take off a layer of Victorian lace or a camisole from the other.

Later as their fiery affair heated up, the governesses were conjured up much like the calm of camomile tea. Each governess always carried a delicate white washcloth, soaked in lemon and rose-petal water; mid-lovemaking this cloth could be called upon to cool the skin and lay across a flushed face or neck aching with heat.

Asking these imagined governesses to meet after the white-hot angry silence of four years seemed a splendid idea to Misha and Helene. They also had agreed each to tell their side of the breakup with the same polite courtesy the governesses had showed each other in their early days. The difference was, now they were not playing a sensual striptease with silken camisoles or lace gowns—they were surrendering to each other their most intimate sorrows.

"Do you know . . ." Misha had written Helene in the month before they would meet again, "that for almost a year after we broke up, I slept in your blue silk nightgown even after your scent faded away? Shall I return the nightgown to you at our reunion?"

"Please keep it," Helene wrote back on a postcard. "I've missed you more than anyone I've ever lost. And now I'm terrified to see you so soon—on Halloween, our anniversary."

Helene saw Misha sooner than she expected. Five minutes before they were to meet in a reserved room of a favorite Japanese restaurant, she stood on a street corner and marveled—for there in a bagel bakery stood Misha, buying her usual week's worth of cinnamon and sesame breakfast bagels, as if this were any other day and not the first meeting with Helene after such long absence.

Fondly Helene studied Misha through the bagel-shop window. Four years had changed her very little; Misha's dark mane of curls was cut short, which gave her round French face the adolescent look of a ga- mine in a Parisian street theater. Helene liked the attitude Misha's small, curvaceous body suggested, like Edith Piaf's elegant waif. Mi- sha's body reminded Helene of her voice—full and feline. Her slight French accent was all but lost in loquacious riffs that had made her one-woman shows such a success.

Unaware that Helene watched her, Misha chatted with the shop owner. Helene recognized her mood—ebullient, on the verge of tears. Misha had always been a high-wire act, more temperamental and the- atrical than Helene in public. But "backstage," as they called their affair, Misha practiced willfull stillness, a monastic and ritualistically simple daily life.

"I'm a potato," she'd always explain. "Underneath my stage makeup, I'm plain and everyday, rooted in the ground. You're the real exotic, my darling."

Helene hid her eccentricities, her deep and mercurial moods, under a veneer of calm and aloof courtesy. "I'm a cat and you're a dog," she'd tell Misha.

"Right, dear," Misha would laugh. "That's why you're beloved by all, possessed by none . . . except me, of course. I take full possession of you. I have a master's degree in jealousy from a respected university."

Misha's onstage casual dismissal and offstage possessiveness had already led to several fights early in their affair. "I know you've slept with your publisher," she'd accuse Helene. "He looks at you as if he's been between your covers!"

"Don't be so vulgar." Helene would try to coax Misha back into bed, or the bath, or to the kitchen table. "Governesses are devoted to each other. All the rest is research."

Where Misha was voluptuous and dark, Helene was pale and slender, with auburn hair and delicate freckles. When they bathed together, Misha would wash Helene's long flame-colored hair, making finger curls on her forehead. "One day I'll cut my hair all off," Misha would say.

"Not while you're with me," Helene laughed.

"If I couldn't be with you, I'd want to cut all my hair off, in memoriam."

Now as they warily met, four years later, in the Japanese restaurant, and were ushered in bare feet to their small room, Helene tenderly touched the back of Misha's shoulders. "You've cut your hair, darling," she whispered.

Misha turned to her. "You weren't with me," she said simply, sadly.

Both women sat down cross-legged at the low table and gazed at each other for the first time in four years.

"I'm so nervous," Misha said, her black eyes wide. "It's worse than any opening night. Maybe I'll throw up."

"I just want to look at you," Helene breathed. "I want to rest my eyes on you."

Helene found herself liking Misha's shorn curls; her black hair had always been so luxurious it distracted from her eyes which were now emphasized—oval and dark as East Indian women's, with that same luminosity. "All you need is a caste mark and you could pass for an avatar," Helene said. "I'd worship you."

"I never let myself remember how beautiful you are," Misha countered, smiling. Deeply she considered Helene—the elegant drape of her jade-green silk blouse with its low, curved cowl collar; its luxurious, brilliant color lent Helene's eyes a cool glow and revealed her long, delicate neck. This sensuous neckline Misha had memorized with her lips; its grace had aroused and captured Misha's imagination from their first meeting. Now she traced that arch of neck with her eyes and remarked softly, "You bare your neck the way some women bare their souls." Misha shook her head ruefully. "That's why I always wanted to dress you in high collars—to keep the vampires away."

"But it's Halloween." Helene smiled. "And here we . . . again."

"All Hallow's Eve . . ." Misha murmured, gazing at her old lover, her eyes brimming. "We're back from the dead." For a moment she shivered visibly, and it seemed as if she might simply bolt from the table.

Then she composed herself, though her olive skin was very pale. "You've haunted me so much all these years," she began, with a trace of outrage. "If I'd known that Halloween night when I invited you to visit after all your parties, if I'd even had a breath of foresight about you . . ."

"I had the foresight, the premonition." Helene laughed, but there was little mirth in her eyes. "It didn't stop either of us."

Misha's grave expression matched Helene's. "You know, the first Halloween anniversary of our becoming lovers—when we'd murdered each other in our minds—I stayed in all night, mourning you."

"I forced myself to go to *The Magic Flute* with George, who knew I was brokenhearted without you." Helene attempted a smile. "We both wore Halloween masks with feathers. But I cried so much, my feathers looked like I'd been mauled by a cat."

"Not by me," Misha protested. "I'm a dog, you said it yourself."

"But you bite." Helene leaned way back but her gaze was so level and cold it had the same effect as a sharp slap to the face.

"And you have the big paw!" Misha tried not to let her voice rise. Without effort her voice, trained to fill a theater, often resounded when she least wanted to be loud. It seemed to Misha that Helene gave her a sly grin. "That's right," Misha couldn't stop herself. "You have the big cat's big paw that comes out of nowhere—slash! Like a tiger. And that's what you struck me with on my opening night." Misha caught her breath and forced herself to sit still. Then she admitted in an almost inaudible voice, "I don't think I have ever forgiven you for that night." Then she covered her face with her hands.

Sighing, Helene studied Misha's small hands, noticing that there was the slimmest of wedding rings beneath the golden fire opal ring Misha had worn when they first met. Helene had worn an Australian fire opal on her ring finger then, too—their rings could have been a matched set. Long ago this had startled them, the first of so many eerie similarities that those of us who knew them believed theirs was indeed a fated affair.

In that Japanese restaurant as Misha noticed Helene's eyes on her own ring, there was a very long silence. At last Misha offered her hand to her old lover. "Did you think I would take my grandmother's opal off when you abandoned me on my most important opening night?" she asked, her voice deepening, her eyes widening until they seemed obsidian, a dark mirror.

"No," Helene murmured, "you never forgave me." Helene quickly let go of Misha's hand and sat back against the cotton cushion. "You married."

"And you didn't?" Misha asked fiercely. "You didn't go out and find in Lila a wonderful partner who is what I could never be for you—attentive and constant—a true mate?" Misha held Helene's eyes, then shrugged and shook her head. "But I always kept you with me. Ross could never replace you. Even he knows that. I've told . . ."

"Tell me this," Helene began, her voice shaking. "I want to know before we go any further"—she waved her hand, her own opal ring flashing fire—". . . that I was a deep love in your life."

Misha gave a surprised start, almost a cry, caught her breath and whispered, "You were an incredibly deep love in my life. Still are." They exchanged a glance that suddenly held all of its old startling intimacy, its humor, its tension and testing. "Was I that for you?"

"You already know that," Helene said tenderly. "We both know much more than we say to each other." Helene studied Misha's familiar face. Even in four years she had not forgotten one detail of its curves and soft slopes. At last Helene offered, "You want me to say it, too?"

"Yes," Misha asked humbly. "Yes, please."

As Helene repeated the words, she felt a dizzying echo in her head, a light-headedness that reminded her of that Halloween Eve four years ago when she'd finally made it to an agreed-upon midnight meeting with Misha. There she stood on the studio landing, listening to the boats off the Harlem River, the Spuyten Duyvel bridge lights blinking like jack-o'-lanterns. Misha had carved her doorside pumpkin with a lopsided grin and vampire teeth, a proper lady's church hat and prim veil crumpled atop its orange face—the effect was of a Victorian prude vanquished by an older feminine tradition of mischief, sheer high spirits, and power.

The pumpkin had made Helene laugh with pleasure, but she still couldn't shake her sense of tension and resistance like an otherworldly foreboding that once she crossed this threshold, she would be changed. Helene was used to change, in fact prided herself on her flexibility, the flowing way she had of moving from city to city, friend to friend, book project to book project, sometimes lover to lover. She often told herself she was a shape shifter, moving between the worlds of sexual boundaries with the naturalness of an androgyne. "We're the future," she'd told one of her past lovers, that time a man. "Everybody is bisexual, it's just the person you choose, not the gender. Someday, the whole world will claim what we're living now."

But the change she intuited that Halloween night felt different, less an internal shift than a radical meeting with another person who already drew her so far out of herself that here she was hesitantly delivering her proffered treat of a foot massage for Misha who had just gotten off a road tour and was exhausted. "Let me, *mea culpa*, offer you a foot massage and pedicure by way of apologizing for missing all your performances I'd promised to attend. Ever yr. *pénitente*, Helene."

"I accept with open feet," Misha had written back from Atlanta. "How about Halloween, midnight, my place?"

So here Helene stood, so light-headed she had to hold onto the banister before ringing the doorbell. She told herself it was climbing all those stairs to Misha's riverfront studio. But even then Helene knew she was crossing over into territory at once terrifying and seductive. She knew that missing all of Misha's performances had been more than a coincidence, even though there were valid excuses. Helene did not want to be just an audience for Misha; she wanted to meet Misha alone, backstage, where Helene would better trust her. Helene distrusted anyone's public persona. She'd seen her father—a successful actor who'd made a name for himself as a leading man in New York theater—succeed in seducing his audiences into what Helene called the "false intimacy" of the stage. While her father was lauded for his commanding warmth onstage, offstage he scrupulously avoided any bond which might threaten his deep solitude. After Helene's mother died when she was seven, her father disappeared into the theater, leaving his three daughters not only motherless, but fatherless as well. As if to compensate for this desertion, he began dragging his daughters along on every tour like small steamer trunks or props. Helene sensed even as a child that this touring together was the illusion of closeness. Her father's reputation as a leading man actually increased with the publicity portrait of a widowed father and family man gathering his motherless girls close to him.

As a teenager Helene refused to attend her father's plays. "I'll see you at home," she always told him. "If we had a home." When he tried to coax her into supporting his art, she countered, "All we're really supporting is your image. There's a big difference between being a star and an artist." In their final argument before her father sent Helene off to a girls' boarding school, she told him, "It must be hard to come home to the sound of only three children clapping."

Now as Helene stood on the balcony outside Misha's door, watching midnight Halloween party goers make the Manhattan streets below into a citywide carnival, a stage, she was very scared. Why had she agreed to meet Misha in private? How could she ever have thought she had the upper hand offstage? Misha was a one-woman show; now she would also be an audience. Helene let her fear hold sway only a few more minutes; then she gathered her considerable wits and reminded herself that she was here for a simple foot massage, a gift she'd given her friends for decades. She was good with her hands, had learned massage growing up with actors and dancers; she'd keep control—everything, including herself and Misha, under control.

For her part, Misha awaited her Halloween rendezvous with Helene with a mixture of pleasure and perturbation. Really, this sister artist was too maddeningly aloof and even a bit dim. Didn't she see that for more than a year, since they'd finally met at that theater party, Misha had been pursuing Helene with postcards and suggestive, ever-so-subtle hints? Misha had waited over a decade to meet Helene at last, and feared she would disappear again into her elusive patterns. Yet Helene had responded to Misha's postcards this past year with reciprocal delight and playfulness. But, Misha wondered, did Helene understand that Misha's notes from every corner of the continent were in fact a seduction? From the moment they'd met—long ago on the phone and in person at last year's party—Misha had sensed that here was not only a playmate, but a peer. Misha had read all three of Helene's novels with respectful pleasure and imagined that someday soon Helene would read Misha's own final draft of the novel that had just been accepted by a small, elegant New York publisher. But Misha wanted more from Helene than a working relationship; Helene's cool, long-limbed grace, her natural red mane and changeable gray eyes had aroused Misha from the first moment when she'd met Helene at Ivan's coed slumber/theater party.

While awaiting reviews of the show Ivan had directed, Helene had generously volunteered to put a dark henna rinse on Misha's hair. Misha felt Helene's hands on her head like a benediction—this lovely woman's touch was somewhere between a physical prayer and a sensual blessing. In the early morning hours when most of the cast dozed, drinks in hand, Misha and Helene were still talking animatedly. To wake everybody up for the morning *Times* review, Misha and Helene had played an impromptu duet. Sitting side by side on the piano bench, Misha turned to Helene—who was also just a wee bit blotto —and leaned close to kiss her lips. Misha smelled the salty, sweet scent of Helene's suntanned, sweaty skin, her light gardenia perfume, a female musk lingering like the music between them.

Just at the moment when Misha leaned near to kiss Helene, the other woman sat way back, her eyes softening, the freckles on her high cheekbones turning a deep rose shade as she blushed. "I think . . ." Helene's words were slightly slurred from drink and confusion. "I think we will help each other with our work." She shook her head as if waking from a trance. "Yes . . . our work."

Misha had practically boomeranged back, stunned at the rebuff. Perhaps, Misha had told herself darkly, Helene was punishing her for being so successful in her own right. While Helene was a critical literary success, Misha was more than obvious star, the center of attention at most parties. Maybe, Misha mused, Helene was resentful of Misha's ease onstage, a place Helene seemed to purposely avoid, even though she was quite charismatic. If this was true, then perhaps Helene had missed all the performances of Misha's last show in Manhattan because she was deeply jealous. Well, Misha understood jealousy; she would forgive Helene, if the woman ever showed up for their Halloween date. As she waited patiently, Misha half-expected Helene to stand her up for this private tête-à-tête. Too bad if she did, Misha decided, with a baleful glance at the chilled champagne; this was her last invitation to Mademoiselle.

Yet there it was, the knock on the door. Her guest didn't gaily call out, "Trick-or-treat." She didn't make one of her innocently seductive remarks. Helene simply stood there, paler than any of the Halloween ghosts who'd trooped up the five flights of stairs to Misha's studio. Helene seemed very young, her gray-green eyes wide, translucent.

"I won't stay long," was the first thing she said. "It's so late." Then Helene seemed to summon all her courage. Holding her bag of massage oils and the pumice stone like a protective shield, she entered.

"I've heard about your foot massages, Mademoiselle, everywhere I've traveled." Misha laughed and swept her inside. "Champagne?"

"Oh, no," Helene said, "I rarely drink."

"Even on the night when all the shadows and all those still living dance together?"

"It would interfere with my work." Helene set down her bag and appreciatively scanned the room—the Japanese silk screens, the African masks Misha had collected, the bird and animal mobiles that fluttered from the high ceilings, some with tiny bells like wind chimes. Everywhere were photos of Misha, in costume, onstage.

"Work? But surely this is play?"

"My massage work, I mean." Helene laughed nervously. Then she seemed to really notice Misha for the first time.

It was a warm night for so late an evening in October and a breeze off the river wafted through the studio, sending all the mobiles and chimes tinkling their melodic, thin music. Misha was dressed in a silken kimono aflame with wild birds. Her black curls, still damp from the shower, draped down across her small shoulders.

"You've hennaed your hair again." Helene laughed, and this time there was more fondness than fear. "It's darker."

Sitting together on the couch, they talked for a time, small talk that was light and easy, especially with the champagne. But at one point Misha's face darkened and she said, "Halloween is such a strange night. It's my favorite holiday of all—Samehedin, the old Celtic New Year, very holy and haunted. Being a pagan at heart, I like that. But it's also a hard time for me."

"Because . . . ?" Helene prompted gently, settling her legs under her on the couch. For the first time since entering Misha's festive studio she felt at ease, disarmed by Misha's confidences.

"Because it is also very near the anniversary of my little sister's death." Misha hesitated, then continued with some effort. "When I was fifteen, Anna was killed in a motorbike accident. We had never gotten along, in fact we had a huge quarrel about my wanting to be a nun, the night before she died. Never made up. As children Anna and I were extremely close, but when I supposedly deserted her for convent school she never forgave me. She said she was going to take a secular vow of silence herself—against her false saint of a sister!" Misha paused with a rueful sigh. "You see, I starred in every convent pageant. I didn't really want God, just the drama of good and evil and me and all those doting sisters!" Misha sipped her champagne thoughtfully, frowning. "Even now sometimes onstage I can look down and see my sister Anna glaring at me, as if she alone sees my black soul. Sometimes I feel her near me, nights like this, when the veils between worlds are so thin. Don't you think the dead can cross over?"

"Does she scare you?" Helene asked very softly, her hand on Misha's. "Tonight, does she scare you? Is that why you asked me to come on Halloween?"

Misha looked at Helene and said without thinking, without stopping herself, something she realized only that moment. "No. It is you who scare me."

Helene did not ask why. She recognized the fear, had sensed it at Misha's door. But strangely now she did not feel it so strongly. Perhaps, she told herself, it was Misha's turn to be scared. "I know," Helene said at last. "But I'm still here."

"Yes . . ." Misha turned to her. *"Merci, ma chérie."*

She fell into her native language as naturally as if she were returning to herself, a safe territory. "And now I think we've talked enough. I know I've danced enough. Please, my poor feet need your good hands." Misha lay down on her futon, covered with a bright purple velvet comforter. She sighed wearily. "You know, sometimes I am onstage, even in my dreams."

"Not here," Helene said. "Never with me. We're backstage girls now. We can always be backstage with each other."

"I'm glad." Misha smiled up at Helene. Misha's face without makeup was surprisingly thoughtful. All that was boisterous and captivating in this woman could quiet down into contemplative lines of cheekbone and jaw. When Helene saw Misha take off her powerful, dramatic mask and lie down on her bed, surrendering, Helene felt she was witnessing a depth and vulnerability almost startling in its openness. Surely Helene had never been so unguarded, so humble, even with her lovers.

Helene tenderly spread the apricot oil over Misha's tight dancer's feet, along the high arches and in between the toes, whose nails were painted a shocking pink.

"Pandora's Pink," Misha murmured, sighing deeply. "Be careful what you open, my mademoiselle."

Helen smiled. She did not answer, preferring to massage in silence so that there were no thoughts, no more words, just hands and bones and such beautiful stretches of skin—taut over the heels where hard little blisters of healed skin made a delicate, calloused circle. Then the private hollows of sensitive ankle which hid so many aches and longings. Secrecy in the spaces between the toes, creases that suggested sorrows and delicious pleasures. Helene concentrated on this foot as she would any foot, all her years of massage training lending her that impersonal and calming trance of the bodyworker. "No book is ever written with the mind," she was fond of saying, "it is created with the hands." Just as she was creating, from flesh and bone, another story between herself and this woman whose vulnerability and need touched Helene as deeply as she was touching.

Misha moaned slightly every time Helene's hands eased away the old aches and private imperfections—the despair of any actor who dances on hard, flat, wooden stages. Now no amount of clapping, no standing ovation, no cherished role could make her move from this bed and this tender ministry. For that was what this was—a ministration, like those Bible stories when Mary dried Christ's feet with her luxurious hair. The nuns in convent school had taught Misha this was humility, but now she knew more. This was the purest, most elemental ecstasy, like a chemical broken down to its basic elements. All the chemicals inside her blood and sweat and tears and skin distilled into this pure scent—a smell of apricot and this woman's perfume, flowers and light salt of sweat.

"Do you remember on that piano bench?" Misha said groggily. "Did you know I wanted to kiss you right then?"

Helene's hands paused only slightly on Misha's foot, then she answered with a long stroke of her thumb up Misha's Achilles tendon like sliding along a gully of soft, warm clay, sculpting not a foot, but a bowl. Misha didn't have feet anymore. She had mud and roots and earth at the very end of her body.

"I didn't know . . . then," Helene answered.

"Do you now?" Misha didn't open her eyes. It was enough to have said it. Her feet said it, too; they were open like another way of seeing, of knowing.

Helene let out a sigh; but that was not her only answer. With one oiled hand, Helene lifted Misha's foot up and placed its high arch against her own breast; Helene heard Misha's heart beating deep echoes up through the very bottom of her foot. "Listen," Helene said. "Do you hear two hearts beating?"

At first Misha heard only her own heartbeat, thudding wild and fast. Somewhere along Misha's thighs, her deep pounding was joined by Helene's pulse; it was distinct, different—like electricity. This radiant heat lightning shimmered up into Misha's pelvis, her belly, along her spine, spiraling around her neck, until that warm, flashing electricity was a high singing in her ears. Under her eyelids, Misha watched lightning inside her head like fireworks—hundreds of bright, syncopated bursts.

Opening her eyes, Misha regarded Helene's long, lean, and delicately sculpted arms silhouetted against the jack-o'-lantern's candlelight. Misha lay very still, her whole body hummed. "The way to my heart," Misha breathed, "is obviously through my feet." Misha was aware that she was wildly aroused, open; but she dared not let her hips dance as they longed to, for fear of frightening this woman off.

Helene still held Misha's foot against her heart, her eyes closed. "I have never felt this before," Helene breathed, her voice full of wonder and some bewilderment. "This is . . . this is . . . I don't know what this is . . ."

Misha leaned up on her elbows, smiling, her kimono falling open to reveal generous breasts. "This is you and me." Misha held out her arms, and Helene kissed her warm foot before tenderly letting it go and stretching her long body to lie alongside Misha. Wrapping her legs around Helene's, Misha opened her arms. "Now . . . now I will take that kiss, Mademoiselle!"

Each sought the other's mouth. Helene's lipstick tasted of warm citrus and Misha's of lavender. Where Helene was slender and small-breasted, nipples pink and hard, Misha was all curves and bosom, her dark nipples like another mouth, poised, presented. Their bodies fit perfectly, soft and rounded, skin smelling of apricot oil and sweet sweat. When Misha's hands stroked along Helene's belly and up her long thighs, Helene shuddered and pulled Misha's naked body on top of hers so that they lay belly to belly, nipple to nipple, mouth to mouth, moving slowly and in synch. Helene's palms cupped Misha's silky buttocks, then pulling aside the kimono, she kneaded and molded those high cheeks as if the warm muscles were molten skin. Misha moved in a trance dance, undulant, and sliding her wet pelvis up and down against Helene's belly.

Then Misha tenderly opened the other woman, whose warm, wet membranes parted like a veil revealing flesh so sensitive and secret. Deep inside, Helene sunk open like sand slipping away beneath surf. Within her was a graceful hand fluidly stroking, fingers searching every shivering, hidden curve.

Helene felt the trembling first along her inner thighs, incandescent and interior as if someone were moving from the inside out. Slopes and ridges within her opened like the spun shell of a chambered nautilus. She was made of sand, not skin, and these tides were her own salty, inland sea. A long shiver flowed up her spine and her back arched high with heat and pleasure from this woman's lips between her legs. Fire and water, steam inside, and at last, the waves. Then this pulsing center that sent her pelvis shuddering, driving deep into the cotton bed. Crying out until the flowing fire faded and left her spent, Helene wept softly. Her hands held the top of Misha's head, Helene's fingers intertwined with Misha's dense, long curls.

Helene lay, the other hand thrown across her eyes, panting, heart beating so hard Misha could see it throbbing through her breast.

"My," Misha said with an admiring smile, "you look like you've fallen from a great height."

Helen sighed and slowly sat up, her camisole wrinkled and wet, one strap falling down over her sloped shoulder. She looked sloe-eyed and dazed. "Polishing mirrors," she murmured. "That's what the Chinese call this loving . . . two women." She stretched, smiling.

Misha laughed at Helene's feline languor. "We will go slow, like a slow dance . . ." She leapt up and her kimono fell to the floor showing her taut dancer's legs, her shapely curves of belly and buttocks. "Listen . . ." She put on an Otis Redding song and sang along in her French accent. Leaping gracefully back in bed, Misha said, "I've got an idea. Let's do a slow dance lying down. May I have this dance, at last, offstage, dear sister of my heart, and my foot?"

"But who will lead?" Helene laughed and slowly let Misha pull off her camisole as if she no longer needed any protection, as if it were old skin.

"You were an incredibly deep love in my life," Helene repeated now, these four years later as she leaned across the table in the Japanese restaurant and took Misha's small hand. "Still are . . ."

Misha nodded, her eyes brimming, unable to speak. She sat back on the futon cushions and carefully took off her kimono, folded it, and set it aside. It was the same bright red silk adorned with wild birds from their first lovemaking.

Helene noted the kimono with a slight, wistful smile, then said softly, "Many times I wished you were just an affair."

"But you knew I was not," Misha insisted, resting her chin on her hands. "We're more trouble than that. What always frightens me is the latitude of our love, that knows no gender, that engages so many deep parts of me. It's too . . . too much homework."

Helene agreed with a grin. "I swear I'm going to write a book. This one will be a best-seller. I'll call it *How to Avoid Your Soulmate* —with the premise that twin souls rarely can be mates—it's overwhelming to meet one's match." Helene paused. "I'll never forget an old boyfriend saying, 'God forgive me, but as long as I can find a wife, I will. I couldn't stand two typewriters in the house.'"

"You know how I hate hearing about your old lovers." Misha bristled, then added wryly, "Besides me, of course."

Helene took this in with a wry nod of her head, then she sat back, arms folded. "We agreed to listen to each other's side of the breakup. Well, I'm listening . . ."

The Japanese waitress slipped in shyly, delivered their bottle of champagne, and disappeared with a faint odor of rice wine. When she left, Misha took a deep breath and began softly, "Do you know how much you hurt me when you canceled all your tickets to my opening night? I always expected that you would be there for *this* performance—at last you'd witness me onstage and . . . and love me there, too!"

Helene dropped her eyes. "I'm so sorry, Misha, I've told you that over and over. I canceled those tickets and went for your jugular because it was the only way I knew to get your attention, to get you offstage again, with me! Remember, I hadn't laid eyes on you in six weeks and you were only thirty blocks away. I felt completely abandoned by you."

"But I am not your papa, the famous *acteur*," Misha said with a flourish. "I wrote you postcards every day and begged you to pretend I was out of town."

Helene sat back and crossed her arms defiantly. "It's simple, Misha, you chose the theater over me, over our backstage love."

Misha sighed. "Yes, I did. And I paid dearly for it. I lost you." She fell silent, staring down at her hands, the bright fire opal atop the slim wedding band. "I never thought you'd leave me by myself up there on that stage. None of my other lovers ever had—some of them even preferred me as a star. But you, you always wanted more."

The two women were quiet, each studying the other with open curiosity and something else—respect. At last Misha broke the gaze and took a deep breath. "You are even scarier to me now than when we were lovers," she said softly. "At least as lovers we could now collapse into each other's arms and change this, whatever this is, into passion."

"But then after the lovemaking, we'd still be here, you and I, looking at each other and wondering what we ever did to deserve each other!" Helene laughed and sat back. "Listen, Misha, maybe we'll never figure it out, ever think of that?"

Misha smiled with her whole body—a delighted, forward movement that startled Helene and reminded her of another language they'd once shared—a language of limbs and lips and eyes. Misha registered Helene's pleasure, the slight flush beneath those freckles she had once named, connected like dot-to-dot, and she said impulsively, "I just want to tell you that I am so grateful you let me be your lover all those years ago, because I know about your body and the way you move through space and your deepest privacies that I could never know as sister or friend. It is secret, privileged knowledge that you only give a lover. Even if we are never again lovers, I will always possess this privacy about you and it is . . . a treasure to me."

Moved, Helene leaned forward and held Misha's hand. "I will never forget our backstage girls. And I thank you for taking off your makeup to be with me, to let me really see you . . . offstage."

Misha held Helene's elegant hands within her smaller ones. "Dogs and cats both have them," Misha whispered. "Paws, pretty paws." Then she let go of Helene's hands and sat back, composing herself. "All those four years of our divorce, when we hated each other so, when we could only write letters, I could still feel your hands on my feet sometimes, your heart beating next to mine. I knew you were alive, not some dead saint or sister. And beneath all our blame and judgment there was, well, I'll say it, some mercy between us . . ." Misha stopped, tears spilling down her face.

Tenderly Helene unrolled her cloth napkin and dipped it in ice water. "Mademoiselle." She offered the cool, white cloth to Misha. "For your face . . . for your beautiful face."

Misha smoothed her forehead and throat, then on an impulse, she proceeded to dip the washcloth in her water glass and cleanse her face of all her makeup. "*Voilà,* I am all yours, your plain potato. And now, it is your turn, Helene, to tell me your side of the story. I want to listen, not like your ex-lover, but like your sister."

Helene hesitated only a moment, before gathering steam. "Two things: first, just what I've said—that you mistook me for a stage wife, a supporting cast. I won't ever just be in your audience."

"I know that only too well," Misha countered, "because you've never been in my audience, not once!"

"Oh, but you're forgetting," breathed Helene, her eyes darkening. "You forget that time I came to rehearsal and brought you those silly scalloped potatoes. You know I hate to cook and here I did a wife-slave thing and made you that casserole."

"My favorite, *ma chérie*."

Annoyed, Helene pushed on. "And what do I see? But you onstage acting out our foot massage scene, from our first night together. I mean, dialogue and everything! It was shocking!"

"That must be the second thing, yes?" Misha flushed. "And I suppose you've never used real life or lovers in anything you've ever written?"

"That's not the point!" Helene burst out, then immediately made an effort to calm herself. "You never asked me, never told me you'd take our love and memorialize it onstage, except of course, you portrayed it as being between a man and a woman—I don't mind that so much. I understand gender was not your point in this play. But it was later, later, when I heard that you'd let it be known that Ross—who was, after all, a musician onstage with you—was really the inspiration for that foot massage scene. It's not your decision to disguise our love, Misha, it's your betrayal—by intimating to everybody that that foot and heart belonged to Ross instead of us, instead of you and me . . ." Helene faded off, tears starting in her eyes.

Now Misha leaned across the table and offered the same cool washcloth to Helene, who held it up to her flushed cheeks, then lay it across her wrist like a bandage.

"I never meant to give that foot massage to Ross," Misha tenderly soothed. "He has never loved my feet as you once did." Then Misha chided Helene, "But you never should have listened to gossip and innuendo. People who knew about us also knew that was our scene, including Ross and even my director—she loved hearing about our romance. Maybe everyone else in the world didn't know, but what's important is that I knew it was you I was remembering. There wasn't a performance when I didn't see your face or feel your hands on me." Misha paused, then added in a subdued voice, "I'm very sorry there are not footnotes in a play like in a book."

"There are acknowledgments," Helene said evenly.

Misha met her direct gaze and nodded. "I acknowledge you, with all my heart and a little late. I acknowledge you." She smiled, then said in a deep voice, "And my feet will always footnote you."

The waitress ventured another appearance, saw the women were no longer arguing, but were in fact cozy. She took their order. Helene and Misha decided to exchange their Halloween presents. They were not at all surprised to see they'd bought each other the exact same earrings—skeletons; one set made of silver, the other bronze.

"Do you know," said Helene with a laugh, "during our divorce I actually consulted a psychic who told me that you and I had been twins in a past life, Roman times; we existed in our own fantasy world and feuded terribly, when we weren't fascinated by one another. During our worst moments, we'd demand of each other, 'Why do you have *my* face?' "

"Why do you have *my* earrings?" Misha grinned as they both placed the dangling skeletons in their ears.

"Because I'm dancing with the undead." Helene laughed.

"I prefer the word *resurrected,*" Misha said and Helene nodded, rolling her eyes.

The dramatic movement was so uncharacteristic of Helene that Misha noted for the first time how very self-assured her old lover had become, how unconsciously dramatic. Whereas four years ago Helene had struck her as aloof and inward, this Halloween she seemed to have come into her own. Perhaps the last two successful books and reading tours had lent Helene the innate grace and self-possession of a natural performer. She was, after all, her father's daughter, Misha mused. She was also surprised that this recognition of Helene's own charisma in the larger world did not arouse her jealousy. Instead it simply aroused her.

"Can we be friends now, do you think?" Misha asked urgently and took Helene's hand. "I want to be best girlfriends and invite you to sit on my balcony every summer. We'll sing and play and watch old Perry Mason reruns together. You still love mysteries?"

"I love you, don't I?" Helene smiled. "But, but what will we do with our bodies, or for that matter, with Ross and Lila?"

"I'll always feel aroused in your presence," Misha admitted. "I will always desire you, even long for you. But we are adults, yes? We can make some ground rules. And with all we have to figure out between us, lovemaking will be no help!"

Helene agreed. "We could be passionate friends, like women in other times and cultures who swore lifelong allegiance to each other, like a 'friend of the bosom.' "

Misha laughed delightedly. "You are so much like a British governess, a perfect part we cast you in. But yes, darling, I accept your soul upon my bosom as years ago I took your heart into the sole of my foot." Misha paused, then said tenderly, "Did you know that I broke that foot you loved so well?"

"Yes," Helene said softly. "I swear I could almost feel the moment you broke it. I was on the uptown express when suddenly I felt sharp pains in my chest. Thought I was having a heart attack, but then it subsided. Next morning I read you'd broken your foot performing and would be out a week."

"Did you also know that this foot which was so sore without your touch, is now permanently damaged—from dancing upon it while broken? The show must go on." Misha wrapped her arms around herself. "If you had been with me . . ." Misha began again, then caught herself, with a sigh. "No, you are not that powerful or my personal healer. But maybe you might have stopped me from dancing on a broken foot."

Helene slowly uncrossed her legs from under the low Japanese table. She stood up, stretched, and then moved to the other side to sit next to Misha—at last embracing her, burying her face in that familiar, fragrant neck. For a long time they held each other, weeping quietly.

"Oh, I still love your smell," Misha whispered.

"Show me where you broke your foot, love," Helene said.

Misha slipped off her kid-leather dancing shoe. "Here," she pointed to the soft ball of her foot. "These little bones that hold up the whole body."

Helene shook her head. "There's a massage technique that focuses only on the foot, reflexology. Each section of the foot is divided into corresponding organs."

"And what inside me did I break here?" Misha asked softly.

Helene hesitated, then cupped Misha's foot in her hand. "Your heart."

"Brokenhearted," Misha breathed and kissed Helen's forehead very tenderly. "Aren't you tired right now, couldn't you just lie down with me here on this futon and sleep another four years, sleep together so chastely, without struggling so much with each other? Don't you get so tired of it?"

"Of what?"

"Of trying to outstrip and outstep and stomp each other into the ground—to win out over one another once and for all?"

"Yes," Helene said and rested one arm around Misha's narrow shoulders. "Oh, yes."

"Then let's try to keep our sibling rivalry in check. Isn't the love between us deeper than the poison?"

"I think so," Helene ventured with a rueful smile. "Let's make a pact right here on Halloween, the old New Year."

Misha laughed. "Yes, we will. But before we make all our good resolutions, you have to tell me a story like old times. But I won't undress you. I'll just listen. Tell me a dark and scary story to honor this All Hallow's Eve."

Helene smiled and stood up, returning to her side of the table. As the Japanese waitress served their dinner of sashimi and miso, of green tea ice cream and melon liqueurs, Helene told Misha how on opening night her publisher had called with last-minute tickets for Misha's show. "Who knows what he was up to," Helene admitted when she saw Misha's famous flash of jealousy in her black eyes. "But I said, yes, I would go with him. They were front-row seats, for God's sake, and I knew you'd see me there with him, that it would hurt you so badly . . . as you'd hurt me. I wanted to wound and punish you. So I stood there ironing my white silk dress . . . remember? It was the one the governesses bought together, vintage high-collar and yet sexy. I was ironing it and imagining my sweet revenge, when suddenly I just started sobbing. I cried so hard that my tears were like sprinkling water under the iron and it steamed up in my face. Right then, I knew that what I was plotting for you was evil, pure evil. The cruel desire to inflict pain on someone I supposedly loved."

"But you weren't in that front row," Misha breathed, her face wide and white. "And . . . and knowing this now I'm glad, very glad you weren't in my audience that opening night."

"I promise you I'll be there next time," Helene swore. "I will truly try."

"And I will try not to break my own or your heart ever again."

"You know we will." Helene laughed, shaking her head. "It comes so naturally to us."

" 'They who have the power to harm and do none,' " Misha quoted, her voice full and deep, " 'they are the master of their faces.' "

"And feet," Helene suggested.

"And fates," Misha finished.

It's been five years since the Halloween reunion of Misha and Helene. In that time those of us who are their friends have had the pleasure of playing with them together, rather than going between them as warring lovers. The first years after their Halloween reunion were a languid honeymoon phase of their friendship. Because both Helene and Misha had secure relationships with mates who approved and encouraged their renewed friendship, and because both women were caught up in successful careers that seemed to keep an eerie evenness of mutual accomplishment, those first reunited years were a kind of idyll. Helene's mate, Lila, is an anthropology professor often doing fieldwork in far-off rain forests; Misha's husband, Ross, is a musician on tour with various recording artists. Both mates agreed that life with Misha and Helene was easier now that the women had reconciled. Misha and Helene had promised their partners sexual fidelity. Sometimes the couples socialized together and often joined larger groups for holiday celebrations. An easiness developed all round so that these gatherings often had a kind of family reunion sense—that familiar bond beneath which there are always lingering, old wounds.

Last fall Helene sent me one of her many invitations to come join my old friends back East: "Misha and I promise not to put you through any more post-divorce pyrotechnics," she wrote. "Did Misha tell you that we've actually managed to work together these last years? So I wasn't wrong after all—we *have* helped each other with our writing, going so far as trusting each other to edit our final manuscripts. In fact, we're being so brave as to have a double publication party, to celebrate both our books coming out. Won't you please come join us?"

As I flew to New York on the Seattle red-eye, I thought about my long friendships with Helene and Misha. Their struggle to find out just exactly who they are to each other—lover, friend, sister, lifelong soulmate—has taught me that deep love between two people persists whether they are spouses or not. Once having loved, Helene and Misha have sought to honor a bond many couples, after the marriage is over, decide to deny or attempt to replace.

In a Manhattan theatre club, I interviewed Misha and Helene and asked why they didn't simply move on or give up on each other if the relationship was so difficult.

Misha retorted, "You're an environmentalist, and you haven't heard of recycling? Well, Helene and I make divine compost; we're recycling fools! My own sister's loss taught me long ago that only death is final."

Helen smiled and added, "Once an old German woman told about her husband; he was still in Europe, she in New York. They saw each other only twice a year, but wrote letters every day. She said, 'As long as he is in the world, I am not alone.' That's how I feel about Misha."

"Sometimes in my darkest times," Misha confessed in a subdued voice, not looking at Helene, "I've wondered if Helene and I have made a terrible, terrible mistake—that we should really be with each other forever."

"What would that mean for our current marriages?" Helene mused, and shook her head in some bewilderment. "I can't imagine leaving Lila."

"Or Ross," Misha murmured. "Besides, imagine us living together. Horrors! There we are, cozy as can be. Suddenly the phone rings. Helene and I dive for it. No matter who it's for, the other will be resentful!"

Helene shook her head with a sigh. "No, better to live across town and loving than that daily drama and despair."

Misha summed up. "I think what we've both learned is that there is no protection from each other. No protection in silence, in blaming, in idealizing, and certainly not even in making other marriages!"

Helene grinned. "The nursing home, that's our goal. I can only hope we'll be too decrepit to make love or war!"

It occured to me as I attended Misha and Helene's joint publication party that night that their attempt to find some kind of sisterhood, to grow and contain all the highly charged erotic and competitive energy between them, is a rare and brave venture. Theirs is a long love, a deep study, a sisterhood worthy of a book or several lives itself.

On Halloween of this year, Misha sent Helene a Rilke poem to honor another anniversary of their bond.

> I want to be with those who know secret things
> or else alone.

I want to be a mirror for your whole body,
and I never want to be blind, or to be too old
to hold up your heavy and swaying picture.
I want to unfold.
I don't want to stay folded anywhere,
because where I am folded, there I am a lie.
And I want my grasp of things
true before you. I want to describe myself
like a painting that I looked at
closely for a long time,
like a saying that I finally understood,
like the pitcher I use every day,
like the face of my mother,
like a ship
that took me safely
through the wildest storm of all.

By return mail, Helene penned in her best governess hand, "How many lifetimes? Yours in perpetual dismay and delight and deep love, Helene."

Part Five

Healing Our Sisterhoods and Reuniting with Our Brothers

14

Our Civil War:
Sisters and Abortion

I have saved the story of my little sister Marla until last because ours is a troubling bond, one that has required much mutual understanding and healing. Whereas I've always had a closer, peer relationship with my middle sister, Paula, an often effortless intimacy and interdependence, with Marla, neither of us has yet quite escaped the roles of big sister-little sister. Though I have relied upon Marla in times of physical sickness or stress, she is not the sister to whom I would turn to seek counsel. And Marla usually consults me second after Paula when she needs sisterly advice. But this was not always so. There was a time when Marla called upon me first.

When Marla's call for my help came, I was living cross-country from her in Colorado. Marla was working as an intensive care nurse in Philadelphia. I'll always remember that call because I was walking with a water dowser as he bent over the dry prairie soil, his gnarled stick trembling like antennae. "There's water here," he murmured, his ancient face smooth as a trance. "But she's deep down."

Deep down was where I was just about to find myself with my sister. On the horizon of this farmland my family had inherited in 1976, that I'd left New York City to work on, I saw my grandmother waving her red shawl, a signal to hightail it to the dilapidated house that none of my siblings would live in, but which I considered a true homestead, especially after leaving Manhattan. It was 1980 and after four years in Colorado, right smack dab up against the adolescent thrusts of the Rocky Mountain range, I had settled in fiercely; I'd fallen into the natural rhythms of a childhood on a forest lookout station in the High Sierras.

"Telephone . . . long distance!" my grandmother shouted across the cornfield I'd worked all summer. Now my corn stood withering in the late October light, dried husks whispering in the cool winds.

"Who is it?" I asked breathlessly, taking the phone.

"Think I'd haul you all the way in here if it wasn't family?" my grandmother demanded in a huff. She was visiting this old farm, which had belonged to her eccentric brother and sister-in-law, and felt herself aswirl in their ghosts.

"Oh, Behba . . ." On the telephone line, my sister Marla's voice was also haunted, as if she were calling me not from cross-country, but from another territory I could barely fathom. I sensed only that she was inconsolable; I would be no help. I knew all this even before she told me. "I just can't believe it . . ."

I knew exactly what she was telling me without the words. We three sisters have talked in a sister telepathy for so many years that we only notice we aren't explaining ourselves if a stranger is around. Our tendency toward telepathy was only increased by our mother's landing a job at the CIA to cap her career of spying on her children over the intercom, the phones. And here again, we had to be secret. My grandmother stood right next to me in the farmhouse kitchen, trying to catch every unspoken word. "You sure?" I asked softly.

"Of course I'm sure! I'm a nurse, remember?" Marla reminded me tersely. "And the father is a doctor. You know it's so hard for us medical professionals to figure out birth control." Then she laughed, but it was not her usual wacky black humor.

"What are you going to do?" I asked softly and saw my grandmother's head cock sharply to the side. She suspected, I realized; her face took on an expression of disdain. She had never much liked her granddaughters; we all knew that. She'd doted on my brother instead.

"Is Grandma standing there?" Marla suddenly asked. "You can't let her know, please. Just tell her you have to come East for publishing business and stop off in Philadelphia to be with me. Will you, Behba? Will you do that for me?"

"Oh, yes," I said loudly so Grandmother could hear. "I have to come back to see my editor, anyway. It'll be . . . fun."

"Can you fly back tomorrow?" Marla asked.

"How long have you known?" I began and then stopped as I saw my grandmother furiously washing dishes, running the precious well water as if we had no drought. "I'll be there by the weekend," I promised. "We'll have . . . a good time."

Before I could even set the phone down in its cradle, my grandmother spun on me. "She's in trouble, isn't she? That Marla . . ."

"We've been planning this for weeks," I lied. "And you're going to run that well dry before we can get a new one dug."

"You girls are going to give your mother a nervous breakdown." My grandmother sent me a direct look, rare for her. Her scowl let me know that she suspected girl trouble and that no less could be expected from one of her granddaughters. I realized in that moment that I didn't like this grandmother. Once I had loved her dearly, even spent part of the first grade with her in southern Missouri, where she taught me Chinese checkers and told me intricate stories. But this grandmother had no attention left for us; instead Grandmother lavished upon our mother a fierce devotion that was at once dependent and cold. Grandmother's doting was not physical; she disliked touch the way a queen will push away her subjects, as if every embrace is a request for favors. I've often wondered if growing up the only girl in a family of five brothers left my grandmother physically isolated, without the companionable sensuality of sisters. She saw us as an unregenerate girl gang.

Our grandfather, on the other hand, loved his granddaughters and called us his "girlie girls." He was always crushing us to his stubbled chin and singing in a pure tenor he could make falsetto to match our high voices. We noticed that every time he tried to kiss Grandmother, she pushed him away with her apron. Years later, when I was in my twenties, she would tell me, "I just don't like the closeness. People get too close, don't you know?"

Grandmother had no girlfriends and disliked socializing. There was about her a melancholy she belied with a churchgoing cheerfulness. The time she was teaching college, during World War I, was the happiest in her life, she said. At the war's end, she was relegated to teaching kindergarten and raising her family. This pattern of feminine authority sought after, captured, and surrendered, runs deep in both my family lines. My other grandmother also taught college, astronomy, during the war, only to be fired when the men returned. And my mother had her heyday during World War II on the railroad, only to decide to leave the Wabash and follow my father into the wilds of the Forest Service where she, a town girl, languished. My mother wrote her first and only book when she was pregnant with me; it was read by New York City publishers and she received several handwritten rejection notes, which she was too isolated and inexperienced to recognize were invitations to revision. She put away her book and fell into writing long letters-to-the-editor.

From all the women ancestors in my family—a gallery of schoolteachers, poets, brilliant spinsters, and bright women blunted by tradition—my generation of sisters has inherited a strong storyline: Marriage can be creative death, or at least a detour. Don't take it; but if you do, never divorce.

That October day on my family's farm, half a continent away from my sister, I watched my grandmother putter around the farmhouse kitchen. She was much too busy, waiting for me to confide to her the real reason for my East Coast trip to see Marla. In the tense air between us I felt the weight of my grandmother's judgment against us, as if she had never been a young girl herself. Grandmother could not know then that the sister she proclaimed trouble would twelve years later take the most trouble with her as she lay dying. Marla would welcome Grandmother into her own home after she had lived with my parents for more than a decade; Marla would bathe and nurse her and, when she was dying, suction the bloody froth that continuously flowed from Grandmother's throat. During my Grandmother's last days, in the emergency room with Marla at her side, Grandmother grasped my sister's hand and said, "I think this is the end."

"Not necessarily, Grandma," Marla offered.

Still holding my sister's hand, Grandmother breathed, "Honey, I love you so much. I couldn't love you more if you were my own daughter."

But that October afternoon as I made my airline reservations, all I heard was my grandmother telling me how messy girls were, how they were always unpredictable, how you could never count on a woman. And yet it was on sisters that we sisters counted. That's what I thought days later when I sat beside my little sister in a Philadelphia women's clinic. Everywhere around us sat women in couples or triads, some teenagers knotted together in what seemed like a sorority: soft, treble whispers, heads leaning together, every color of hair and skin and eyes imaginable. Next to us sat an African-American trio with bright orange and fuchsia flowing dresses; these young girls wore their African trade-bead necklaces and dangling earrings as if they waited backstage for some high ceremony—a dance, a choir. There was a gravity about them, a mournfulness beyond their youth, and they held one another's hands tightly, in terror. Everyone in this clinic was so young, I suddenly thought. Where were the elders? If we all had been part of some women's society, or primitive tribe, there really would be ceremony, there would be wise women witnessing and helping us in this ancient and awe-inspiring sacrifice.

But instead there were white, sterile walls and a busy brusqueness about the nurses as they ushered the women in, not unkindly, but as if we were simply there for a routine medical procedure. We were processed expertly and when my sister was handed her ultrasound photo she tried to borrow that same clinical expertise as she studied her own embryo.

"Look, Behba," she said quietly, "it's so small."

I nodded, gazing at the obscure black-and-white squiggle. "Yes, I see it," I said.

Marla was silent a long time. Then she said, her voice full of wonder, "It's amazing."

"Yes," I echoed, "amazing."

I watched her tears make splotches on the ultrasound and I put my arm around her shoulder. We were surrounded by other sisters, mothers, and friends who waited with arms around each other's shoulders. This was the last time during my visit that I would be allowed to embrace Marla. Our last day together we had a terrible fight as I continued to plead with her to get an abortion.

"So how will you support this baby?" I demanded. "Move back to Virginia with Mom and Dad? Mosby, that's a nightmare!"

"Do you know one of my earliest childhood memories?" she shouted. "It's Mother in one of her bad spells locked in the bathroom and me—I'm so little I can't even reach the doorknob—standing outside howling and crying for her to let me inside. I would never consider asking Mom and Dad to help me raise this baby."

We sat in somber silence for several minutes. Then Marla said quietly, "You know, you were always Mom's favorite."

No one had ever said it aloud before, even in our sibling skirmishes, though we sisters knew that because I looked so much like Mother, because she had stared into my eyes as if into a mirror, I somehow bleeped on her very vague radar. Paula (with whom Mother fought) and Marla did not break through my mother's moodiness. We sisters also knew without ever speaking about it that my brother, Dana, was the most favored child, being the last, the end to Mother's childbearing chores, and a boy. Mother, unlike her mother, liked the company of other women, had many girlfriends, but she, too, had fallen into her mother's misogyny and turned to the males around her with the charm and dependence of the traditional Southern belle. At the same time she deferred to and served my father and my brother, Mother also had a subversive and cunning contempt for men. It showed in making fun of them behind their backs. Often, she escaped my father's reign by making the church her career, and once she ran off with her girlfriends to lobby for women's rights at the Southern Baptist convention. When we lived in California, she moved a woman friend who was studying for her Ph.D. at UC Berkeley right into our home, where she happily pitted my father's rather authoritative intellect against her friend's philosophical brilliance. We sisters always got the message from our mother that if she'd had the courage, she would never have married, would have led her life on the stage or on the railroad. But she had been trapped by her times, she suggested; and now that she was so ensconced, she staunchly defended her position, much the way a servant will identify with the masters and punish all insurrection from below. Below, of course, were her daughters.

"Yes, all right." I gave Marla a level look. "I am Mother's favorite of us girls. But have you ever thought what it might be like being a vampire's favorite? I feel like I've had to be Mother's feeling-eye dog and I've finally resigned from that. Or haven't you noticed?"

"I've noticed!" Marla shouted. "And now you're trying to lead me on a leash in my own life. Give it up, Behba! Give up this big-sister crap and stop telling me what to do!"

"You asked me to come here." I grabbed her arm with sisterly authority. "If you don't want to be a little sister, don't act like one."

Marla glared back at me with a look of determined defiance and shook off my grip. She faced me and said darkly, "This is *my* life and my decision! And I won't have an abortion!"

Once before I'd felt this dismay and disorientation when my big sister's physical authority and benevolent tyranny over my siblings was overthrown, but it had been years ago when I was eight and Paula was six. I'd commanded her to fetch me a Coca-Cola and she'd turned to me with a wondering look on her face and stammered, "Nnnnn-no!"

In disbelief I faced Paula in my eldest-sister majesty and pronounced steadily, "Co-ca . . . Co-la . . . *now!*"

As if amazed by her own mutiny, Paula had stood her ground. "No," she said again, this time without any tremor in her voice. "You got legs. Get it yourself."

With the predatory grace of physical omnipotence, I stretched, and then leapt onto Paula, each hand pulling her ponytails. This little lion-cub tumble was all it usually took to stifle any insurrection. But Paula shocked me with a resounding punch to the belly and then she bodily picked me up and threw me over a hassock which rolled over and over like a wagon wheel with me around it. When I finally bounced to a stop against the bookshelves, I gazed up at my sister with the true respect of deep alarm. "Wow," was all I could say. Only then had I noticed how much bigger-boned she was than I; her sturdy biceps easily outflexed my thin arms. Compared to her solid rib cage I was birdlike, fragile. We were both very thin, gangly, with strong, athletic legs. But there was no contest anymore in wrestling, as there would always be in sprinting or sports.

But this fight with Marla over abortion was more than a childhood tussle and tumble. We were adults and we were very angry, capable of doing real harm to each other. We had spent so many of our years bonding against the common enemy of our parents, especially our abusive mother, that we had never imagined or explored our own capacity for violence. I knew that I was perfectly capable of becoming abusive myself, that it was patterned into my body. What mattered was that we both deeply registered our rage and pain.

"Oh, Behba." Marla turned back and held me. "Let's not fight."
She started to cry.

Then I wept, too. I sobbed because I knew something was broken
between us. Even as we embraced each other we were separated by
our beliefs and choices. And that deep philosophical distance would
in the next decades divide Marla and myself more surely than the
continent between us.

As children growing up in the South, no matter what our personal
squabbles, my sisters and brother and I were always on the same side.
Our parents were akin to Yankees. Not so anymore. As I stand in my
Seattle voting booth casting my liberal pro-choice ballot, I know that
in Virginia my little sister Marla is vigorously voting for a pro-life
candidate after having spent six months as an anti-abortion lobbyist
in Washington, D.C., and is now active in pro-life state politics. Then
there is Paula down in Florida who, though more conservative than I,
is a staunch supporter of a woman's right to choose. And my brother,
Dana, volunteers at a Christian pro-life crisis counseling center.

Recently, when Marla was interviewed on television for her pro-life
views, I decided to give a reading in support of abortion rights, and
Paula countered by commenting in one of our three-sisters' conference
calls, "Hey, Mosby, I just wrote another big check to NARAL [Na-
tional Abortion Rights Action League]. Call it checkmate, sis. Your
move."

Marla's move was to tell us casually that she'd just returned from
the Virginia State Republican Convention where she and other Christian conservatives schmoozed in hospitality suites as if attending a
high-school reunion. It was only the next day when I opened my *New
York Times* that I realized their platform was one of the country's most
extreme far-right agendas—vowing to restrict abortion, limit homo-
sexual rights, and defeat gun control measures. We sisters try to find
our usual light tone when talking about abortion; the feelings are so
deep, humor is the only balm. And sometimes I swear I can hear us
grinding our teeth when we talk on the phone. We sisters often make
the dark joke that all throughout childhood we played Civil War,
reenacting Confederacy vs. Union, brother-against-brother battles;

now we spend our adulthood engaged in a civil war that separates us as sisters.

It is one of the great ironies of my sisterhood that Marla, whose childhood was one of conciliation, angelic sweetness, and temperance, would grow up to be a passionate activist in the anti-abortion movement. I often wonder, is Marla's crusading a comment on her own sisterhood?

"Where did we go wrong?" I often ask Paula, only half-teasing. I feel such dismay and guilt when I hear of Marla donning her white nurse's uniform and counseling other women outside abortion clinics, that it seems as if I have indeed failed her somehow. So I feel compelled to counteract and balance her in the wider world.

When did it begin, my little sister's righteous advocacy? Certainly some of Marla's activism had its roots in our religious upbringing. But in those days Marla was too sweet-tempered to fight for her faith. Often Paula and I worried that our little sister was really The Littlest Angel or actually that "angel unaware" the cowgirl Dale Evans memorialized in the book our mother read us at bedtime. We suspected Marla was a secret angel because she was always smiling serenely, as if she knew something we didn't; or worse, because her soul was originally sweet, never sinful like Paula's and mine. We were often listed as Top Ten on the church's weekly prayer list for various sins —playing hookey from Girls' Auxiliary or sneaking into the church to steal grape juice and crackers used for communion. We had a secret hiding place under the baptistry where we rendezvoused with the preacher's boys. There we held bubble gum-blowing contests, exploding each bright pink puff with forbidden kisses.

Marla was so sweet she didn't even snitch on her older sisters. Now, that was really scary. So how did this model of saintly childhood grow into the woman who once at an abortion clinic sit-in was carried off to jail, wearing her green nursing surgical scrubs?

"Maybe pro-life activism is Mosby's idea of sainthood," I suggested to Paula recently when we were trying to fathom Marla's strong campaigning against abortion.

Marla's child, whom I first saw in that women's clinic in 1980 as an ultrasound tadpole, is now fifteen and has two brothers. The doctor father, who first deserted my sister, repented, became a born-again

Christian, and they eventually married when their first son was three years old.

In 1983, they moved back to Georgia. When their oldest son was in first grade my sister began home schooling because they believed the public school system was a total failure, both academically and morally. Now they are back in Virginia, living near my parents, and Marla is deeply involved in right-wing conservative politics through her work with the Christian Coalition. Marla is a brilliant strategist and speaker for her cause.

What keeps us three sisters from each other's throats is a complicated and continual negotiating pact not to trepass on one another's political territories. There is a certain sister sovereignty, a respect for "otherness" that for us, as for many other siblings, is hard-earned. We have shaped our identities by defining our differences, as well as our shared realms—compare and contrast, the age-old discipline of delineating character. It is one way of learning about ourselves and the world around us.

I remember showing a picture of my family to a psychologist friend. He stared at the snapshot a long time, then let out a sigh of recognition. "Every time I look at a family photo, I expect to see maybe one, at the most two, family members who are what I call *awake.*" He shook his head and laughed. "But every damn person in this family is wide awake and staring straight out at you. Look at those faces, full of passion and conviction. Yikes! How are your family reunions?"

"When all the relatives get together, we've had fights over whose religion gets to say grace," I answered. "And we argue issues and talk about politicians as if they were far-flung relatives. We take everything personally, especially current events."

"A family of true believers," he murmured. "And every one of you believes something different. What a nightmare!"

It's not a nightmare, but the continual dance of the political and the personal in my family can at times take on a certain dreamlike and dark quality.

In the dog days of August 1993, my sister Paula called with one of her weekly "Family Flashes." She is Communications Central among us siblings and we rely upon her for the latest bulletins.

"Listen to this!" she breathed. Even though she was cross-country, her tone was as intimate and confiding as a tête-à-tête. "In one week all of us sisters have had national coverage! Right after your cover story on abortion in *New Age Journal* hit the stands, I'm sitting in my bedroom sobbing over these horrible divorce mediations with my soon-to-be-I-hope ex-husband. I'm crying into the phone to a girl-friend when I see out of the corner of my eye this woman on my TV. The sound is turned down and I'm eyeballing the stock reports when I think, 'That woman looks familiar . . . that woman looks really familiar . . .' Then I scream and drop the phone. That woman was our dear sistuh!" She said this last in her best shocked Southern aristocratic lady accent.

"Marla on national news again," I groaned. "Her campaigning against fetal tissue research on that TV sound bite was bad enough." But some part of me is smiling and I realize that I am proud of her, my little sister, making news—even though I don't agree with the news she's making. It is a strange mixture, these two opposite feelings of sibling pride and dismay. "She's at it again," I said. "What is it this time?"

"Well, I called Mosby and she's taped it . . . will send. I'll copy it for you. Apparently CNBC called her about the Christian Coalition's stand on tax issues. Right after her TV appearance, there was a note on the new pact between the Christian Coalition and Pope John Paul, who are joining forces to fight abortion at the 1994 Cairo conference on population."

"How can Mosby join forces with the Anti-Christ of our childhood?" I demanded, laughing. As Southern Baptists we were taught the Evil Empire was not just in Russia, but in Rome. I well remember people in my parents' church promising that if John Kennedy were elected, he would hand his presidency over to the Pope like a Communion wafer.

"Politics makes strange bedfellows," Paula continued. "Thank God, the Pope is celibate. Can you imagine the offspring of such a union? And there'd be no aborting the little monster, of course."

"Speaking of little monsters, let's call Mo when I'm in Florida with you and tease her about the Pope."

Days later driving up from the Florida Keys, Paula and I called Marla from the car phone and put her on speaker phone. Outside the car, the hurricane-wasted landscape south of Homestead spoke eloquently of Hurricane Andrew's visit a year earlier.

"Hey, Mo," Paula began, shouting over the van's engine and air-conditioning. "We're here in Homestead, scene of total devastation. We thought of you and the Pope."

Marla laughed heartily. "How appropriate you two call when Hurricane Emily is headed toward our coasts. How are you, and, oh, the Pope is fine."

"So what did you wear on CNBC, Mosby?" I demanded as withered trees and palms propped up by two-by-fours whizzed past the windshield.

"Oh, a silk blouse and skirt. You know, conservative, but . . ."

"Elegant!" we all three finished with a flourish. We have a sister joke about silk blouses since we can wear the same size and lend one another our best silk shirts whenever we're together. We also have a tradition of freely "borrowing" one another's clothes, like the time I temporarily stole Marla's white satin teddy, a shower gift to her, which I wore to her wedding.

"What color silk blouse?" I ask.

"Blue. You know, our color, looks good with our eyes."

"Can I borrow it?" Pooh chimes in. "I'm going to call all the television stations and ask for equal time for my rebuttal."

Paula was also on television that week quite unexpectedly. Walking out of the local courthouse the morning her divorce was final, she was swarmed by a CNN film crew.

"Are you aware that in the 1962 Cuban missile crisis, President Kennedy conducted his embargo strategy from a secret island bunker right off the coast here? What do you think of that?"

"That's fine," Paula said. "A president needs to be calm and safe to make national security decisions. Besides, I think you should turn that bunker into a Cold War museum."

The reporter asked her what she was doing in the courthouse.

"I was finally getting divorced," Paula said. And the reporter gave her a high-five.

"I wanted to go on and add that I felt like I was in the twilight zone, Behba," she told me later. "There I was, just out of a marriage to a crazy Cuban and a survivor of our family's Cold War . . . when here this reporter is sticking a microphone in my face and asking me how I felt about some civil defense bunker. I wanted to tell him, 'Hey, Bucko, where was that bunker when I needed it?'"

"So," Paula took up again. "Don't you think it just a little bit odd that I walk out of my divorce court to be asked to comment on the Cold War's Cuban missile crisis after the Armageddon of my marriage?"

Together, without any signal, we both hum the theme song to "Twilight Zone." I remark, "It seems only right that CNN would film that historic moment when you can walk away from a Cold War and reemerge from your bunker."

"Well, at least it was upscale CNN and not the *National Enquirer*. You know, like those photos of pasty-faced people who've been buried in fallout shelters for decades thinking they were the last people on earth and wondering if it's safe to come out?"

"It's safe," I tell her, hoping that it's not a lie.

Then she falls quiet and we give way to a companionable stillness, even though it is long-distance and the phone bill is ticking away. Paula and I often fall quiet on the phone, but the conversation continues, telepathically. This time, we both know we have again fallen into the mystery that is our little sister.

Suddenly I ask, "Do you realize that we three sisters all came of age in different places?" I scraggled into my adolescence somewhere between Virginia and Berkeley, California. Paula was the only one of us sisters who finished high school in one place, California. And Marla got her high school years divided like me, but between California and Georgia.

Paula has stayed in the South (in Florida) ever since she left California in her freshman year in college to go to Emory University in Atlanta. She is very Southern in her graciousness and sense of class, but her adolescence in California's 1960s still informs her open nature. Though Paula and I disagreed on the Vietnam War (she was for it) and she considers herself a moderate pro-choice Republican, she still escaped the fundamentalism that reunited Marla with the Southland.

I remember the stifling summer of 1971 when my father upped and moved us once again, to Georgia. And once again it was cross-country—it might as well have been cross-culturally. Every move of the many we made as children (on the average, every year and a half) was drastic, most of them coast-to-coast: from the wilds of the High Sierras on a Forest Service lookout station to Harvard and the amusement park slum of Revere Beach, Massachusetts; from Boston to the

vast horizons of Missoula, Montana (where we moved into three houses
in eighteen months); from Montana to Northern Virginia and the
nation's nearby capital; from aristocratic, conservative Virginia to Berkeley's People's Park. We three sisters stuck together in every move,
bewildered and often lost.

"Moving was like dropping acid," Paula said ruminatively. "Except
the trip never ended. You were stuck in the hallucination of a new
place and never got back to what was normal or familiar."

In Georgia in 1970, Marla and I were without our third sister for
the first time ever. Paula was promised that if she changed colleges
and followed the family south, she could take the summer to say good-
bye to her California friends. I was under quite a different dictum
from my father: My longed-for return to the University of California,
where I'd just finished my sophomore year, was directly dependent
upon how well I helped the rest of the family adjust to Georgia. "Your
job this summer, Brenda Sue, is to settle this family down here in the
South." My father laid down the law in the voice we call his Chief
Peterson command tones. "If your mother, brother, and sister don't
adjust well, you'll just have to stay and go to school here. You can
forget ever going back to California."

It was during that endless, desolate summer that Marla and I
bonded deeply again, as we would sit in the hot, black Georgia nights
and talk. Years later Marla would tell me, "If you hadn't been there
with me that summer, it would have been unbearable."

The pressure of my father's threat hung over me as profoundly as
the Georgia humidity—a heat that was so intense and foreboding that
many nights I awoke with the sheets wrapped around me like a
mummy shroud. And no matter how often we soaked our sheets in
cool water to sleep (we had no air-conditioning for three months), the
nights were a never-ending swelter. My mother, a dyed-in-the-wool
Southern Baptist, was mortified to play hostess to a plague of fundamentalist visitors who believed she must have backslid from her years
out West. No matter how hard she tried, Mother couldn't convince
these women who came "witnessing" that she was saved and truly one
of them. Neither Mother's Southern accent, which had survived decades outside the South, nor her credentials as church organist in such
far-flung outposts as a Southern Baptist church that met in a garage
in Missoula, Montana, convinced these missionaries that she was still

among the sistership of the believers. Miserably, Mother wept after each visit of various churches' Women's Missionary Unions.

"I used to be the president of my W.M.U. group," she'd proclaim.

The visiting harpies would look at her and shake their heads like a Greek chorus. "Sister, isn't it time you rededicated your life to Jesus?" they'd insist.

"It's because you've been living in California, Mother," I'd try to soothe her. "That's like living in a whole state of sin to these people —Sodom and Gomorrah. Don't let it get you down. Just join a church and then you'll be in with the in-crowd again."

Put in the position of helping my family make a happy transition to this strange and violent Georgia landscape, I was helpless to heal my little sister's and my mother's pain. I had my own. Just before moving I had suffered a miscarriage and broken up with my boyfriend. That blistering, shadowy summer of 1970 in Georgia, I lived in terror that I would also lose my college life if my father condemned me to stay in the South and never return to California. It was during those dreary, humid days when Mother spent afternoons locked in her room weeping and my little sister Marla and I sat downcast in our bedrooms mourning the losses left behind that we found some refuge in our sisterhood. I did not confide to Marla the story of my own recent miscarriage. Nor did Marla confide to me her despair, at seventeen, over losing her first boyfriend. We didn't talk about our personal lives; instead we found refuge in artistic discussions and trying to fathom this Southern society.

This was a strange new world, this rural Georgia high school in which Marla was seen as an alien because of her Western accent and the "hippie clothes" she wore. That summer I remember sitting with Marla every day down by the Yellow River in the backyard, skipping stones over the pale, shining currents. She was reading Shakespeare and *Look Homeward, Angel*, in which she would later star in the high school production. That was the summer Marla began writing, a talent that she still uses today in her own pro-life activism. But that Georgia summer when just we two sisters were together was like getting to know Marla all over again.

We found that we shared a dark sense of humor and a wacky playfulness, even about our grim situation that summer. I found my youngest sister unexpectedly philosophical and dreamy. I had assumed she was as pragmatic and earthy as Paula. But those days down by the Yellow River we drew closer to each other than we have ever been since—when we fell back into our roles of the three sisters with Paula the intermediary.

I remember leaving Georgia at the end of the summer, given permission to go by a father who pronounced my summer job of "The Transition" a C-plus grade. Leaving Marla in that kudzu-ridden Southland of fundamentalists and humidity, I felt I had betrayed her. That sense of having deserted my sister simply by going on with my life—remains with me today.

To continue with my life, I left my sisters at home. That's the way it should be, but during the next decade, Marla went through nursing school; she lost her "hippie" stigma and became a Southern belle, star of senior plays, and gained a reputation as a high-school intellectual, a budding writer. Our parents still dragged her to their Southern Baptist Church, and she was briefly engaged to a churchgoing Georgia boy. What would my little sister's life have been like if she'd stayed and settled in the West? For that matter, what would any of our lives have become if we had settled in anywhere, instead of enduring such transience?

Now, as adults, we are scattered all over the country. The childhood pattern of moving has continued into our adulthoods, with the exception of myself who has fiercely rooted in here on the shores of Puget Sound for more than twelve years. Paula is in Florida, Marla in Virginia, and my brother, with his navy career, is jetting around between Virginia and Monterey. By comparison, my parents seem downright grounded in Virginia, where they've stayed for the past fifteen years.

In 1989, after my grandfather's funeral my sisters and I decided to take a trip together back through the South. As we barreled along the back roads, I began to notice that other motorists were waving at us, some shaking their heads, others flashing the raised fist, right-on sign. Few cars passed us without comment. Some drove by grimly avoiding eye contact, and some honked as if we were all in the same wedding party. "Hey, what's going on?" I asked my little sister.

"You'll see," she said slyly and grinned.

At the next gas station, I took the notion to check Marla's bumper stickers. There, emblazoned in neon letters, was the sign IF YOU CAN READ THIS—THANK THE DOCTOR WHO DIDN'T ABORT YOU!

I stood there silently, feeling both shocked and bemused. It was disorienting and oddly comical to be driving around inside my sister's opinions.

"Kind of like getting stuck inside my mind, isn't it, Behba?" Marla laughed. "Enemy territory."

"But we're not really enemies," interjected Paula, always the peace-maker, the Great Communicator, as we call her. "Enemies can't sing perfect three-part harmony."

"Or play on the same baseball team," I said, referring to our child-hood years in Virginia when we kids played softball on our own home-made field, complete with dugout, wooden bases, and even an announcer's stand atop our tree fort.

"I never played on your team," Marla said sadly. As Paula and I turned to her in shock, she continued, "Don't you remember? You both and the neighbor boys wouldn't let me play. You said I wasn't old enough or good enough to hit and throw the ball. You made me sit in the announcer's stand and call the games."

Paula and I were aghast. We didn't remember excluding Marla from our play. How else had we unthinkingly excluded her?

"But at least you were allowed in our tree fort," Paula said lamely.

"Oh, yeah, right." Marla made to smile, but her face was serious, resentful. "The little fort with its play-by-play announcer's stand was my place. But you and the other guys never let me into your real fort, the one hidden in the woods with a secret lock and rope ladder. I never saw the inside of that secret hiding place."

"Maybe you're lucky." Paula said, trying to make light of it. "The magic password was that you had to kiss Butch Horton, Mr. Juvenile Delinquent himself, to be allowed in. You didn't really miss much, Mosby."

But she had. Both Paula and I knew our little sister had missed out on a secret tree fort that was the envy of the neighborhood. It was complete with shag rug, sun roof, canned food, flashlight, and even magazines for lazing about on the lookout. As big sisters, we had never allowed Marla up into our tree fort, not admitting her to our club.

It occurred to me as we drove along Southern back roads singing together that Marla had indeed found her own club, which again separated us three sisters. In describing her pro-life allies Marla has called these sister-travelers her "philosophical comrades." As we drove down those humid Georgia back roads in our Sisters' Express, I looked over at my sister Marla and said, "You know, Mosby, we got thrown out of that fort, too, our own tree house. Some of the big boys in the neighborhood conquered it and made it their headquarters."

"Oh, forget it," Marla said from the back of the van and pulled my hair lightly, as if I still had pigtails. "It's all right that you two big sisters shut me out of all your secret games and forts. I know I was the lost child."

She said it so matter-of-factly, it broke my heart.

"Ain't we all lost children, sistuh?" Paula intoned.

I couldn't laugh. I was remembering a scene from our childhood: we three, two years apart in age, sitting in a makeshift Montana church. The preacher shouts, "It was Eve who ate that apple from the Tree of the Knowledge of Good and Evil. And in going against God's will, in eating the fruit poisoned with mortality, that woman condemned us all to exile from God's sweet Garden. Eve listened to the serpent and her own sinful self, instead of her precious Lord!" We shuddered, we three terrified sisters, little descendants of Eve.

It was 1958, and we little sinners were living that year in the shadow of glacial ranges and yawning green wilderness; we sisters and brother spent most of our days running through the woods playing like primitive tribes. Those days we lived so far away from other kids that it was just us kids together. We played wild horses with an elaborate caste system that included my brother as a small stallion. At Sunday school, our teacher, as if sensing the unbroken, fine horseflesh of such high-strung fillies, would glare at us girls as if her lectures were lassos. "Little women have to work especially hard for our Lord's redemption. We were the first in all creation to go against His Divine Will."

Sometimes it seemed hopeless to a nine-year-old. I often had trouble covering my utter bewilderment with my big-sister authority when my sisters asked me to explain our Sunday school teacher's "sermonettes," as she called them.

"Do you think God will ever forgive us for eating that stupid apple?" Paula asked once as we all loped along the open range.

"Nope," I said, and suddenly felt a strange happiness within. At that moment I knew that, no matter what I did, as long as I was female I would always be Eve's daughter. I somehow intuited that being forgiven by this angry Father God might be the same as being broken—the sharp bit of blame always turning me this way and that. Better to be a wild filly with no righteous rider.

That day, when I felt the happy hopelessness of an unforgiven female, I wondered if this feeling was an echo of the "still, small voice" the preacher was always talking about. But when I asked my Sunday school teacher whether my still, small voice belonged to me or to God, she corrected me soundly. "Nothing about you belongs to you," she pronounced. "Except for your sin."

After that I kept my voice quiet, except with my sisters. The only time we opened our mouths in church was to sing the prescribed songs. One song stays with me:

> On a hill far away stood an old rugged cross
> The emblem of suffering and shame
> And I love that old cross . . .

This is not a hymn we three sisters sang three decades later as we cruised along in our Sisters' Express on the Southern back roads. That Baptist hymn would have stirred us up into an abortion debate with me demanding to know how the fetus had come to replace Christ on the symbolic cross of pro-life marchers. During this trip we declared ourselves in a neutral, demilitarized zone.

In Atlanta we all got dolled up in our best evening clothes for a fancy restaurant date together. At that time my two younger sisters were indulging in forbidden territory—cigarettes. We all also drank alcohol, which is rare for us, since we have inherited zero tolerance from six generations of teetotalers and Indian blood. All of us were off guard when Paula suddenly cozied up to Marla and asked sweetly, "How did you get so . . . so right-wing, Mo?" She lit Marla's cigarette with a tipsy flourish and laughed. "Or maybe I should ask, where did your big sisters fail you?"

"Oh, yes," Marla joked, "it's been a living hell putting up with two sinners like you all my life."

"Three sisters," Paula took up, "two sinners and one saint. Remember when we believed you were really an angel unaware?"

Marla fell silent and bowed her head. All levity was gone now among the three of us. Marla sighed and said, 'None of us is an angel. We've all made personal decisions which ended up hurting us."

As she spoke we three exchanged knowing glances. We'd all been through so much, sometimes together, sometimes feeling very much alone. I often feel completely alone in my own family. There are times when I cannot even confide in my closest sister, Paula, for fear that she will be confused or critical of my beliefs. I do not feel judgment from my siblings as I do from my parents, but I do feel at times deeply unknown and unmet.

Once I told my little sister Marla that I felt very alone in our family, to which she responded with sympathy and a kindly "Oh, I'm sorry, Behba. Sometimes I feel alone too."

"But how can you when the whole family is so . . . so Republican and conservative and . . . traditional . . ." I said.

My sister said nothing, just listened patiently. What could she say? If she was the lost child in our family, I am in the tradition of that mythic ugly duckling who, upon maturity, recognizes that her own wingspan is simply different. Perhaps now as adults it is these differences which most define us, rather than our shared childhood.

As we three sisters sat in that Atlanta bar, a candle's glow illuminating our faces—these family faces that share the same eyes, slope of cheekbone, and strong jaw—I reflected again upon our profound differences. How difficult it was to learn and understand the delicate steps in our lifelong sister minuet. Often we could not help but sometimes step on one another's toes just by being who we really are, while also seeking sisterhood.

That Sisters' Express marked an important journey for us. We have not traveled together alone as sisters since that post-funeral 1989 road trip. We have seen each other separately and sometimes burned up the cross-country phone lines so that it often feels that my sisters live right next door. Other times there will be lapses when we three sisters connect less frequently. Recently, there was another occasion for sister conferences and what I've come to call "Sister Summits" by phone.

In the fall of 1993, after I published my "Sister Against Sister" cover article in *New Age Journal*, there was a family cataclysm in response to my story of our family's infighting over the issue of abortion. Marla let it be known through the sibling hot line that she was furious with me for my portrait of her as pro-life activist.

"But how in the world did Mosby ever find out about that piece?" I asked my brother, who was the first to break the news to me that Marla was on the warpath. My little brother also feels strongly against abortion, but he is not a political activist like Marla. He is as conservative as she is, and yet they share a wonderfully dark sense of humor, which keeps us siblings all talking. "I never expected Mosby to read *New Age Journal*. I mean, after all, Dad says that Mom thinks I've gone cult for publishing in magazines like that."

"You aren't going to believe this, big sis." My brother laughed, obviously bemused. "But Marla got wind of your abortion piece when a pro-life friend of hers called to say she'd read an excerpt of your article in a California pro-life newsletter. Seems your article bleeped bigtime on their radar!" joked Dana Mark.

"What did Mosby do?"

"You know Mo." Dana laughed. "She immediately went to her local library and looked it up for herself. She was really angry at you." My brother's voice dropped and he sighed. "You know, sis, I think she's just hurt you didn't talk to her before publishing it. She just wants to be included, don't you think?"

"But she'd censor everything!" I protested.

"Sure she would." My brother laughed softly. "So would I, if I had the chance. You know what I thought after you sent me the article?"

"I'm afraid to ask."

"I thought, well, there's one simple solution to your writing." He paused for effect. "I decided I just won't teach my girls to read and write!"

We laughed together and again I felt that odd mixture of dismay and delight when dealing with my younger, more conservative siblings. "Oh, little brother," I sighed. "How did we get to be on opposite sides? We were always such little soldiers together. Rebels."

"We grew up," he said simply. "We've gone our different—and some might say—weird ways."

"But we've never gone over to the Yankees, although your navy's pretty damn close."

He laughed. "Call your sister," he suggested. "She's standing by."

When I called Marla Mosby she told me she resented most that I'd published her story and described her beliefs without checking it all out with her beforehand. "How would you like it if I wrote about your life in my conservative publications?"

"I'm sure it wouldn't be a flattering picture," I admitted.

"Listen," she said, "you know I'm not an extremist . . ." She paused. "For example, I think killing abortion doctors is a terrible violation of all that the pro-life movement stands for. But you make me out to be some kind of fanatic."

I was quiet. At times my sister has seemed fanatical to me, but I'm sure I often appear the same way from her point of view. How could we be such anti-matter to each other? Where I am gray and ambiguous, Marla is sure and straight. Where I am passionately concerned about the natural world, its environment, and animals, my sister is devoted to preserving the inner world of womb and baby. Sometimes I wondered if the fundamentalist focus on a woman's womb as a kind of Garden of Eden before birth (and on original sin) wasn't a poignant wish for a return to paradise.

And yet my sister and I did share that same sense of longing for what was violated to be healed—she, any aborted baby, and I our ravaged natural world. On the phone with Marla I had to smile. She and I were alike after all—both devoting ourselves to the rights of the Other, whether it was unborn or animal.

When I was working on the chapters of this book about my own sisters, I called upon both Marla and Paula for readings and critiques—and I got much more than I ever bargained for, in the form of impassioned letters, frank disagreements, and helpful corrections. With both sisters I spent hours on the phone comparing our versions of childhood, our memories of exact events, and our different philosophical points of view. Once, after an all-day phone session with Marla, trying to present a portrait of her that was both true to her own sense of self and to my point of view, I found myself realizing that Marla had not asked me for direct counsel since that time long ago in 1980 when I flew back to Philadelphia to convince her to have an abortion. That fetus we first studied in an ultrasound is now a teenager and a gifted artist. I send him art magazines and he sends me stunning wildlife drawings that have earned him awards.

"Is that abortion fight really the last time you called me for my sisterly counsel, Mosby?" I found myself wondering, saddened.

"I think so," she murmured, trying to remember. "It's not that I didn't ever ask your advice, it's just that . . ." She sighed. "Well . . . we're so different philosophically. But you're wrong when you say that I substituted my pro-life philosophical sisterhood for you and Paula. I always knew who my real sisters were." Then Marla laughed good-humoredly. "I just knew that philosophically we're going such differ-ent paths, I can't exactly ask you-all for directions on how to get where I want to go!"

Marla reminded me that she did not get involved in pro-life activ-ism until about six years after she'd given birth to her first son. So she relieved me of some guilt I'd been carrying about my long-ago abortion counsel sending her reeling off into pro-life activism. "It was a slow and deepening commitment that had very little to do with my own sisters and everything to do with my own soul's work," she explained.

"So you don't think that we . . . that I somehow failed you, Mosby?"

"Get real!" She laughed. "Do you think success is someone being just like you?"

There she had me again in a philosophical checkmate—what I've come to expect from my debates with my sisters. But as I've worked on this book I've come to understand again that between my little sister and myself it is not as much a point-counterpoint chess game as a dance—truly a minuet.

A dance is not a march or a rally or a battle in which sides must be clearly aligned or nothing is ever won or accomplished. A dance goes in circles and is an intricate mirroring of only graceful steps, not philosophical solidarity. The solidarity is in moving in synch with the music, not the message. No one can dance to a political speech or battle cry; dancing is what is done in the trenches between the wars, or when one is resting and embracing the Other with gladness, some-times wariness, and often recognition.

I thought about this sometimes tense, sometimes wonderful dance between my sisters and myself when I read the phrase "intimate en-emy" in the work of Gnostic scholar Elaine Pagels. If I had to portray myself under any philosophical label it would be, I suppose, as Taoist/ animist/pagan, and Marla has described herself as a fundamentalist Christian. There was a time in early centuries when orthodox Chris-tians, Jews, pagans, and mystical Gnostics all danced together in a chaotic, exhilarating plurality, before monotheistic religions took hold.

Today we often see an angry divide between the orthodox and mystical traditions.

The best way I've learned to describe myself in relation to my little sister, brother, and parents is to say with more respect than judgment, that they follow an orthodox path and I a mystical one. There are, of course, orthodox and mystical traditions existing within one religion, as the Kabbalistic exists within Judaism, the Zen practices within Buddhism, or the Sufis within Islam. I remember a friend telling me once that she suspected the next war in the twenty-first century would be not between rich and poor or different countries, but rather between the universal and fundamentalist minds, whatever the nationality.

But that war will only come if each tradition demonizes the intimate other. In Pagels's work, she traces the evolving, intertwined histories of God and Satan to explain the philosophy of the "intimate enemy" that is so much with us today. In an exploration of Pagels's writing, David Remnick in *The New Yorker* illuminates Pagels's concern over the "literature and the rise of demonization, a practice that has haunted two thousand years of history. For Pagels, demonization is a crucial and terrifying component of Christianity." It has led Western civilization to portray the world as a battle with "the great Other in a cosmic war . . . Us and Them." When the New Testament writers created a "psychology of cosmic war . . ." it then "influenced the course—the tragic course—of Western history."

I do not want the story of my sisterhood to be a tragedy. We will have tragedy enough in knowing that as siblings we will see each other through life—and death. Nor do I want to see my little sister, who is so philosophically opposed to me, as an intimate enemy. We must be very careful, and that means we must take great care with each other, we must not demonize the other to prove ourselves right-eously right. We were both raised in a fundamentalist tradition and so our mutual training is this Us-Them intimate war.

"You know, Mosby," I said as we again talked over this book to-gether, arguing, changing, refining it so we both could agree at least on this portrait, if not on anything else, "some sisters don't talk for years when they disagree. I'm glad we're still talking, even if I really don't like what you're saying!"

"I can't imagine not talking with you, Behba, even when sometimes every word that comes out of your mouth drives me up a wall!"

Then I had to tell her, though I didn't want to, though I wondered if I might regret it, "Well, I do feel closer to you after all this. You've actually, well, I think you've made this book . . . better."

"Well, being a frustrated writer myself, I've always wanted to rewrite other people's books. This is fun, isn't it? In a masochistic sort of way."

There was a silence on the phone and I realized how healing it was to talk with her, how much I had missed her those years when we kept a polite distance, neither of us confronting the other on our own abortion beliefs. It was like dancing with someone who no longer steps on one's feet, because we have practiced the steps until we know instinctively how to find some common movement, some shared music.

Already we are planning another family reunion—with fear and trembling and pleasure. This year it will be in Nashville, Southern bastion of churchfolk. But there is also music in that town and we intend to go out dancing with our kissing cousins every night. Who knows what arguments will break out over Sunday services—but some of us plan to worship with our dances and songs.

Though it feels like a final act for this book on sisters, it is a continuing drama and dance between my siblings, one that mirrors a larger schism in our society. I believe that if I can understand my own siblings, then perhaps I learn compassion for the wider, diverse world—for that is what siblings also teach us, from birth to death— how to be fully together while also individuals, how to heal and accept our differences without easy answers or denial. It is a healing and a reunion which begins first at home, then translates into all the sister- hoods and brotherhoods around us.

Recently I found myself talking about abortion again on the phone with my little sister. She had just signed on to direct a state campaign for another pro-life presidential candidate.

"I want to acknowledge something, Mo," I began, hardly knowing what I was going to say myself. "All this time you've been fighting against abortion, maybe you were unconsciously carrying some of my own ambivalence about it."

Marla was flabbergasted. "But you *believe* in abortion." She was very quiet and I could feel between us a deepening alliance, something I hadn't felt with my little sister since those Georgia days as teenagers down by the Yellow River when we spent hours skipping stones and talking philosophy. "It's funny, Behba, I haven't been to an anti-abortion march in almost six months. In the past, I was more involved in the social protest pro-life movement. Now I've moved into a more political advocacy role."

"This is all news to me," I marveled. "Have your . . . have your views really modified, would you say?"

"Not really," she said. "I'm still very much against abortion, but I believe it's more effective to get out the message to women that there is a caring network of people who will help them in their crisis pregnancies—so they won't feel forced to choose abortion." She paused thoughtfully. "For years, we pro-lifers were the only women talking about abortion, you know, Behba, while you feminists acted like it was as simple as getting wisdom teeth taken out."

"I never believed that abortion was simple," I said quietly. "You know I've always thought it was a deep moral decision needing much solace, spiritual and emotional . . . and a real sisterhood."

There was a deep silence between us. Was it acknowledgment, at least, of our separate political and spiritual sisterhoods, each offering its own succor to those women who face the painful realities of abortion?

At last I found myself asking my own sister, "Well, is our civil war over? Or is this some kind of a truce?"

"It sure ain't a surrender," my sister said, laughing. Then she was quiet. "Do you remember what you said to me a long time ago down by the Yellow River?"

"Funny, I was just remembering that river too."

"You said, 'I love you for breathing.' Remember?"

"Of course."

"Well, I've quit smoking," she said. "For good."

"I love you, sis," I managed to say, my eyes filling. "I love you for breathing."

We listened to all that was not said between us, all that we have still to discover about each other—where we stand, how we'll change. It will never be easy, this sister bond. We are not on the same side, but we are also not anymore in such a polarized civil war. We are, like the rest of the bewildered world, looking for survival skills without an easy enemy.

Epilogue:
The Sisterhood of Man

I was driving along the freeway listening to NPR's "All Things Considered" report that the *L.A. Times* had just released its revised stylebook with updates to counter the sexism inherent in our English language. One of the changes was the suggestion that editors and writers sometimes consider using the phrase "the *sisterhood* of man." I was so struck by this simple switch from brotherhood to sisterhood; it seemed more radical than anything I'd heard in ages.

For centuries women have heard ourselves referred to as existing within the brotherhood of all mankind; the idea that we might also exist within a wide and diverse sisterhood was a welcome balancing act. I found myself wondering, what would a sisterhood of man look like? Immediately I thought of my little brother, the boy born after three older sisters. We've always joked that Dana Mark is our honorary sister, not only because he was raised in a house of women, but also because he himself is now proud father of four daughters. His latest license plate reads, "MY GIRLZ." That next week on a road trip from Monterey, California, to San Francisco, I teased Dana Mark about being ahead of his times, since he has always existed in a sisterhood of man.

"Even the navy couldn't drum my sisters out of me," Dana Mark laughed. "But if they heard me even mention the *sisterhood of man*, I'd probably be shot!"

In his aviator squadron my brother was often chided by the other fliers for leaving the air base punctually every afternoon so that he could be home to baby-sit his little daughters while his wife was starting up her own business. My brother often jokes that in marrying Renée, he combined all the best and none of the worst of his elder sisters. We sisters each take some credit for our brother's good marriage. As a boy he was a quick study when it came to the ways of women and as a result he was one of the most popular boys in high school and college. Girls sought him out because he could talk with them like a friend, and yet he understood romance from both male and female points of view. It was no wonder that when the phone rang, it was often a girlfriend calling.

"Do you remember," I asked Dana Mark as we drove over the blond California hills, through garlic groves and artichoke fields, "how we programmed you to behave on dates?"

Dana Mark laughed. "I'd come home from a date and the three of you girls would grab me and give me the Grand Inquisition. You girls were always with me." Dana Mark shook his head, grinning. "At the drive-in, I could just imagine my three sisters in the backseat like sports commentators or worse yet, critics. But I don't know how I could be a good father to four daughters now if it weren't for my sisters. In the navy I'm surrounded by macho guys, and then I come home to all these *girls*." Dana Mark paused. "But it . . . it brings me back, all these sisters and daughters, it brings me back to myself somehow."

As he continued talking about his four daughters, I gazed fondly over at my younger brother, smiling at his strong, sensitive hands that know how to change diapers in the dark.

"I love being a father," he said firmly. His other love is flying and navigating one of the world's most technologically advanced and expensive military jets.

I remembered when these two loves collided and he made a very painful choice. Dana Mark was one of the youngest naval lieutenants ever to work with the Joint Chiefs of Staff in the Pentagon. His career was off to a spectacular start. There he was in the Defense Department hub working in politico-military affairs. My mother, who has spent the last seventeen years in the CIA, and my father, whose love of the military shows in his lifetime naval reserve captain status, both believed my brother was not only in the stratosphere of the skies, but also that of the military hierarchy. Then came the promotion offer that would have sent my brother on the fastest track to the top—with the condition that he spend six months of every year at sea.

We sat in the Pentagon cafeteria, my brother and I, talking over his decision. He was giving me a proud tour. But his face was grave and pale. "I told them 'no,' " my brother said softly. "And it was so hard to say it. I told them I had no memory of ever playing with my own father."

"You told your commanding officers *that?*" I marveled.

He gave me a military nod, then continued. "I told them that I remember all the guys on ship who played tapes their wives sent them of their kids, who had their children's drawings on the inside of their lockers and above their bunks. I talked about how it was to come home from a long tour of sea duty and meet your own kids for the first time—how they were afraid of their own fathers and shrank back on the dock when the guys tried to reach out and embrace them. I said no, understanding that the navy would never approve, that they'd slot me into a lower career path, that I'd be seen as a fool by most of the other soldiers . . ." He shook his head sadly. "But I never wanted to reach out to one of my girls and have them shrink back in fear because they didn't know my face, they didn't even know their own daddy."

I sat in that Pentagon cafeteria with tears streaming down my face. My brother's eyes were full too. All around us was the scurry and hustle of men in uniform. I felt for a hallucinatory moment that he and I stood on a great battlefield that was history itself; we were eating pie and chatting as if we were not part of the fray, were in fact occupying some invisible camp pitched near all the fighting. There we were talking about children and staying home from the crusades and how to keep our daughters from being afraid of their absent fathers—what we might well call the more traditional "herstory."

Every now and then in the march of khaki and white and blue uniforms I'd catch the stride of a military skirt, modest in length, but just as ambitious in its pace. I wondered to myself, now that women are marching and flying into combat alongside our brothers, and more men are staying home to nurture children than ever before—shouldn't our stories change to reflect our brave new roles? There is a new world we've just begun to explore between the sisterhoods and the brotherhoods; it is a world beyond holy wars, and the war between the sexes or other gender skirmishes that so distract and prevent us from the more death-defying, courageous work of peer relationships.

We know all about sibling rivalry, just as those animal behaviorists have overly focused their research on aggression and dominance in other species, to the exclusion of those survival skills of group cooperation and long-term nurturance. What we don't know as much about, what may well be the work of our future, is *sibling alliances*. As the population shifts to a disproportionately large aging population of those with more siblings than children, we are given an opportunity to learn the survival strategies of the sibling bond: negotiation, sharing, and peer partnerships. All successful peer relations are based on mutual respect, not dominance, on the give and take of equals. If research shows us that happiness in old age is directly related to past good sibling bonds, then a reunion of brother- and sisterhoods is crucial to our species' survival and happiness.

If we are to reunite sister with sister, brother with brother, and brother with sister, some old ways between us must die; new relationships must be created. What is dying now, is in fact in its final, violent death throes, is the patriarchy. I believe it may take the patriarchy another fifty to one hundred years to truly transform into a world where brothers and sisters stand side by side. But our global politics are already making the shift. In the way that the Cold War was based on a totalitarian model, much like an oppressive parent-child dynamic, we now have a post–Cold War world with the old oppressor-over-oppressed, all-powerful parent model becoming increasingly obsolete. Where we once had the motherland or the fatherland, will we now learn about the sibling-land? Because sisters and brothers are true peers, we continually seek the balance of contemporaries over any notion of final dominion. Siblings define themselves by their differences and learn to tolerate diversity, to live with competition as well as cooperation. We learn the power of heeding one another's counsel and authority, just as we also find ourselves as siblings caught up in a complex minuet of shifting alliances. The world of the twenty-first century may be more about partnerships than superpowers, about the unexpected dance between former enemies, and the reclaiming of peer relations. For all of this, our sibling bonds, biological and chosen, will be an important element in our global survival.

This vision of a new world order begins on the personal level and moves into the political and collective—and that is why healing our own sisterhoods and bringing back our brothers is so essential. All of us know we cannot return to the patriarchal ways that have brought us this far. But of course, that doesn't keep us from backlash or re-gression or yearning for a myth that has almost destroyed our species.

Even my brother finds himself sometimes longing to be a patriarch, just as his wife lets him soundly know that she won't be dominated and that he must share equally all the work, just as his sisters once insisted that he do his chores alongside us. We cannot divide the labor anymore—there is too much to do together.

As I searched for myths to support my vision of a world in which the sibling bond is a successful working model for partnerships, I found the ancient Sumerian myth of Ianna (5000 B.C.), the Queen of Heaven, who descended into the underworld to reunite with her male counterpart Anu. Then there were those Egyptian myths of Isis also braving the underworld for her dismembered Osiris; she pieced her partner back together and restored wholeness to the world. This an-cient mystery rite of woman resurrecting and reuniting with man is echoed in the later Biblical story of the siblings Mary, Martha, and Lazarus.

We might call this moving myth "ourstory," after all the divisive-ness of past *his*tory and *her*story. The story begins with a brother's death. Lazarus has been buried in the family tomb for four days by the time Mary and Martha beseech their friend Jesus to bring back their brother from the dead. Unlike Isis or Ianna, Jesus does not jour-ney into the land of the dead at this time; it is not himself he is going to resurrect here in this small village. It is not a savior, but a brother who will return to these grief-stricken sisters. Weeping, Christ goes to that cave-tomb and asks that the great stone be taken away. Into that dark, earthen mouth, Christ calls, "Lazarus, come forth!"

Trailing dank, winding sheets and still bound head and foot with graveclothes, Lazarus slowly emerges from his cave, that earthen womb, reborn. Imagine his sisters embracing their brother, their deft, sure hands stripping away the burial cloth with which they had so recently wrapped him. Imagine that his death stench does not keep them from kissing that pale, shrunken face or clasping his beloved body close to them. Does he walk painfully between his sisters, an arm around each of them as they steady him? Or does he—miracle that he is—leap and even dance when he finds that he is restored to his life, and to his sisters?

Mary and Martha are sisters who remind us we do not want to lose our brothers even as the patriarchy dies. We want to grow old together, sisters with brothers, and learn again the enduring secrets of sibling love and survival. This beautiful myth of the sibling bond is played out everywhere in our culture, but it has not been our focus, so it has been almost invisible.

In my own neighborhood I found myself thinking of those reunited Biblical siblings sharing their old age together when I moved into a beach cottage on Puget Sound several years ago. One of my neighbors was Rachel, a woman in her eighties. Our kitchen windows faced each other and we met often in our gardens. For all I knew she was an aging widow living that solitary, slow slide into isolation. I pitied Rachel and tried to bring her little gifts to cheer her up.

"Cheer her up!" my housemate Gloria corrected me. "Rachel doesn't need cheering up; she probably needs to take more naps just to cope with all the hubbub around her."

"What hubbub?" I demanded.

"Oh, you never see it because you're not an early riser and you're always out in the evenings," Gloria informed me with a grin. "But Rachel has a gentleman caller every morning about dawn; he stays until about nine A.M., then returns for supper."

"You mean Floyd." I tried to cover for my lack of attention. "I know about him. But he's married and lives up the hill. He's not her lover."

"Of course he is," Gloria countered. "They're going to Hawaii together this winter and if you ask me, every morning is a vacation for those two lovebirds."

I was stunned at how I'd missed this lovers' bond; I was even more stunned when one midnight I awoke to the sound of music, not loud rap music, but Big Band music. In my darkened kitchen I spied into

Rachel's kitchen and witnessed to my wonder not just Rachel and Floyd with raised martini glasses, but also another man and woman I'd never seen before. They were having a wonderful party, dancing and drinking and laughing as if it were early evening. I could barely keep my eyes open and felt like a child watching the adults party while I peeped down from the bedroom stairs.

As it turned out, the other man and woman were from Australia, both in their late sixties. For the past decade this couple, Dexter and Sally, had come to live with Rachel six months out of every year. So, during the spring and summer, what I'd assumed was Rachel's solitary life, was filled with surrogate siblings. They shared suppers, gardening, cleaning, laundry, and so much good nature I was envious.

"No nursing homes for us," Sally would often tell me in her robust Australian accent. She slapped her blazing white laundry and hung it on the line between our houses.

I was slightly embarrassed at the ladies' bloomers and big bras billowing in the wind. It struck me that I rarely saw underwear in public anymore; my generation's preference for dryers precluded this cozy intimacy flung out for all to see. "They wouldn't let you hang your beautiful clean laundry on the clothesline in a nursing home," I nodded.

"They hang *you* out to dry in a nursing home!" Sally snorted. "Then after they drain away all your money, they bury you." She shook her head firmly. "Dearie, when you've lived as long as we have you realize that the simple *couple* is not enough—someone always dies and leaves the other alone. So you find sisters and brothers in self-defense; they'll take care of you, when your children might rather put you away."

Dexter and Sally have very fine relationships with their own children, but they do not intend to be a burden or to be cooped up in a government pensioners' home in Australia. This half-yearly sojourn to stay with Rachel has benefited all of them. Because Rachel is ten years older and more frail, Sally and Dexter take care of the heavier work, with Floyd's help. This sibling household is an image that has stayed with me strongly, and even though I've left that neighborhood, I keep in touch through walks and visits. Their alternative to the isolation and despair of what Sally disdains as "old folks' homes," seems so sane and simple a solution. "Whoever dies first," Sally says in her matter-of-fact voice, "we'll still be in good company, you know, like having your brothers and sisters back. But this time you choose them," she said, and laughed.

As I drove with my own brother on our road trip to San Francisco, I felt deep comfort in knowing that when I am old I will continue to choose the company of my sisters and brother, as well as that larger brother- and sisterhood I've created during my long life. I found myself playfully asking my little brother, "So, sweetheart, would you say you're still living in the sisterhood of man? First surrounded by sisters, then by daughters?"

He was as startled by the term as I had been when I'd first heard it on the radio. "Would it be any different?" he wondered. "Would just changing the words change the world?"

"What would a sisterhood of man look like to you?" I asked, eyeing him curiously.

He shifted in his driver's seat and stretched. "Remember when you and I drove across the Mojave Desert?" He flashed me a smile. "We took turns at the wheel, we sang two-part harmony, and you gave me all that advice on my life; then I told you how to solve all your problems, too!"

"But did we take each other's advice?" I teased.

"That's not the point, sis," he said. "Point is that we sought each other's counsel and no one had the last word."

"Or the word from God," I finished for him. "Or the *one way*."

My brother didn't even wince when I used the phrase that has often defined the fundamentalism in my family as in the world. Where my little sister has chosen to picket abortion clinics and lobby legislators, my brother is also involved in anti-choice activities. His take the more subtle and life-supporting form of counseling pregnant mothers through a Christian-sponsored group, which then helps sponsor or adopt babies once they're born. Like my sister Marla, Dana Mark has also at times chosen home schooling for his children so that they might be insulated from public schools and instead be taught a traditional Christian curriculum. The home schooling came to an end when my brother was transferred to California and my sister is now sending her three boys to a conservative Christian school.

When my brother and I fall into our spiritual sibling discussions, they are markedly different from the volatile dialogue between us three sisters on the subject of abortion. Both my younger brother and sister deplore the rash of murders and other violence against doctors and clinics who support abortion. And yet both my younger siblings still firmly believe that the right to choose abortion does not naturally belong to women.

"What about all your daughters?" I asked my brother as we ruminated on what the sisterhood of man might look like in the future. "Would you support your daughter if she chose to have an abortion?"

Without a moment's hesitation, my brother answered. "Yes, I would support her." He paused. "But I would also counsel her in all the alternatives."

"Fair enough," I said. "And what if she didn't seek your counsel?"

Here, my brother took a long time to consider his answer, which seemed to surprise even him. "I would feel . . . I would feel left out."

I turned to my brother and saw so much bewilderment and pain on his face that I said nothing for a time. I wondered, had he often felt left out as a boy among all these girls? Had he felt excluded from all our feminine ways? Had he been as lonely, surrounded by females, as women are now in a society so long dictated by males?

"You would feel lonely for her," I suggested softly, "for your daughter, if she didn't talk to you about something so serious as birth and death. Right?"

"Yes." He nodded. "I would feel like I was missing in action, like I'd missed out on a big part of her life."

On an impulse I asked, "Do you think the brotherhoods ever long for the sisterhoods? Are the brotherhoods at last lonely enough to share the power and all the pain?"

My brother laughed, but his eyes were serious. "You remember that football player, sis?" he asked. "The New York linebacker who was fined $125,000 dollars for missing a game, so he could be there at the birth of his child?"

"Amazing, wasn't it?"

"I don't think he should have been fined, and you know, even in my squadron, I'm not completely in the minority. That football player was acting not in the line of duty, but in the line of love." He laughed, then continued thoughtfully, "You know, it was you, my sisters, who first taught me how to love."

I smiled. "What would we ever do without one another?" I asked softly, touching my brother's face lightly, familiarly. His is the same jawline and bright, deep-set eyes of all us siblings; as much as we differ, we all share this family face. And it is repeated now in a new generation of seven sisters and three brothers—another sisterhood of man. In fact my sister Paula is now engaged to a man whom she describes as "like a best girlfriend." He is also a doting father and brings two more daughters to their shared household. "Five girls under one roof," Paula marvels. "It's sisters in spades!"

When I first began this book on sisters, all seven of my nieces were thrilled. Even as little girls (with no brothers), they had already glimpsed the way our societies trivialize and dismiss groups of females while according male bonding—whether it is in sports or religion— more legitimacy and attention.

Already my nieces are a strong sisterhood. They declare that they've watched the movie *Beaches*, which is about girls who grow up together and remain best friends, at least twenty-two times. "Girls are just as important as boys," my niece Lindsay advised me. "I'm glad I've got so many sisters. We're lucky that way."

Her older sister Lauren went a step further and wrote a theme paper on sisters. Lauren, Lindsay, and Lissy, my sister Paula's children, proudly call themselves "The Three L's," and at their school they sign their papers L1, L2, and L3. Thirteen-year-old Lauren wrote this about her sisters:

> Though Lindsay was "given to me" (and I still claim this, of course), we often fight. I have tortured her, and she has tortured me. We have said the word *hate* too many times, but we love each other. We will tease and hurt, but we are close. . . . I remember the nights when I huddle up next to a sister, after a horrid nightmare or when upset. When I break out in tears, I always look for a sister to put my shoulder on. I remember when deep into the night we would (and still do) chat and play, steal covers and spy.
>
> And then there is Larissa. Lissy is six years younger than I. We call her "Delicious" and "Pate Shu" [sic] or creampuff in French, because she is so cute. I have scars from Lissy. She is probably stronger than I. With her hot temper and mine to match, we have bit, clawed, and pulled. But I would not change sweet Lissy for the world. . . . She is willing and helpful, honest

and kind. If it were not for my sisters, I don't know what I would do. . . . It comforts me to know that I have two sisters to cry with, laugh with, yell at, fight with, and love.

Lauren is the same sister who at the age of eight, while listening to her mother and me talk around the kitchen table, gasped in sudden epiphany, "Oh, I get it! Grown-ups can feel two things at once— happy *and* sad!"

Feeling two or more things at once, juggling roles from sister to mother to wife, balancing the need for Self and sister societies with the demands of family and career—these are the complicated skills of nurturance and long-term survival which women bring to the world, both personal and political. We are complex creatures who have been too long denied our wide spectrum of vision, emotions, and bonding abilities. Where the brotherhood alone might become preoccupied with hierarchy, dominance, and aggression, the sisterhood at its best can bring egalitarianism, cooperation, and mediating compassion.

Perhaps a better title for this final chapter might be "Bringing Back Our Sisters," because it is this sisterhood which must be fully restored, in all its complex shadows and lights, before we can completely embrace our brothers as equals. Recently I had a dream that my own sisters and I came upon our little brother lying dead. In that odd, trancelike state of the dream, my sisters—even though they are both highly trained intensive-care nurses—did not try to resuscitate my brother. Instead, we all three turned and went on our way, very preoccupied with something we were solving together. When we all returned, we found to our deep pleasure that our brother had somehow resurrected himself and, like Lazarus, we welcomed him back.

This dream tells me that as we sisters reclaim our self-worth, our dignity, our complex and sacred feminine skills, we can leave it to our brothers to resurrect themselves. Our job as sisters is not to save the brotherhood, but to redefine and embrace the sisterhood. In doing so, there will be a new world waiting when our brothers, who have also survived the ravages of the patriarchy, can return to the living.

But meanwhile, there is so much to be done, to remember, to create. And the journey has just begun. There will be many sisters like way stations along the path to help point us toward one another, as well as toward our proper place—a place which includes rest and reunion as well as work and play. And along our journey, we can use the vision of a vast sisterhood of man through which to better see the entire world.

Like my niece Lauren, I do not know what I would have done without my own sisters beside me. Both my sisters, for all our differences, agree. Recently my sister Paula reminded me of her long-ago suicide contemplation. She wrote, "In the end, it was my sister who made me grab onto the world that I had already abandoned."

By not abandoning our sisters or ourselves, we grab onto and hold a world which needs so much embracing, so much heartfelt vision and healing. Perhaps now it is time for the sisters to try their hand at the survival of our species—and the animals, the tribal women's societies, and sisters of a new generation can show us the way. The journey may be difficult, and we will need all the skills of alliance and bonding that are in our nature. As the German poet Rilke wrote, "A storm is coming/and I hear the far-off fields say things/I can't bear without a friend/I can't love without a sister."

I have found myself recently part of several new sisterhoods. One of these sister societies is a group of women who are established writers and advocates. We have been meeting together privately to talk about our lives and our work as we enter a new millennium, which will perhaps be remembered as one in which "the sisterhood of man" returned to the wide world.

At the end of one of our weekends in a small island retreat, we women formed a circle. We said thanks and blessings on the trees and water that surrounded us; we spoke of our sisterhood bond and deep pleasure in finding ourselves in one another's company. We talked about growing old together. As we held hands, eyeing one another with grave, grateful faces, someone said simply, "It's not really about power, is it? It's about connection."

"The power is *in* the connection," another sister said, speaking for us all. And everyone in that small circle of powerful women smiled.

Selected Bibliography

Alcott, Louisa May. *Little Women*. New York: Thomas Y. Crowell, 1955.

Allen, Paula Gunn, ed. *Spider Woman's Granddaughters: Traditional Tales and Contemporary Writing by Native American Women*. Boston: Beacon Press, 1989.

Allende, Isabel. *The House of the Spirits*. New York: Bantam Books, 1986.

Alvarez, Julia. *How the Garcia Girls Lost Their Accents*. New York: Plume Books, 1992.

Anderson, Lorraine, ed. *Sisters of the Earth: Women's Prose and Poetry About Nature*. New York: Vintage Books, 1991.

Austen, Jane. *Pride and Prejudice*. New York: Dell Books, 1959.

Bank, Stephen P., and Michael D. Kahn. *The Sibling Bond*. New York: Basic Books, 1982.

Barstow, Anne Llewellyn. *Witchcraze: A New History of the European Witch Hunts: Our Legacy of Violence Against Women*. London: Pandora, 1994.

Bell, Quentin. *Virginia Woolf: A Biography. Volume One: Virginia Stephen, 1892–1912*. London: The Hogarth Press, 1972.

Berkinow, Louise. *Among Women*. New York: HarperCollins, 1981.

Buchanan, Christina, and Celina Spiegel, eds. *Out of the Garden: Women Writers on the Bible*. New York: Fawcett Columbine, 1994.

Cahill, Susan, ed. *Among Sisters*. New York: Mentor Books, 1989.

Campbell, Joseph, and Charles Muses, eds. *In All Her Names: Explorations of the Feminine in Divinity*. San Francisco: HarperSanFrancisco, 1991.

Chekhov, Anton. *Three Sisters*. New York: Broadway Play Publications, 1991.

Chernin, Kim. *The Obsession: Reflections on the Tyranny of Slenderness*. New York: Harper & Row, 1981.

Codren, Mary. *The Serpent and the Goddess: Women, Religion, and Power in Celtic Ireland.* San Francisco: Harper & Row, 1989.

Coontz, Stephanie. *The Way We Never Were: American Families and the Nostalgia Trap.* New York: Basic Books, 1992.

Croutier, Alev Lytle. *Harem: The World Behind the Veil.* New York: Abbeville Press, 1989.

Davenport, Kiana. *Shark Dialogue.* New York: Atheneum, 1994.

Delaney, Sarah and Elizabeth A., with Amy Hill Hearth. *Having Our Say: The Delaney Sisters' First 100 Years.* New York: Kodansha International, 1993.

Downing, Christine. *Psyche's Sisters: Reimagining the Meaning of Sisterhood.* New York: Continuum, 1988.

Eisler, Riane. *The Chalice and the Blade: Our History, Our Future.* San Francisco: Harper & Row, 1987.

Eliot, George. *Middlemarch.* New York: New American Library, 1964.

Fossey, Dian. *Gorillas in the Mist.* Boston: Houghton Mifflin, 1983.

Galdikas, Birute M. F. *Reflections of Eden: My Years with the Orangutans of Borneo.* Toronto: Little, Brown, 1995.

Gaskell, Elizabeth. *The Life of Charlotte Brontë.* Middlesex: Penguin, 1975.

Gelernter, Cary Quan. "Crone: Women Growing Older with Passion, Purpose." *Seattle Times,* May 23, 1993.

Gibbons, Ann, Toomas Koppel, et al. "Is There a 'Female Style' in Science?" *Science* 260 (April 16, 1993), cover story.

Gilligan, Carol. *In a Different Voice: Psychological Theory and Women's Development.* Cambridge, Mass.: Harvard University Press, 1993.

Gimbutas, Marija. *Language of the Goddess.* San Francisco: HarperSanFrancisco, 1995.

Goleman, Denise. "Men at 65: New Findings on Well-Being." *New York Times,* June 16, 1990.

Gonzalez, David. "Religion Journal," *New York Times,* Feb. 4, 1995.

Goodall, Jane van Lawick. *In the Shadow of Man.* New York: Dell, 1971.

Goodrich, Norma L. *Priestesses.* New York: HarperPerennial, 1989.

Green, Rayna. *Women in American Indian Society.* New York: Chelsea House, 1992.

Green, Rayna, ed. *That's What She Said: Contemporary Poetry and Fiction by Native American Women.* Bloomington: Indiana University Press, 1984.

Harjo, Joy. *In Mad Love and War.* Middletown, Conn.: Wesleyan University Press, 1990.

Herzing, Denise Lore. "Dolphins in the Wild: An Eight-Year Field Study on Dolphin Communication and Interspecies Interaction." Ph.D. dissertation, Union Institute, Cincinnati, Ohio, 1993.

Hogan, Linda. *The Book of Medicines.* Minneapolis: Coffee House Press, 1993.

Hrdy, Sarah Blaffer, and George C. Williams. "Behavioral Biology and the Double Standard," in Margery L. Oldfield, ed., *Social Behavior of Female Vertebrates.* New York: Academic Press, 1983.

Johnson, Robert A. *Femininity Lost and Regained.* New York: HarperPerennial, 1991.

————. *She: Understanding Feminine Psychology.* New York: Harper & Row, 1977.

Kirkevold, Barbara, and Joan S. Lockard, eds. *Behavioral Biology of Killer Whales.* Vol. 1, Zoo Biology Monographs. New York: Alan R. Liss, 1993.

Klagsbrun, Francine. *Mixed Feelings: Love, Hate, Rivalry, and Reconciliation Among Brothers and Sisters.* New York: Bantam Books, 1992.

Koppelman, Susan, ed. *Women's Friendships: A Collection of Short Stories.* Norman: University of Oklahoma Press, 1991.

Kunene, Mazisi. *Anthem of the Decades.* London: Heinemann, 1981.

Kuzwayo, Ellen. *Call Me Woman.* San Francisco: Aunt Lute Books, 1985.

Leder, Jane Mersky. *Brothers and Sisters: How They Shape Our Lives.* New York: Ballantine Books, 1991.

MacKenzie, Rachel. *The Wine of Astonishment.* New York: Viking, 1974.

Matthews, Caitlin. *Sophia, Goddess of Wisdom.* London: Aquarian/Thorsons, 1992.

McIntyre, Joan. *Mind in the Waters.* New York: Charles Scribner's Sons, 1974.

McNaron, Toni A. H., ed. *The Sister Bond: A Feminist View of a Timeless Connection.* New York: Pergamon Press, 1985.

Metzger, Deena. "Re-vamping the World: On the Return of the Holy Prostitute." *Utne Reader,* Aug./Sept. 1985.

———. *The Woman Who Slept with Men to Take the War Out of Them and TREE.* Berkeley, Calif.: Wingbow Press, 1983.

Miller, Alice. *The Drama of the Gifted Child: The Search for the True Self.* New York: Basic Books, 1990.

Miller, Jean Baker. *Toward a New Psychology of Women.* Boston: Beacon Press, 1976.

Monaghan, Patricia. *The Book of Goddesses and Heroines.* Saint Paul, Minn.: Llewellyn Publications, 1990.

Moss, Cynthia. *Echo of the Elephants: The Story of an Elephant Family.* New York: William Morrow, 1992.

Mylonas, George E. *Eleusis and the Eleusinian Mysteries.* Princeton, N.J.: Princeton University Press, 1961.

Neumann, Erich. *The Fear of the Feminine.* Princeton, N.J.: Princeton University Press, 1994.

———. *The Great Mother.* Princeton, N.J.: Princeton University Press, 1963.

Nicholson, Shirley. *The Goddess Re-Awakening.* Wheaton, Ill.: Quest Books, 1989.

Pagels, Elaine. *The Gnostic Gospels.* New York: Random House, 1979.

———. *The Origin of Satan.* New York: Random House, 1995.

Paris, Ginette. *Pagan Grace: Dionysus, Hermes, and Goddess Memory in Daily Life.* Dallas: Spring Publications, 1990.

———. *Pagan Meditations: Aphrodite, Hestia, Artemis.* Dallas: Spring Publications, 1987.

———. *The Sacrament of Abortion.* Dallas: Spring Publications, 1992.

Payne, Katharine. *Elephants Calling.* New York: Crown Publishers, 1992.

Perera, Silvia Brinton. *Descent to the Goddess.* Toronto: Inner City Books, 1981.

Powers, Ann. "Queer in the Streets, Straight in the Sheets," *Village Voice,* Nov./Dec. 1993.

Pryor, Karen, and Kenneth S. Norris. *Dolphin Societies.* Berkeley: University of California Press, 1991.

Qualls-Corbett, Nancy. *The Sacred Prostitute: Eternal Aspect of the Feminine.* Toronto: Inner City Books, 1988.

Ranke-Heinemann, Uta. *Eunuchs for the Kingdom of Heaven: Women, Sexuality, and the Catholic Church.* New York: Penguin, 1991.

Raymond, Janice G. *A Passion for Friends: Toward a Philosophy of Female Affection.* Boston: Beacon Press, 1986.

Rountree, Cathleen. *Coming into Our Fullness: On Women Turning Forty.* Freedom, Calif.: The Crossing Press, 1991.

Shepherd, Linda Jean. *Lifting the Veil: The Feminine Face of Science.* Boston: Shambhala, 1993.

Shepsut, Asia. *Journey of the Priestess.* London: Aquarian/Thorsons, 1993.

Sjoo, Monica, and Barbara Mor. *The Great Cosmic Mother: Rediscovering the Religion of the Earth.* San Francisco: Harper & Row, 1987.

Small, Meredith F. "A Reasonable Sleep." *Discover*, April 1992.

Smiley, Jane. *A Thousand Acres*. New York: Fawcett Columbine, 1991.

Smith-Rosenberg, Carroll. *Disorderly Conduct: Visions of Gender in Victorian America*. New York: Alfred A. Knopf, 1985.

Sovatsky, Stuart. *Passions of Innocence: Tantric Celibacy and the Mysteries Eros*. Rochester, Vt.: Destiny Books, 1994.

Spretnak, Charlene, ed. *The Politics of Women's Spirituality*. New York: Anchor Press, 1982.

Stanton, Elizabeth Cady. *The Woman's Bible*. Boston: Northeastern University Press, 1993.

Stone, Merlin. *When God Was a Woman*. New York: W. W. Norton, 1980.

Tan, Amy. *The Joy Luck Club*. New York: Ivy Books, 1991.

Thomas, Elizabeth Marshall. "Of Ivory and the Survival of Elephants," *New York Review of Books*, March 24, 1994.

Thomas, Warren D., and Daniel Kaufman. *Dolphin Conferences, Elephant Midwives, and Other Astonishing Facts About Animals*. Los Angeles: Jeremy P. Tarcher, 1990.

Ugwu-Oju, Dympna. "Pursuit of Happiness," "Hers" col., *New York Times Magazine*, Nov. 14, 1993.

Ulufudu. *The Zulu Bone Oracle*. Berkeley, Calif.: Wingbow Press, 1989.

Vollenhoven, Sylvia. "South Africa Through Women's Eyes." *Ms.*, Sept./Oct. 1993.

Walker, Alice. *The Color Purple*. New York: Harcourt Brace Jovanovich, 1982.

———. *Possessing the Secret of Joy*. New York: Harcourt Brace Jovanovich, 1992.

———. *Warrior Marks: The Sexual Blinding of Women*. New York: Harcourt Brace Jovanovich, 1993.

Walker, Barbara G. *The Woman's Dictionary of Symbols and Sacred Objects*. San Francisco: Harper & Row, 1988.

Wasson, Gordon R., Carl A. P. Ruck, and Albert Hofmann. *The Road to Eleusis: Unveiling the Secret of the Mysteries*. New York: Harcourt Brace Jovanovich, 1978.

West, Rebecca. *Cousin Rosamund*. New York: Viking, 1986.

———. *The Fountain Overflows*. New York: Viking, 1956.

———. *This Real Night*. New York: Viking, 1984.

Wharton, Edith. *Madame de Treymes*. New York: Charles Scribner's Sons, 1907.

Williams, Hector. "Secret Rites of Lesbos," *Archaeology*, July/Aug. 1994.

Woodman, Marion. "Marion Woodman on the Crone," *Crone Chronicles*, Spring Equinox, 1993.

Woolf, Virginia. *Orlando*. New York: Harcourt Brace Jovanovich, 1973.

———. *Women and Writing*. Edited by Michele Barrett. New York: Harcourt Brace Jovanovich, 1979.

Zweig, Connie. *To Be a Woman: The Birth of the Conscious Feminine*. Los Angeles: Jeremy P. Tarcher, 1990.

Zweig, Connie, and Jeremiah Abrams, eds. *Meeting the Shadow: The Hidden Power of the Dark Side of Human Nature*. New York: Tarcher/Putnam, 1993.